YEARS OF HORROR, DAYS OF HOPE: RESPONDING TO THE CAMBODIAN REFUGEE CRISIS

Edited by
Barry S. Levy, M.D., M.P.H.
Professor
Department of Family and Community Medicine
University of Massachusetts Medical School
Worcester, Massachusetts

and

Daniel C. Susott, M.D., M.P.H.
International Health Specialist
New York and Honolulu

ASSOCIATED FACULTY PRESS, INC.
Millwood, N.Y. ● New York City ● London

Library of Congress Cataloging-in-Publication Data
Main entry under title:

Years of horror, days of hope.

   1. Refugees –Cambodia. 2. Refugees –Thailand.
3. Refugees –Health and hygiene –Cambodia. I. Levy,
Barry S. II. Susott, Daniel C., 1951-
HV640.5.C35Y43   1986   362.8'7'09593   85-21441
ISBN 0-8046-9396-X
ISBN 0-8046-9399-4 (pbk.)

To the people of Cambodia:
the millions who have suffered and died,
and the millions more who have struggled to survive
and to rebuild their lives and their culture.

CONTENTS

PART 3: PUBLIC HEALTH, NUTRITION, AND EDUCATION

PART 4: AID BEYOND THE HOLDING CENTERS IN THAILAND

PART 5: BROADER PERSPECTIVES:
PAST, PRESENT, AND FUTURE

PART 6: EPILOGUE

ILLUSTRATIONS

FOREWORD

John H. Bryant

This book makes two important contributions to refugee assistance and disaster management: its portrayal of the minute-to-minute, person-to-person events embodied in the Cambodian relief operation; and a series of fundamental principles and lessons to be learned from this response to a historic human disaster.

The political turmoil that eroded Cambodia from within and the international forces that wracked the country from without are not ignored, but the focus of the book is on how those caught up in the events—international organizations, private agencies, volunteer health professionals, Thais, and the Cambodian people themselves—coped with both the small details and the larger practical problems of that tragedy.

It would be a mistake, however, to think of this book as only a collection of anecdotes. While many scenes, interactions, and concerns stand by themselves as useful and often memorable contributions to our deeper understanding of these events, it is the general observations—the principles and lessons—that will affect the ways people and agencies operate under such circumstances.

John H. Bryant is a physician who, during the height of the Cambodian relief operation, was Deputy Assistant Secretary, United States Department of Health and Human Services. He is currently Chairman and Professor, Department of Community Medicine of the Aga Khan University in Karachi, Pakistan.

ix

Personal experiences and lessons learned are closely related. The impressions and reactions of people to their individual predicaments and opportunities provide the basis in reality for more general observations, and the principles and lessons show the importance of maintaining a broad perspective, of keeping the most fundamental human values to the fore as individual problems are faced.

Examples abound in this book, of both the illustrative personal experience and the general principle to be drawn from it. Readers can choose for themselves among the impressions and reactions. Let me suggest some of the principles and lessons to be learned from the Cambodian refugee crisis:

UNHCR and similar organizations are working at those intersections of international affairs where the value of human life is protected and maintained, or demeaned and subjugated to the personal and institutional needs of agencies that make their way at the expense of the refugees. The most fundamental human values must be acknowledged and maintained as guidelines in the midst of what will often be chaotic events. Here are four examples:

Unaccompanied children. UNHCR is implacably opposed to trade that would place children separated from their parents in Western countries; first priority must be given to protecting the basic principles of family life.

Resettlement. While there are times when resettling members of families in other countries is the only way to reunite separated families, wholesale resettlement endangers the chances of Kampuchea surviving as an independent nation.

Voluntary repatriation. The surface view of simply enabling Khmers to exercise their right to return to their home country was complicated by vested interests—Khmer Rouge interests in regaining followers; Heng Samrin's concern for fresh guerrillas being launched from a safe sanctuary. In the end, UNHCR saw to it that those who went, did so voluntarily.

Level of services. Services should relate to the standard of living of the surrounding population, but this is made difficult by the limited willingness of agencies to contribute to affected Thai villages, and by the invasion of a vast aid circus.

* * * * *

In an area of military conflict, aid organizations have a moral and practical obligation to assure that aid goes effectively and efficiently only to noncombatants. If they use their resources unwittingly to advance particular political or military objectives, they can readily forfeit their moral and practical standing and the possibilities of playing a useful role.

Extensive negotiations were required to allow a consortium of aid agencies to function inside Kampuchea, serving only noncombatants and with full facilities for monitoring the use of resources. Some lessons were learned from this collaboration:
–One or a few agencies should take the lead, and the others yield some of their autonomy and independent action.
–Collaboration yields more even and balanced approaches to aid with less foreign penetration.
–Collaboration can create synergistic effects in field administration, host-government relationships, media effects, and fund-raising.
–The crucial issue that contributed to interorganizational unity in Kampuchea was interdependence in monitoring.

And some principles:
Self-help. The people should be viewed as partners, not as victims. Capacity building, supporting their natural resiliency, and focusing on appropriate technology contributes to this end.
Equity. Aid should be fairly distributed to all people in need.
Appropriate technology. Sensible and useful materials should be sent and used—hoe heads, for example, not high-heeled shoes or potato chips.
Leveraging impact. In desperate and chaotic situations, aid can be targeted on leverage points to achieve quantum increases in the impacts of aid. An example is the opening of the barge operation from Singapore to Kompong Song in Kampuchea, which broke a bottleneck in moving supplies.

Reconstruction and development. While it is important to deal effectively with the emergency stage of such a crisis, it is also important to shift the orientation as early as practicable to reconstruction and development.
Communication about disasters. Explicit strategies for communication should be developed. Aid agencies should cooperate, consult and share information, they need to recognize a responsibility for helping the public sector—national and international—to understand the problems and how to address them sensibly.

An important lesson in the planning, preparation, and distribution of food was that of having the Cambodians directly involved. They understood the taste preferences of their people and could negotiate acceptance of foods modified to increase their nutritional value.

A number of important comparisons can be made between the Cambodian relief operation and other relief efforts:

Unusual aspects of the operation included high levels of funding, a large supply of experienced personnel, manageable numbers of new arrivals, adequate supplies in neighboring countries, a good transportation system, a supportive host government, and the strong role of the UNHCR.

Similarities to past operations included lack of preparedness, competition between agencies, inequities in the distribution of aid, overemphasis on medical aid, poor execution of nutrition programs, overemphasis on charity, a failure to assess long-term impacts.

Welcome innovations were management and coordination of an unusually high quality; the development of a children's center for unaccompanied minors with surrogate mothers; a shift from institutional approaches in feeding to decentralized arrangements; and greater use of sanitarians.

Although refugee relief has improved substantially, alternative approaches are needed: better documentation of experiences, better training, more programmatic research, and deeper understanding at a sociological level of the reactions of the refugees to their experiences and to life in the camps. In particular, relief organizations need to expend more effort to move away from pure relief and towards more developmental activities.

There are ample other lessons as well, in medical administration, in education, and in surveillance.

The dominant characteristic of this book is its persistent attention to the immediacy of human events, unfolding in the midst of larger forces and events that are both paradoxical and bizarre. Humanitarian aid goes to victims and victimizers alike. People at the extreme edge of human need seem to attract both sensitive nurturing and ruthless exploitation. A carefully built system of refugee assistance seems to have had virtually no impact on the ultimate issues of the future social well-being of the refugees and the political future of the country. (The last is the most painful of the book's paradoxes.)

A central lesson, therefore, of *Years of Horror, Days of Hope* is that large numbers of caring people can deal with the immediate effects of a great human tragedy, but all the while, the larger world may be failing to deal effectively with the very forces that gave rise to the tragedy. Nonetheless, those who work in the hot glare of human need persist, care, and help—and are themselves at the same time helped—to build a personal and then an international capacity for assisting others to survive under seemingly impossible circumstances.

PREFACE

A young man burned himself to death outside my dormitory at the University of California at San Diego in 1969. Near the place where he began his flaming panic-stricken sprint into oblivion remained the sign scrawled on a piece of cardboard: "In God's name, end the war!" The world had just learned that the United States was bombing "Vietnamese bases" inside the gentle land of Cambodia; Ronald Reagan, then governor of California, closed the university to quiet the growing protests.

Sadly, the horror continues. 1986 begins. These are hopeful days for the few fortunate ones, but hundreds of thousands of Cambodians cannot awaken from the nightmare of their lives.

People would rather forget. The years of the involvement of the United States in Southeast Asia, the Vietnam War years, ended for most Americans—and gladly so—in 1975. For the Cambodian people, whose history seems an endless succession of wars and occupations and suffering, 1975 marked the beginning of an era of terror unknown in previous times.

In 1979—10 years after the self-immolation of my fellow student in San Diego, when I was finishing my internship at a hospital in Massachusetts—Cambodia was being seen on TV in everyone's living room. To the horrors of the years of gradually dawning awareness of the Cambodian bloodbath was added more terrible news: 40,000 starving refugees had been forced out of their Thai haven, forced to claw their way back through the mine fields and malarious foodless jungle to the devastated homeland they had fled. Starvation became synonymous with Cambodia as the world witnessed suffering it would never forget.

In creating this book, we wanted to record for the world the events of the years since 1979—to depict the overwhelming response to a catastrophe of shocking magnitude, in the hope that any such interventions in the future would be more effective. Years since 1979 have brought, at times, brief periods of euphoria and joy and hope such as few Cambodians ever thought they could know again after the horrors of the Khmer Rouge years. We wanted to illuminate the relief effort in its most human aspects.

D.C.S.

* * * * *

A surgeon from Washington, a pediatrician from India, a medical student from Minnesota, a nutritionist from Oslo, a sanitarian from Oregon, and a dentist and a businessperson from Phnom Penh—these seven individuals as well as 45 others have contributed the chapters that comprise this book, the purpose of which is to describe the Cambodian relief operation from many different personal perspectives. We believe that an understanding of this operation provides not only specific insights about such relief activities but also helps to define the spirit of humanity, which is so well demonstrated in such a crisis.

From 1975 to early 1979, Cambodia endured a holocaust of unbelievable magnitude. After the Vietnamese overthrew the Pol Pot government, many Cambodians fled to the Thai border. Meanwhile, about five million people within Cambodia faced a bleak existence as attempts were made to begin rebuilding the country.

The Cambodian relief operation took shape in the Thai and border camps and also inside Cambodia. Although the focus of most of the chapters in this book is on the activities and life in the Thai camps, it is important to recognize that much relief work also took place on the border and within Cambodia itself.

The book is divided into six parts. Part 1 describes the early days of the relief operation, focusing on the larger Thai camps of Khao I Dang and Sa Kaeo, and the development and coordination of the volunteer response from the United States and elsewhere. Part 2 describes medical activities from the perspectives of physicians and others from the United States, Great Britain, Australia, Cambodia, and India. Part 3 describes public-health (from epidemiology to family planning), nutrition, and education activities. Part 4 describes relief activities for populations other than the Cambodians in the Thai camps: those Cambodians remaining in Cambodia, poor Thai villagers, Cambodians who had emigrated to third countries. Part 5 puts the relief operation in the context of other relief operations and develops the concept of an "institutional memory" to preserve the lessons learned in such situations for improved responses to such crises in the future. Part 6 is an epilogue that brings the status of the relief operation and life in the Thai and border camps and inside Cambodia up to date.

We are aware that there are some gaps and some overlaps in our account. We have attempted to minimize these to the extent feasible. In reality, however, the relief operation itself had both gaps and overlaps, and to present it otherwise would be misleadingly simplistic. We also recognize that the book tends to emphasize the relief activities in the holding centers inside Thailand more than it does the important activities on the Thai-Cambodian border and those within Cambodia itself. We acknowledge that the book places much emphasis on the role of the United States in the relief operation, reflecting both the major part our country played in it and our own more numerous contacts with the American relief community.

In addition to describing the relief operation, an underlying purpose of the publication of this book is to motivate—and inspire—health professionals to participate in such activities in the future. Such activities require both knowledge and commitment, and one of the aims of the book is to generate the commitment to assure that critical needs are met. We wish that such relief operations would not be necessary—and perhaps someday they will not be. But man-made and natural disasters have actually increased in recent years, making our understanding of the needs and appropriate responses to such situations all the more important.

The Chinese word for crisis has two characters: one stands

for danger, and the other for opportunity. Clearly the relief operation reflected the dangerous period during the previous Pol Pot regime and the continuing dangers that Cambodians faced in Cambodia, on the border, and even to some extent in Thailand and third countries. But equally clearly, the relief operation reflected opportunity—opportunity for people from around the world to join together in relieving the suffering and meeting the desperate needs of the Cambodian people.

This sense of a shared humanity was strongly experienced by most expatriates who participated in the relief operation and by many of the Cambodians themselves. A final purpose of this book is to re-create—regenerate—that shared humanity, evident in such crisis situations, and to use it to improve the quality of life on this planet.

B.S.L.

ACKNOWLEDGMENTS

The development of this book has been a very complex task, necessitating the assistance, cooperation, and support of many. We wish, first of all, to convey our deep gratitude and to acknowledge all those whose written contributions appear in its pages and to thank them for their willingness to have their writings edited and condensed to fit the format of this book. We are also grateful for the assistance of many other people, including some who wrote draft chapters for us that we were unable to use for lack of space.

We gratefully acknowledge Richard Koffler, President of the Associated Faculty Press, for his expert advice and guidance in condensing and improving the structure of the original manuscript, and his assistance and encouragement throughout the long process of bringing this manuscript to publication. We also express our deep appreciation to Mrs. Elizabeth Bigelow, who performed outstanding work in copy-editing the manuscript.

Marion Dorscheimer typed, modified, and remodified the text on word-processing equipment, and we thank her for her outstanding and untiring work. We also wish to acknowledge the additional secretarial support of Pam Brown, Laura Ugrinow, Elizabeth Allen, Terry Perry, Marcia Knoll, and Nagwa Abou-Seif, and the support of Patricia Dillon.

John H. Bryant, Bruce Wilcox, Florette Rechnitz Koffler, Robert M. Davis, Damaris Kirschoffer, Janet Yang, and P'ing Collis reviewed the manuscript in draft form and deserve our deep thanks for their helpful and perceptive comments and suggestions. We are grateful to Jerrold Hickey and Datus C. Smith, Jr., who gave helpful advice; to Sue Morton, who provided much background information; and Connie Schick, who translated two chapters from French, their original language. We are highly indebted to the International Rescue Committee and the American Refugee Committee, with whom we served in Thailand. We also acknowledge Randy McNamara, Joan Holmes, Chan Thy Yi, Lim Huy, Lim Ang, and Sue Campbell.

B.S.L. especially acknowledges Nancy, Laura, and Benjamin Levy, Bernice and Jerome Levy, Robin J. O. Catlin, N. Lynn Eckhert, and Werner Erhard; and D.C.S. especially acknowledges Kathryn and John Susott and David DiPietro for their support, guidance, and inspiration.

HISTORICAL CONTEXT AND BRIEF OVERVIEW OF THE RELIEF OPERATION

Barry S. Levy and Daniel C. Susott

Civilization in Cambodia began thousands of years ago, although written records exist only for the past two thousand years. Its ancient temples reflect an advanced civilization with an intriguing culture and magnificent art. Bridging Southeast Asia between India and China, Cambodia was greatly influenced by these two other cultures. Over hundreds of years, there were numerous wars among the countries now known as Thailand, Vietnam, and Cambodia.

In the mid-19th century, Cambodia became a colony of France and remained so until 1953, when it won its independence. From then until 1970, Prince Norodom Sihanouk was chief of state and managed to maintain the nation's political neutrality among the superpowers. During the late 1960s, the Vietnam War increasingly encroached on Cambodian territory, including aerial bombing, causing death and destruction as well as political instability.

In 1970, the Sihanouk government was overthrown and was replaced by a pro-Western government headed by Lon Nol. In the ensuing five years, the forces of the Communist Khmer Rouge led by Pol Pot gained increasing power. Finally, in April 1975, the Khmer Rouge toppled the Lon Nol government. They renamed the country "Democratic Kampuchea," or the "People's Republic of Kampuchea." [We, the editors, use the more traditional name of Cambodia, but we respect the right of others, including the contributors to this volume, to use the name of their choice.]

Within days, the Pol Pot regime emptied the cities in an attempt to return the nation to a more primitive condition, free of "parasitic," foreign, and modern elements. In the process, anything and anyone representing present-day civilization—particularly Western civilization—was destroyed. Thousands of people died at the hands of the Khmer Rouge troops for such "crimes" as wearing eyeglasses or a wrist watch,

Hongly Khuy, John J. Naponick, and the ICRC supplied some of the information for this chapter.

symbols to the Khmer Rouge of Western civilization. Others were murdered after having been falsely accused of being Western spies.

During the next four years, much of Cambodia was, in effect, a forced-labor camp. Everyone—young and old, healthy and sick—was compelled to work, usually in the fields with primitive farming techniques. They had very little to eat, marginal housing and clothing, poor sanitation, and virtually no medical or health-care services. During this period, it is estimated that approximately two million of Cambodia's eight million people died—as a result of murder, disease, and starvation.

In late 1978, the Vietnamese army invaded Cambodia, ostensibly to protect the security of their border. They overwhelmed the Khmer Rouge and installed a new government under the leadership of Heng Samrin. People could now freely leave the communes where they had been enslaved and seek their lost families, homes, and villages. Hundreds of thousands of Cambodians fled to the Thai border in hope of finding refuge there. The Khmer Rouge troops in disarray also headed west. They took shelter in the jungles of western Cambodia, where many of them remain, some 30,000 strong at the time of this writing—January 1986.

In 1979, Cambodia was in a state of devastation. Although the Vietnamese had overthrown the Khmer Rouge, the country remained in a desperate condiiton. Warfare and social upheaval had prevented the planting and harvesting of the rice crop and a major famine loomed. Only a massive and immediate relief effort could avert further catastrophe.

Thailand, itself a developing nation with a population of close to 50 million, had already experienced several waves of refugees. In 1944, about 70,000 Vietnamese had fled into one of its northeast provinces. In the late 1940s, Chiang Kai-shek's irregular Chinese army troops moved into northern Thailand following their expulsion from China by the Communists; they are still living there. In 1954, another wave of Vietnamese refugees reached Thailand after the Communists overtook the French at Dien Bien Phu; they, too, remained there, becoming somewhat—but not completely—integrated into Thai society.

In 1975, there was a large influx of refugees into Thailand with the fall of the governments of South Vietnam, Cambodia, and Laos to Communist regimes. Almost half a million people, mostly Laotians, fled from their native land and were accommodated in 24 camps in Thailand along the north and northeastern border. These people were gradually resettled in third countries under the coordination of the United Nations High Commissioner for Refugees (UNHCR) and the cooperation of these countries, mostly in North America and Europe.

During May 1979, more than 40,000 Cambodians fled into southeastern Thailand at Kao Larn. In June, some 40,000 Cambodians were forcibly returned to their native land by the Thai military at Preah Vihear. In September and October, another 50,000 Cambodian refugees arrived near Ta Praya, north of Aranyaprathet.

The relief operation, discussed in this book, consisted of medical, public-health, and development activities. It was coordinated primarily by the International Committee of the Red Cross (ICRC) and the United Nations Children's Fund (UNICEF), in close collaboration with the Food and Agriculture Organization of the United Nations (FAO), the World Food Program (WFP), and the United Nations High Commissioner for Refugees (UNHCR). These agencies, in turn, enlisted the participation of many private voluntary organizations from around the world. The operation itself took place under the supervision of the Thai military.

The relief operation had two related parts: (1) a joint ICRC/UNICEF mission to provide assistance to those in Cambodia; and (2) a coordinated emergency relief and medical effort for the thousands of Cambodians gathered along the Thai border. ICRC also undertook its traditional protective activities, such as tracing lost relatives and visiting prisoners, and the Thai government asked UNHCR to establish holding centers for the care and maintenance of those Cambodians who were permitted to cross from the border deeper into Thailand. The two largest of these holding centers opened in the fall of 1979. Sa Kaeo opened on October 24 and by the spring of 1980 accommodated some 30,000 Cambodians; Khao I Dang opened on November 21 and accommodated up to 150,000 by the spring of 1980. Overall, about 1.5 million Cambodians received assistance at the Thai-Cambodian border. Most returned to Cambodia but many remained in border camps.

In April 1980, at the height of the relief operation, more than 150,000 Cambodians—considered to be "illegal immigrants" by the Thais—were in holding centers. In addition, at this time, there were more than 160,000 Cambodians living in camps on the border and another 900,000 or more were regularly coming to the border for assistance.

As of early 1984, approximately 100,000 still remained in these border camps. Between 1979 and 1984, approximately 200,000 received care and protection in the holding centers (refugee camps) in Thailand. Between 1975 and mid-1983, more than 350,000 refugees who had fled to Thailand from Cambodia, Laos, and Vietnam had been resettled in third countries. About 189,000 of these refugees were Laotian, 120,000 Cambodian, and 44,000 Vietnamese.

Eighty thousand Thai people along the Thai-Cambodian border have been directly affected by the border warfare, the influx of refugees, and the subsequent relief operation. Some of these people have been uprooted from their homes. Many others have been less directly affected.

Within Cambodia, where approximately five to six million people have remained, relief has been undertaken by several voluntary organizations from Western nations and by groups from the Soviet Union and Eastern European countries. Massive relief in the first half of 1980 helped to avert a serious famine. The Vietnamese army, numbering approximately 200,000 troops, has continued to occupy the land.

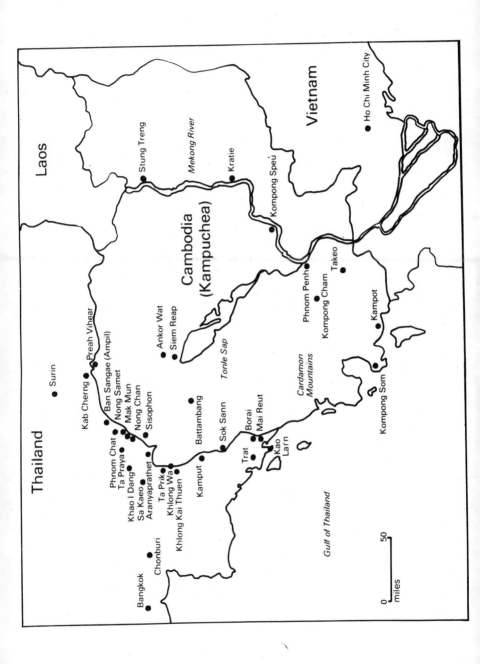

When I don't know who I am, I serve you.
When I know who I am, I am you.

—*The Ramayana*

PART 1

OVERVIEW

ONE PERSON'S STORY

Seang M. Seng

Death. It seems like every part of my story ends in death. I'm sorry.

In 1975, I was a fourth-year medical student at the Faculty [School] of Medicine at the University of Phnom Penh. I was raised in a very poor family. My father had left his parents when he was 2 or 3 years old to stay with a neighbor. My mother grew up in a village close to Phnom Penh and she was "middle class." But after they got married they were really poor. They moved to Phnom Penh when I was 5 years old. My father had a grocery store then. My mother and whole family worked in the store. We were 6 siblings, 5 sisters and me the only boy.

Most of my father's side of the family were rich, unlike my parents. So they didn't communicate regularly, only once or twice a year. One of them was doing business with the government, and another was responsible for forests on one side of Cambodia. My father always taught me to depend on myself.

Seang M. Seng, a Cambodian, was a physician's assistant and translator at Khao I Dang from November 1979 to July 1980. He is currently a second-year medical student at the University of Hawaii in Honolulu.

3

I knew all of my mother's family. By 1970, our family business was doing well, and I would say that by then we were "middle class." Almost all of my mother's ten siblings depended on our family. My mother's parents and some of her sisters worked in our family business. I worked for my family until I started medical school in 1970; my father wanted me to focus then on my studies. My sister Sy married a man who was a secretary to the Interior Minister. They had a boy and a girl, who were born right before the Communists came into power.

On April 16, 1975, I was on duty in Monivong Hospital, an army hospital. They called upon the students to help the army. There was so much shelling that the school was closed. I had been on duty every other night since the medical school closed in January, though I was not in the army. That night the shelling was so terrible that I did not want to stay in the hospital; the ambulance took me home. Early the next morning, I told my parents I wanted to visit the hospital to help in case they had a lot of emergency cases coming in. As I walked out at 8 or 9 o'clock, I saw a lot of people showing white flags, hoping that peace would be coming. I too thought the war was over.

As I walked on the road to the hospital, I saw some Khmer Rouge banging cars into trees; they didn't know how to drive. Many people were standing outside, but their houses were closed. Before I got to the hospital, I saw Khmer Rouge soldiers shooting open the door of a grocery store and then carrying out food and wine—especially wine—and putting it on a truck. I thought this was very strange since I had heard that the Khmer Rouge were very disciplined, and this was not discipline at all.

When I got to the hospital and spoke with the nurses who were on duty with me the night before, they told me that the Khmer Rouge asked us to move everybody out of the hospital. There was no movement yet, and I thought this was very strange. On the way home, I saw that people were beginning to move out of the city. When I got home I told my family, "We have to move out." We packed what we could into the car and moved out to the house of my uncle, one of my mother's brothers who was a controller in the financial ministry. We all considered him well-educated; he was the only one in the family in government office. He believed that the Khmer Rouge were not going to harm us and that we should go back to Phnom Penh. He knew one family related to the Khmer Rouge, and for this reason we were able to live within 18 kilometers of Phnom Penh.

On the road it was like the movies, a million people fleeing at one time, everything going crazy. Tanks were moving in front of us; we had to move to the side for the tank would not stop for us. And I saw people from the hospital in wheeled beds, with intravenous fluid hanging, their families pushing them along. Some of these people died along the way. There was no time to bury them. I saw about five or six bodies when I moved to the side of the road, usually though I stayed in the middle of the crowd. One of my friends covered his car with the Red Cross flag, thinking the Khmer Rouge would not harm him, but I think they took his car. I was with my family all this time. There were 24 of us, all following my uncle. All that we thought to bring with us was rice; my father also brought out money and gold. During the evacuation we bargained for food. Normally, a pound of meat cost 3 or 4 riels, but then it cost around 1000 riels. After the evacuation, there was no more trade. It took us about a week to cover the 18 kilometers to our destination. When two million people walk, you cannot go fast; also my uncle said to move slowly so we could stay closer to the city.

During the first 3 months, we didn't work much, but filled out the forms and attended political meetings telling us that Angka would take care. About 3 months later, we were pushed out; the Khmer Rouge asked us to tell what we did in the Lon Nol government. My brother-in-law said he was in the Interior Ministry; they took him away. We never saw him again. I guess they killed him.

My uncle was happy when he heard that we would move after 3 months, but I thought it was strange that we had heard nothing from my brother-in-law. But I was happy to move, since I couldn't stand those people where we had been living; they always called my family Chinese since we had pale skin. I thought it would be better somewhere else. My father told people that he did not want to stay there and that we should go to Vietnam. But my mother wanted to stay with her parents, and they all listened to my uncle. Much later we learned that all people who went to Vietnam survived. But we stayed in Cambodia. If all of us had believed my father, my family would still be alive today.

After 3 months, we were put onto trucks and moved to Battambang province. We were only told to pack our belongings and meet at a certain point. Then we were loaded into 13 trucks and moved. My family was still all together, except for my brother-in-law who had been taken away. When finally they dropped us in Battambang, they told us to go through a small path on the other side of the highway. We knew that we would be isolated from other people. The area was very far away from the highway, and nobody stayed there before. They asked us to build our house, and we built a small hut, and a couple of days later they moved us again, saying they would use these houses for the people who came later. They moved us a step at a time farther and farther away from civilization. I think I built huts for my family at least six times, but we never had a chance to stay there for longer than 2 or 3 months. I believe about 30,000 "new people" from the cities were resettled in this region.

At that time I had not done physical labor. I had a bag of medicine which my father had somehow hidden along with my stethoscope and blood pressure cuff. I was trying to help some people. They gave me rice in exchange. In those first few months, the Khmer Rouge were not really strict about forcing people to work, since there was movement of a lot of people going in and out. I did my "business" in secret, and there was a great deal of trust among the "new people"; nobody tried to report that kind of activity. But later on, I ran short of medicine, and wanted to save a little of it for my family, so I went to work.

I met a former law student who was related to the Khmer Rouge of that area. Since most of the Khmer Rouge were illiterate, he was chosen to write down the names and keep track of the people who worked, including how many were in their families, so that the workers could receive rice. Sometimes I stood in line two or three times, and he allowed it; I think we had a good understanding. So for a while we got enough rice. But later when the Khmer Rouge got to know us they did the distribution themselves, and that was over.

After that, they began to divide us into groups. We teenagers were separated from our families and sent to work far away. All of my sisters, except the oldest who had two children, had to leave the village. So I wouldn't be sent out too, I told them that my sister was my wife and the two children were mine. So I was able to stay in the village with my parents.

In only about 6 months, things fell apart. Starvation came. When food became desperately scarce, I felt that we did not need to feed the smallest children. My niece, born just before the Khmer Rouge took power, was only a few months old. My sister ran out of milk, and when food got scarcer and scarcer, there was little for my niece to eat.

The place where we were forced to stay was really bad. Even water was hard to find, and there was almost nothing edible. The rice field was not yet ready, so all we had was what the Angka gave us, one can of rice for one person. My youngest niece died first. I felt that she ate a lot, and I was sort of jealous. And I felt that no matter what we fed the baby, she would die anyway. It was a terrible decision, but I thought maybe we could save some food for the older one, whom I really cared about. I was relieved when the baby died because she had cried all the time because she had always been hungry.

As for the older child, Vimol, one day I was working as a food supplier in the fields far from the village, and I felt that if I could bring him with me he would have more food than the other people, since he would not have to do anything but stay around the kitchen. I took him there. He was really smart, and he quickly learned to call me "Daddy" and people thought he was my son. But in only 2 days, he began to have diarrhea. He knew that that I had medicine and he begged me to give him a shot. He was 3 or 4 years old. He said if I gave him a shot the diarrhea would go away. I told him it was hard for me if he kept having diarrhea, for if I couldn't work they'd send me back to the village and we'd have no food to eat. I really pitied him. I put him on my back, and on the long walk back his chin kept digging into my shoulder and it hurt me and I told him to stop but it kept pressing into my shoulder. I dropped him off roughly and began to scold him. But, oh God. He could not lift his head up. He was too weak. I had not realized this. He was sort of paralyzed. I brought him home, and then I had to go back to work, 10 miles away. After 2 or 3 days, I was allowed to come back to see him. But by the time I came, he sort of became another person. He was so thin. I could not recognize him. My sister had a wound on her leg and could not even take care of herself, let alone my nephew. I found a fish for him and put it into his hand for him to eat, but later that day he died, with the fish still in his little hand. I can't remember this without crying.

I heard from my other sisters once in a while. One of my sisters, the second one, tried to come home. They caught her. They tied her up for one day in the sun. I went to see her. She was swollen. I cry whenever I remember. Her name was Soeur. I heard later from my friend that she died. This was 1975: Christmastime—that's how I remember it. They had a hospital for the teens, and would not send her to the one in the village, or I could have seen her again before she died.

My oldest sister was one of the last of my immediate family to die. She was so skinny when I went to see her in the hospital. My mother had had two pendants worth about a million riels each. One she traded for three cups of rice. The other she gave to my sister. She called me to the hospital, and said, "I'm going to die soon. I don't want them to pick through my things or bother my body after my death, so I want you to have this pendant and Buddha." Amazingly, the next day she died. It's kind of sad when you know you are going to die. I still have that pendant.

I can hardly bear to remember the deaths of my parents. The last time I saw my mother her chest was flat as if she had TB. I stared at her, thinking, "Mom, you have changed so much!" I felt very sorry for her. I tried not to cry. Somehow, my tears flowed out incessantly. My mom begged me to stay and share her meager rice soup with her. At first, I resisted, not wanting to deprive her of extra nourishment. But then I relented and stayed. It was the last time I saw her. I often think of my dad, his dry skin and his fleshless body. He was so emaciated that his cheek bones protruded and his temples were sunken. On looking at his face, I couldn't tell if he laughed or cried. . . .

Within only 16 months of the Khmer Rouge takeover, all members of my family had starved to death except me and my younger sister, Sam Ang, who was 12 years old. We both were left behind in a world with no personal belongings, no radio, no papers, no free communication, no school, no money, no market, no religion, no human rights. Later, Sam Ang and I became separated. I heard that she had joined the teenagers' group in the rice fields. I never saw her again. Her group was moved too far away from my place. I heard she was put in the hospital once. And that was it. [See Seang M. Seng's later brief chapter on hospitals during the Pol Pot regime.]

After my family died I stayed alone. I had only a hammock

and a mattress. The emotion is so strong. I sometimes tell myself I'll write it all sometime, but each time I start, the emotion is too strong. Everything comes at one time in my mind. First I want to write, then my mind slips to something else.

After the Vietnamese pushed the Khmer Rouge out of power in January, 1979, I went back to the city, and first thing I went to see how many of my family was left. We had been separated in the early months of the Pol Pot years, and I found most of my mother's family in the suburbs. Then I heard that a couple of my friends went to work at the French hospital, Calmette. My friend Mituna was working there as a surgeon, and I had a wound on my hand and asked him for some penicillin. I got a few pills, and decided to work with the Vietnamese, since my friend said it was not too bad, and besides it had been so long since I practiced medicine.

On the first day I went to work in the hospital (known as the "Chinese Hospital" during the Lon Nol times but now they changed the name to "17 January" Hospital), they asked me to be in charge of about 100 beds. I was in charge alone there by myself, and it was so scary since it had been 5 years since I had held a book. I went all around trying to find books, first to the Russian hospital and finally to my old house. All my medical books were there, but the window was open and they were all damaged by weather over the years, and unusable. My mattress was torn—I don't know what they were looking for—and, of course, everything of value was gone from the house. But I did find the picture of my mother, now my most precious possession.

It was really spooky to be in Phnom Penh then (July 1979). The city was still really empty. I went to visit the medical school. When I got there, I saw that it was painted red. I was alone in the school and I opened the door like I always did before. I saw all the bulletin boards, empty with no paper on them, and I remembered that was the place we always gathered to see our scores—who did well and who poorly. It was a weird feeling, so empty.

I was transferred to the out-patient department, where we saw over 100 patients a day, with two doctors in charge. Medicines were limited, for example, only six pills of antibio-tics were allowed per prescription. This was controlled by the government; medications were free, though limited. Most of the patients who came to us were swollen and had complications of starvation. The hospital had neither enough food nor enough beds. Some patients had to lie on the floor, or even outside the hospital. Sometimes when the patients overwhelmed the hospi-tal, I put two beds together to sleep three patients. The families of the patients wanted to stay with them, making it even more crowded.

I worked there for 4 months. I did not have an idea to leave the country when I started that job. I thought that if the medi-cal school opened then I would go back to school. But it seemed that the people who controlled the hospital knew nothing about medicine. For example, the woman in charge spoke Cambodian, but her accent was Vietnamese. And she controlled our every action. I also felt very limited by them. A couple of my friends moved out to go to the border. Then I heard a rumor that the school of medicine would not open in Phnom Penh, but they would sent us to Russia or North Vietnam to finish the degree.

Then one of my patients, when I asked him to return for more pills the next day, told me no, he could not. He had to go to the border. I asked how and he said, "By bike." And I thought, "My God, from Phnom Penh to the border by bike?" I asked him if he would take me along. He said he could. On the border, at Camp 007, they needed a lot of doc-tors, and he told me one whom I knew who was there—a fifth-year medical student, Puk Saradath. I thought I would have more freedom than staying in Phnom Penh. That was Sunday, and all the medical students had to visit Tuol Sleng, the school that had been turned into a Khmer Rouge execution and torture center. I took that opportunity to leave with that guy early in the morning, on 18 November at 5 a.m. My new wife, Kimly, asked permission of her parents and she came with me. My aunt gave me the bike, and Kimly's mom gave me a necklace, a part of which we cut to spend for rice on the way to the border. We still have the part left over.

At the border, I met two classmates, Song and Chamnam, who had been there 2 or 3 weeks earlier. Dr. Song worked for the Australian medical team. At the border, we had to buy a house, but we had no money. Luckily, that was the day they started to move people to Khao I Dang, so we only stayed in 007 for a few hours, not even one night. We attached ourselves to a group of 12 or so people who had small malnourished children who were among the first admitted to Khao I Dang. So we all came together. When we got to Khao I Dang, my friend already had a job with the Australian doctors, and although I did not speak English I wanted to work with the Americans. So on my second day there, I went to work with the American Refugee Committee.

The presence of the international teams made me feel safe and comfortable. The waving of the UNHCR flags had replaced the flickering light of the torches, under which we were condemned to work and starve. Eyes full of meanness, glaring at us every second, had been replaced by eyes full of tears of compassion, ready to help and to provide us care. It was the time we all felt that the nightmare, at last, was going to end.

A PERSPECTIVE ON THE START OF
THE RELIEF OPERATION

Robert C. Porter, Jr.

The Thai-Cambodian border was deceptively quiet in August
1979. The Khmer in the old UNHCR refugee camp in Aranyaprathet (Aran) spoke furtively about new and growing, but
still small, military and civilian encampments along the border
several kilometers to the north. In these border camps, there
was hesitancy among the occupants to approach any closer to
Thailand. Fearing a forcible repatriation, such as had occurred
earlier in June at Preah Vihear, most sought only the food,
medicine, and security these camps seemed to offer. Throughout the late summer of 1979, there was a fairly regular secret
movement of refugees between the border camps and the
Aran camp. There were also very small clusters of Khmer civilians and military along Cambodia's northern border with
Thailand.

Robert C. Porter, Jr., worked from August 1979 to February 1980, monitoring the
Cambodian refugee situation and relief operation, particularly activities involving
United States Government funds. He is now a Foreign Service Officer with the State
Department of the United States, assigned to the United States Embassy in Bangkok.
His statements do not necessarily reflect the American government's policy, posi-
tions, or views.

Another deceptively quiet world existed to the south of Aran stretching through the rugged mountains to the Gulf of Thailand. The remnants of the Khmer Rouge army and support groups, as well as any civilian population they could drag along, had retreated to this area following the Vietnamese consolidation of its position in Cambodia during the first half of 1979. In April of that year, the world got a glimpse of what was developing on the Khmer side of the border when a large, decrepit group of Khmer civilians passed through Thai territory escorted by Khmer Rouge soldiers on the run from one village to another.

In August and September 1979, the Khmer Rouge and those civilians living with them were slowly running out of food and medicine. They were decimated by malaria and other diseases. They had been living on severely reduced rations since their retreat to the border and consequently were readily susceptible to disease.

Visitors to Thai border villages at Borai and Ban Laem in September encountered small numbers of Khmer civilians in deplorable condition, who were being temporarily fed and housed at police stations. The sustenance they received from the local authorities was minimal, but at least it was better than that in the areas of Cambodia which they had just left. These were Khmer civilians who could no longer take the deprivation and suffering of life in the border areas still controlled by the Khmer Rouge; they had cast caution aside and fled. Suffering in many cases from severe malnutrition and malaria, they were like animals whose only thought was to find food. They were a warning of things to come.

During one of my visits to Ban Laem to check on a group suffering from malnutrition and malaria, a pudgy, alert Khmer man, with a gold tooth and dressed in the new black clothes characteristic of the Khmer Rouge, approached me. His healthy appearance, which contrasted sharply with that of the suffering crowds around him, made me feel uncomfortable; I walked away. Later, a group of Khmer who had taken refuge there told me that he was a Khmer Rouge official. In the succeeding three months, it became apparent that Khmer Rouge officials and soldiers had first priority in the distribution of food and medical supplies, that a certain portion was kept in reserve for emergencies, and that only then did civilians and support people receive a share. Since there frequently was not enough to go around, such low-priority groups as the sick, the elderly, and the weak suffered greatly.

Throughout the summer of 1979, reliable observers believed that a group of 1,700 mostly unaccompanied minors and former students, was located on the Khmer side of the border in the Borai district, far south of Aranyaprathet. They originally had crossed the border north of Aran and on April 12 had been involuntarily repatriated to a malaria-infested jungle surrounded by Khmer Rouge camps. One of my tasks at the time was to find out what had happened to this group and to determine whether it had enough food. I had no luck. Much later, I found out that most of them had died of starvation and malaria.

The eerie calm on the Thai side of the border continued into the early autumn of 1979, but one began to become aware of the movement of people on the other side of the border and the increasingly obvious signs of the developing crisis. The only foreigners known to me to be working on the Thai-Kampuchean border at this time were several missionaries and a few voluntary-agency people, including Robert Ashe, and me. There should have been more.

The sole UNHCR field officer had left the border during the spring of 1979 following a disagreement with Thai officials. Although UNHCR personnel occasionally visited the area, no one person worked there regularly until the arrival of Mark Brown in September. The ICRC, which had provided food and medicine for an estimated 40,000 refugees at Nong Chan and Ta Praya in May 1979, had suspended its operations on the border on June 13 after filing a protest with the Thai government about the forced repatriation of more than 40,000 refugees at Preah Vihear during the preceding five days.

Throughout 1979, it became increasingly clear to informed observers that the Vietnamese invasion and occupation of Cambodia had unleashed a massive migration of people within the country. Preoccupied with chasing the remnants of Pol Pot's army and establishing an occupation administration, the Vietnamese allowed people to move relatively freely, and most Khmer seized the opportunity to return to their home villages, search for lost relatives, and dig up hidden valuables.

The Vietnamese invasion in December 1978 had virtually halted the harvest of the major annual rice crop, and very little of the normal rice crop had been planted during the turmoil that followed. Severe food shortages developed during 1979. As more and more information became available, many began to speak of the situation with concern. In April 1979, United States Secretary of State Cyrus S. Vance testified before a Congressional committee on the likelihood of Cambodian food shortages. In July, an ICRC/UNICEF mission visited Cambodia and reported conditions of "extreme deprivation."

Realizing that they might well starve if they remained within Cambodia, many Khmer took advantage of the relative freedom and moved westward toward Thailand to seek food, medicine, and security. Others—particularly the urban educated, the former civil servants, and members of the middle class who had suffered so much under the Pol Pot regime and who now felt they would repeat their suffering and not be allowed to live and work the way they wanted in Cambodia under Vietnamese Communist domination—also took advantage of the chance to move toward Thailand; they hoped to be resettled abroad.

The majority of Khmer, moving westward, headed for border areas not under Khmer Rouge control, and clustered there during the summer and fall. These camps soon grew into the massive "cities"—with an estimated population of half a million or more, including a good representation of Cambodian's former urban, educated, official, and middle classes.

Many of these areas were dominated initially by Khmer warlords and pirates engaged in cross-border trade, as well as by a few genuinely nationalistic Khmer who hoped to organize groups to resist the Vietnamese occupation of their country. In search of relative security, the migrating Khmer gravitated toward these encampments, and as the famine spread within Cambodia, they grew rapidly into large population clusters. Their growth was facilitated and fed by the massive amounts of emergency relief pumped into the border area. Food was a powerful tool in the hands of the Khmer. Despite efforts of the international donor countries and the international organizations to oppose such improper use of relief supplies, the warlords and fledgling resistance leaders used international relief to build popular support for their groups, as well as to feed their soldiers.

The Thai attitude at this time was one of extreme caution, and there was no desire to get involved in what was happening on the opposite side of the border. In the past, under the Pol Pot regime, Thailand had had serious border problems. In 1979, Khmer refugees living on the border began to steal food and other items from Thai villages close to the border. Small-scale fighting between Vietnamese and Khmer forces frequently caused damage to Thai villages in the area. With Vietnamese troops so near, the Thai government hoped that it could keep its side of the border peaceful. Moreover, Thailand's international image had suffered because of media coverage of the forced repatriation at Preah Vihear in June. Thai officials believed that the fewer outsiders who knew about the situation on the border, the better.

There were exceptions to this approach. After October 24, 1979, Thailand allowed Khmer to cross the border for "temporary asylum" in specially designated UNHCR-administered holding centers. The first group comprised almost 30,000 Khmer from the Khmer Rouge-held areas south of Aran. One month later, more than 120,000 Khmer from the non-Khmer Rouge areas north of Aran entered. As in other countries, it took time for Thailand to develop a clear policy to respond to the emerging crisis. The early attitude of some Thai officials could make life difficult for those in the international community whose task it was to locate Khmer in need of food, medicine, and security. One could drive along border roads and be told by Thai officials that there were no refugee encampments anywhere nearby, only to be escorted to the same area the next day by another official who felt he could reveal the existence of a group of starving Khmer to a foreigner he trusted and knew. One began to appreciate the importance of cooperation and building good relationships with local officialdom.

Foreigners on the border often discovered the refugee encampments by chance or through a tip-off, occasionally from a Thai villager, but more often from Khmer in the UNHCR Aran camp. We were told of three border camps, and later located and visited them with the permission of the Thai military.

All the border camps continued to grow well into 1980. Throughout 1979 and part of 1980, Non Mak Mun (also known as the Old Camp, Reahou, or 204) turned into one of the most troublesome sites for both Khmer and foreign relief workers. It produced a strange assortment of leaders and residents. At least two Khmer claimed to be relatives of Prince Norodom Sihanouk. One—the notorious, babbling "mad prince," Souryawong—nominally acted as one of the camp leaders. He also seriously abused the camp residents, lined his own pockets with gold, and feuded with other Khmer camps in the area. (He reportedly was killed or returned to the Cambodian interior in 1980.)

By far, the most evil and harmful of the Khmer at Non Mak Mun was Van Saren. A warlord in the worse sense of the word, he had engaged in smuggling along the border for several years and had reportedly obtained Thai citizenship. His citizenship and his wealth allowed him to come and go at will. He had houses in the Thai villages of Aran and Non Mak Mun from where he became deeply involved in the cross-border flow of goods, especially gold and silver. In addition to his commercial interests, Van Saren also was the self-styled leader of the camp at Non Mak Mun. With a band of undisciplined armed brigands, he used the control of emergency relief supplied by Thailand and the international community to turn the camp into a major population and commercial center and to build up his bank account. A hot-tempered, unpleasant man with absurd delusions of grandeur, he continually threatened, harassed, and tried to absorb the other Khmer border camps around him. His motives were predominantly commercial. He wanted to control all the black-market trade in food, supplies, and precious metals. His unpredictability and continual feuding made life difficult for Thai and international relief officials, whom he occasionally threatened with death. His men once tried to drag away and kill my Khmer assistant, but fortunately were stopped by nearby Thai soldiers. (Van Saren later disappeared and reportedly was murdered during the consolidation of the border camps, but few people would be surprised if he were living in luxury somewhere outside of Cambodia.)

The Khmer camp at Nong Samet (also known as the New Camp, Rithysen, and 007) always held the most exotic fascination and excitement for me. Bad roads made it difficult to reach, but upon arrival one encountered what seemed like an endless mass of bustling humanity. A tall forest provided welcome shade. The stone ruins of an old Angkor-style Buddhist temple gave it a particularly Khmer air. While its early military leadership was among the more corrupt, disruptive, and despicable, the camp was usually well organized and tightly run. Astride one of the main trails to the Thai border, it had an interesting population and a lively market. For a time in 1979 and 1980, it was the most populous Cambodian city on earth, far surpassing the then reawakening but still tiny Phnom Penh.

After the involuntary repatriation in June 1979, the area around Nong Chan had remained quiet until September 1979. On a drive through the area in the middle of that month, however, a United States Embassy colleague of mine met an unassuming, rather frail Khmer named Chea Chhut. Chhut told my colleague that he and several hundred other Khmer had just moved to Nong Chan and wanted to start a new settlement that would have no market, be devoid of corruption and turmoil, and be dedicated to ridding Cambodia of all foreign troops (goals which later were changed or proved unattainable). Under constant harassment from the warlord leaders of neighboring camps, Nong Chan in 1979 and early 1980 developed into what many international relief workers considered to be the "best" (i.e., the least corrupt and troublesome) of the border camps. In part because it was a "better" camp, stood along a major trail to and from Cambodia, and by December 1979 had become the site of an informal "land bridge" set up by Robert Ashe and others to pump rice seed into northwestern Cambodia in time for planting, Nong Chan was chosen as a site for the international community's formal cross-border rice distribution programs.

In their effort to eliminate the Khmer Rouge, Vietnamese military units had gradually managed to cut the trails to the border in several places, thereby effectively blocking communication and shipment of supplies between Khmer Rouge positions. Many informed observers believe that because they were unable to provide for their soldiers and civilians and were under intense Vietnamese military pressure, the Khmer Rouge commanders in the area encouraged their civilians and debilitated soldiers to cross into Thailand. The Khmer Rouge leadership made this decision in order to preserve its remaining military and civilian strength in that area. The decision was a calculated risk that someone else would agree temporarily to assume the burden of caring for these people and that after they had recovered, they would be allowed to return to Cambodia to resume the fight against the Vietnamese.

(The Khmer Rouge were under so much pressure at the time that they really had no other choice. The decision, however, was to cause difficulties. While the more hard-core Khmer Rouge soldiers and cadre later did return to Cambodia, forcing a number of civilians to accompany them, a larger number ignored "orders" and physical abuse from the Khmer Rouge leadership and continued to reside in UNHCR camps in Thailand. Many of them now speak of their hopes for a Cambodia under Prince Sihanouk's leadership and without either the Khmer Rouge or the Vietnamese. Some have returned to Sihanouk and Son Sann border camps.)

Interviews in December 1982 with refugees who had crossed the border south of Aran in September and October 1979 indicate that Khmer Rouge cadre may have ordered Khmer Rouge soldiers and accompanying civilians to remain on the Cambodian side of the frontier, and some apparently were prevented from entering Thailand. A general breakdown in discipline, combined with desperation and determination to flee to safety on the part of so many Khmer who had been pushed to the limit of human endurance, made it nearly impossible for the Khmer Rouge cadre to prevent large numbers from crossing into Thailand.

The border first ruptured on October 10, 1979, near a cluster of houses called Khlong Wa, about 27 kilometers south of Aran, when several thousand Khmer entered Thai territory. As I re-call, it was Robert Ashe, head of a voluntary agency called Project Vietnam Orphans (PVO), later known as Christian Outreach (COR), who through his dedication to the welfare of the Khmer and his contacts with the Thai military, was among the first foreigners to discover the crowd at Khlong Wa. It was Robert Ashe and refugee workers from the United States Embassy who first followed up on the initial dis-coveries and helped to publicize the desperate condition of the Khmer and the need for emergency assistance to these and other Khmer along the border.

The first reaction of the Thai military was to contain the group at Khlong Wa and send them back to Cambodia as soon as it was safe, but the flow did not subside. Eleven days later, following a visit to Khlong Wa with his deputies, Thai Prime Minister Kriangsak Chomanan reversed the hard-line policy of sending the Khmer back, and for several weeks there-after the Thai allowed the Khmer to cross freely into Thailand in search of shelter, food, medicine, and security. Prime Minister Kriangsak said he made the decision to grant temporary refuge out of compassion for his fellow Buddhists and assurances from various foreign governments and organi-zations that Thailand would receive assistance in caring for the Khmer.

Within a week, more than 30,000 Khmer Rouge-controlled civilians and unarmed soldiers had crossed the border at Khlong Wa. A narrow stream formed the border, and on the Khmer side was a network of trails linking Khmer Rouge villages and camps to the north and south. A short time later, another 30,000 had crossed into Thailand to the south at Ta Prik, Khlong Kai Thuen, Ban Laem, and other points.

These were the Khmer who had been pushed to the most extreme forms of suffering. Ironically it was this group, among whom were Khmer Rouge probably responsible for the murder of thousands of Cambodians, that the media portrayed so graphically and who seized and held the sympathy of the Western world.

They came in all states of mind and condition. Some young men and women, looking suspiciously strong and healthy, would have made good soldiers for any army. The Thai and the few foreigners present along the border at this time were well aware of the extreme crimes committed by the Khmer Rouge during the previous four years and the possibility that Khmer Rouge soldiers were posing as refugees. It was, however, impossible to screen the group carefully, since people were dying in large numbers. It was also unclear at the time whether there were soldiers in the crowd, and it was the much, much larger group of seriously ill people around them who were our desperate concern.

The majority could hardly have looked worse. It was difficult to see how some had even had enough strength to cross the border at all. They were dying in front of us, emaciated, crying, covered with flies and body wastes, and oozing fluid from every orifice. There were shriveled-up, undersized babies with skin drooping from their buttocks, too weak to cry. They were held by mothers whose breasts had no milk to offer.

Among them were many children abandoned by or separated from their parents or Khmer Rouge production units. On the first day I saw one such boy of 14, obviously suffering from malnutrition and disease, wandering around aimlessly. When I asked him why he had not received any food during the distribution that day, he said that he was not a member of any "unit." I took him to a Khmer in charge of food distribution and asked that he be fed. A few days later, I encountered him again, this time with an even more distended stomach and swollen feet. He still had not been fed, so I took him to a Thai sergeant who immediately gave him food. During my next visit a week later, I ran into him again, only this time his eyes were swollen shut and the skin stretched across his stomach was a raw red color and looked as if it were going to burst. He still had not been picked up by the food-distribution system, and I wondered for a moment whether there was hope for any of us.

In the weeks that followed those first crossings at Khlong Wa and Khlong Kai Thuen, I roamed through the jungle and swamps along a 20-kilometer stretch of the border between Nong Pru and Khlong Kai Thuen in search of Khmer who were in danger of dying from starvation or disease but too weak to reach safety on their own. I had not been trained nor had I expected to do this kind of work, but I was obliged to do what I could in view of the nearly total absence of qualified personnel and the desperate condition of the tens of thousands of Khmer pouring into Thailand. I worked initially with Robert Ashe, my Khmer assistants (who included a former dean of students at Phnom Penh University, a former high-level Phnom Penh bank officer, and an ex-airplane mechanic, all of whom themselves had earlier found refuge in Thailand), and somewhat later the first small contingent of ICRC delegates to arrive at the border. Within a month and after the arrival of the ICRC contingent in full force and of hundreds of foreign volunteers and organizations, this work was taken over by experts.

What I encountered during those few weeks, however, was unforgettable. Every few hundred meters in any direction in the border area, we came upon individuals or groups of Khmer—mostly women—in various stages of dying. These "death camps" contained sick, injured, wounded, weak, or old people who, being no longer of use to the Khmer Rouge, had been abandoned by them as a drain on precious resources. Some groups seemed like patients in temporary hospital camps abandoned because the medics had run out of medicine.

Signs of Khmer Rouge inhumanity were everywhere. In

general, the civilians who had been living under Khmer Rouge control were completely emotionless and acted like robots. The Khmer Rouge discarded people who were in less than perfect health as if they were broken parts of a machine. They were left to fend for themselves. Most of those we came upon were too weak to move any farther. Many were dead when we discovered them lying by the trail. Many others were dying and too weak to chase the flies from their eyes, noses, and mouths. They died in front of us, as we carried them to the road, or on the way to the Thai hospital in Aran or later at the UNHCR holding center at Sa Kaeo.

Unable to cope with the large numbers of Khmer we encountered, we did not know which ones to move and which to leave behind. The kilometers seemed endless as we traversed the trails and fields with bodies slung on our backs or carried on stretchers. I was bothered by the fact that the nearby Thai villagers we encountered seemed so unconcerned and unhelpful, that we alone were the ones discovering all this, and that no one else was there to help. Later, as the ICRC staff grew, we were able to point out the locations of groups in need and to continue our search elsewhere, and it was not long before the ICRC had obtained as much access to the border as we had.

The ability of Robert Ashe and other voluntary agency personnel, the United States Embassy border staff, and later the ICRC to operate along the border in search of Khmer in need of assistance was due primarily to the cooperative and compassionate attitude of many individual local Thai military personnel of every rank. Both before and after Prime Minister Kriangsak's decision to open the border to the Khmer, one could sense a definite unease on the part of the Thai military with the presence of so many Khmer civilians and military on both sides of the border. It renewed one's faith in the basic humanity of mankind to encounter so many Thai soldiers who were willing to help the Khmer survive. Special credit is owed to those who in the early stages of the crisis risked their military careers by assisting when it was their government's policy not to do so.

North of Aran, a turbulent, desperate, and growing crowd of humanity was pressing against the Thai border. South of Aran, tens of thousands of ghostlike, dying people were suddenly straggling into Thai territory in flight from the strong Vietnamese military pressure. It was obvious to the Thai authorities, the officials of the United States Embassy, the staff of the voluntary agencies already operating in Thailand, and the few officials from international organizations then in Bangkok that a massive response from the international community would be needed to cope with the rapidly deteriorating situation.

OPERATING A UNITED NATIONS PROGRAM: A PERSONAL REFLECTION

Martin Barber

On the morning of October 22, 1979, a colonel in the Thai Supreme Command telephoned the UNHCR office in Bangkok and told me his government had decided to admit to Thailand 90,000 Khmers who were at that moment massed on the Kampuchean border south of Aranyaprathet. A site had been found a few miles from the small town of Sa Kaeo, and since the matter was urgent, the Supreme Command proposed to move them over a period of six days, starting in 48 hours. Would UNHCR kindly look after them in Sa Kaeo, in liaison with the local civilian and military authorities?

At the time, I was responsible for programming UNHCR's activities in Thailand and had been in Thailand for about 16 months. After the phone call, I sat still for several seconds, literally stunned, while images flashed through my mind. Then

---

Martin Barber was the Chief of the Regional Office Kampuchean Unit (ROKU) and then Deputy Regional Representative of the United Nations High Commissioner for Refugees from June 1978 to May 1981. He is currently Director of the British Refugee Council in London.

I went to the next office and told somebody, so that if something happened to me in the next five minutes, at least somebody else would know.

Thai government policy up to this point had been clear: No Kampucheans were to be allowed on Thai soil, since they were engaged in a civil war in which Thailand had no wish to become embroiled. Inevitably, however, over so long a border, individuals and small groups managed to cross undetected into Thailand, and a few had even reached Bangkok and walked into our offices.

In some border areas, government officials were reluctant to force back people in such a distressed condition, and this allowed time for temporary encampments to form where voluntary agencies were able to provide food, and contacts could be made with the various foreign embassies by those who believed they had relatives overseas. Since 1975, almost none of these people had had any contact whatsoever with relatives living outside Kampuchea.

During early 1979, the Thai government had gradually been persuaded to agree, on a case-by-case basis, that those Kampucheans whose departure from Thailand to third countries could be guaranteed within 30 days could be moved directly to transit centers in Bangkok, but nobody was allowed to stay on Thai soil longer than that 30 days.

After the forced repatriation of 1,800 Khmer by the Thai military in April and of a further 40,000 in June 1979, the Thai attitude toward those Kampucheans who managed to sneak into Thailand gradually relaxed. UNHCR was able to obtain guarantees of resettlement places, mainly in France and the United States, but all the time the number massing on the border was increasing.

In mid-September 1979, two colleagues and I were able to visit the two vast border encampments of Nong Samet and Non Mak Mun, where the number of new arrivals was growing daily, and also the area south of Aranyaprathet, where remnants of the Khmer Rouge in pitiful condition were spread out among the trees. During September, the Thai government held meetings with representatives of various international organizations and foreign embassies to discuss the situation and to advise them of plans to allow large-scale supplies of food to go through to the border. UNICEF and ICRC began to truck in large quantities. Thai Prime Minister Kriangsak Chomanan visited the border and was visibly moved by the suffering he witnessed. By early October, the Thai government was sufficiently confident of international support and internal acceptance of the need for a humanitarian policy to talk about admitting Kampucheans into holding centers on Thai soil. Initially it had seemed that the government would seek funds from international sources to build, equip, and run these centers itself. A telephone call on October 22 indicated that the Thai military believed this would be impractical, and wished UNHCR to do it—with the centers, of course, remaining under Thai administrative control.

Throughout the months of effort and worry that were to come, the memory of the 1,800 and the 40,000 forcibly repatriated Khmer would return, not really to haunt me but to act as a stimulus. I was determined, and I think most of my colleagues felt the same, to make sure that we did not fail those who now relied on our help.

The site that had been located for the 90,000 Khmer Rouge remnants was a disused rice field in a village called Ban Kaeng, near the small market town of Sa Kaeo, 60 kilometers west of the Kampuchean border. On October 22, we futilely searched our maps to find the location of Ban Kaeng. Within days, pictures of that field were being beamed to most of the television sets in the Western world. Rosalynn Carter, wife of the then President of the United States, came to see for herself [see her chapter, "When Statistics Become Human Beings"].

A year later, it was once again only another disused rice field.

When the first buses arrived, 48 hours after the telephone call, we had just had time to mobilize a basic food supply, the first elements of a temporary water supply and sewage system, and the material for the most basic shelter. Medical teams were converging from existing refugee camps around the country. Field hospital facilities were established for a thousand patients. The site at Sa Kaeo proved totally unsuitable. It was far too small and could not be drained. In the first few days of the operation, it rained heavily, and the Khmer lay in thick mud. The scenes were indescribable. Despite immediate medical help being available, for some it was too late, and on one day in the first week 40 people died.

In undertaking the operation which followed, we had several priceless advantages over situations in which many UNHCR offices have found themselves when faced with emergencies. First, and most important, we had a substantial UNHCR team already in Thailand, including a number of young Thai members on the field staff, who had been working on the program for Laotian and Vietnamese refugees. So when the telephone call came, I was able to call Mark Malloch Brown, our field officer in eastern Thailand, and he took charge of the field operation. I also called Glen Dunkley, our education officer, who was on an inspection trip to schools in northern Thailand, and he came to assist me at the Bangkok headquarters. I was then able to call our field officers in various other parts of the country and instruct them to proceed immediately to Sa Kaeo, and put themselves at the disposal of Mark Brown. Second, there were several voluntary agencies with teams working in existing refugee camps in Thailand that were able to transfer staff quickly from existing operations and to recruit reinforcements. Third, Thailand has an excellent network of roads and a commercial system whereby you can have almost anything delivered to any part of the country within a few days, if you have the money to pay for it.

Funding was not a problem; the sensational television coverage had ensured that. What was needed was people. In this operation, the most important element was the recruitment and organization of human resources. Those who work in the field, apart from those in purely technical jobs, need to be young. It became evident that the ideal age for those in positions of organizational responsibility in the holding centers was the late twenties. Previous relevant experience, more often than not, was a disadvantage. Repeatedly these young men and women showed that things could be done which more experienced heads had either not thought of or believed on the basis of past experience to be impossible. Young officials need older and more experienced advisers and technicians in a number of fields, but they need to be the ones in charge.

In the early days, the Khmer refugees at Sa Kaeo were too dazed and exhausted to do anything much to help themselves. We hired buses and moved up to one hundred volunteers a day from Bangkok: local people, tourists, students from the universities, wives of diplomats, and on the weekends, the diplomats themselves. They did anything and everything from passing out food to putting up tents, digging latrines, and removing the dead for burial. Some of these original volunteers stayed on and on, and eventually became UNHCR staff members.

When organizing an operation of this kind, it is tempting to spend a lot of time out in the field, checking that everything is all right. This is a mistake. One should go just often enough to be able to visualize and describe the situation in some detail, and otherwise only as often as the field staff feels it is useful. If things go wrong, one hears about it soon enough, and personal visits to "sort things out" are only rarely helpful .

Khao I Dang, the next camp to open in Thailand, was

everything that Sa Kaeo was not. The site, covering an area of 2.3 square kilometers on a gently sloping hill, had good drainage. It opened on November 21, 1979, after just four days of preparatory work spent in establishing the overall design of the camp and developing the basic infrastructure (roads, water tanks, and latrines) of the first "chunk." On the first day, 4,800 people arrived, and by December 31 there were 84,800. By mid-1980, the population had reached its maximum of 150,000.

The Kampucheans who entered Khao I Dang in the last six weeks of 1979 were in immeasurably better physical condition than those in Sa Kaeo. Shortages of food in Kampuchea had been patchy, and those caught in the Khmer Rouge retreat had suffered particularly severe privations. In Khao I Dang, a surprising number of well-educated people began to emerge who for four and a half years had hidden their identity from the Khmer Rouge. For them, the opening of Khao I Dang meant an extraordinary opportunity to express themselves freely after years of silence. It was, above all, a chance to read and write again.

Within hours of arriving in camp, which they were having to build themselves, a number of Khmers approached Mark Malloch Brown for permission to build a school. In Bangkok, we were fortunate to find a Thai educationalist who had a Khmer mother and could speak and read the language. The most exciting aspects of the program were the search for Khmer texts in libraries around the world; the rewriting from scratch by the Khmer themselves of Khmer language textbooks, all of which had been destroyed by the Khmer Rouge; and the art and essay competitions organized among the children, which exposed the horrific things going on in their minds.

It somehow always seems to be assumed that the people most needed to deal with disasters are doctors and nurses. This is rarely the case, and when it is, it usually is so for a relatively short time. If a refugee camp like Khao I Dang is established with adequate water, sanitation, shelter, an adequate supply of basic food, and a proficient preventive public health and hygiene program, then after two or three months there is no reason why it should need substantially more doctors and nurses than any other portion of the population. One of the most wasteful features of the whole relief effort was the enormous amount of money spent on flying in doctors and nurses from all parts of the world, many of whom were unable to find any work at all to do while others were not fully employed or at most provided services of peripheral importance. While the 140,000 Kampucheans in Khao I Dang were overwhelmed with medical attention, the five million people left in Kampuchea had virtually none. The political imperatives meant that a Kampuchean refugee could obtain the most sophisticated treatment free of charge, while his brother living in a village 50 miles away had to pay an exorbitant amount to buy an aspirin on the black market.

Almost as soon as the work in Sa Kaeo began, we created a special unit in the UNHCR office in Bangkok to deal with the new emergency. It was called the Regional Office Kampuchean Unit (ROKU), and I was appointed to head it. We believed that the work for Laotian and Vietnamese refugees in Thailand should continue with as little interruption as possible from this inevitably more glamorous new program. It was to ensure this that we established this separate unit.

The basic organizational plan which we developed was simple. Each holding center had its own UNHCR field officer who, within general policy guidelines, was in charge of everything that went on there in the name of UNHCR. He or she reported to me and my deputy in Bangkok. This worked reasonably well, except possibly in the procurement of supplies.

At the outset of the program, the needs were so desperate and unpredictable that the field officers were sent out literally with suitcases of banknotes, so that they could obtain supplies immediately and as close to the holding center as possible. When this phase passed, all substantial orders had to be channeled through the Bangkok office and obtained by the procurement officer in accordance with accepted United Nations procedures. This inevitably took more time, but our staff in the field did not have the experience to operate such a system locally. With hindsight, we should perhaps have moved more quickly to develop formal agreements with voluntary agencies to operate specific parts of the program on our behalf. It is unusual for UNHCR to be as directly "operational" as we were in this program, and given the systems within which the United Nations is obliged to work, it is normally preferable to operate through one or more "implementing partners." This gradually began to take shape as the program developed, and we concluded agreements with more than 20 different voluntary agencies to provide services ranging from food supply and nutritional work to education, vocational training, and welfare support for vulnerable groups.

Conditions of work were never easy in the centers for either the UNHCR or the voluntary-agency staffs. In Sa Kaeo, in particular, the presence of a number of Khmer Rouge cadres, keen to ensure the continued allegiance of even their most reluctant recruits, made the job of field officer in that center probably the most sensitive post of all, and one where we were obliged to change personnel every few months.

The question of "protection" was therefore a constant concern. We appointed one protection officer at the ROKU headquarters and several protection assistants working for the field officers in the centers. Under the constant threat of Khmer Rouge intimidation, Sa Kaeo was their toughest assignment.

The specialist officers in ROKU Bangkok, covering protection, health, education, construction, children's projects, procurement, finance, and personnel, were joined by two information officers and a consultant on disaster management. Information is a vital and often underrated commodity. We found it difficult to define clearly what the information officers' role should be. Naturally they were responsible for liaison with the press. If, however, the information officers were located in Bangkok, the press bypassed them and interviewed the harassed field officers in the centers; if the information officers were in the centers, then we in Bangkok were bedeviled with press queries and general inquiries from all sorts of sources. Embassies, voluntary agencies, academics, potential volunteers, Khmers with relatives in the camps, individuals writing from every corner of the earth, parents hoping to adopt a child—all these and many more required information regularly and quickly. In addition, information on the constantly developing situation in the field needed to be gathered and transmitted to UNHCR headquarters in Geneva and other UNHCR offices around the world. Full, accurate, and well-presented information is essential for successful fund raising as well as retaining public support. A substantive record of programs is also necessary for long-term evaluation and comparison. Being obliged to submit regular detailed reports on a variety of topics was one of the aspects of the work that the field officers, frequently exhausted by their operational responsibilities, found most difficult. Faced with the same situation again, I would look much more carefully from the start at the ways in which information can be gathered and disseminated more effectively.

Zia Rizvi, who arrived in Bangkok at the end of October 1979 and subsequently took overall control of UNHCR's entire operation in Southeast Asia, immediately retained as consultants for our Kampuchean program the firm of Intertect, experts in disaster management [see the chapter, "The Cambodian Border Relief Operation in the Context of Other Relief

Operations," by Frederick C. Cuny]. This proved to be a great asset. Nobody on our staff had ever been through anything like it before. The Intertect consultants did not tell us what to do, but they made us consider things that had been used in other disaster situations. Above all, Everett Ressler made us think through contingency plans. He developed scenarios that looked at three or four different sets of circumstances. There is a terrible temptation in an emergency situation to spend one's whole time dealing with the immediate problems at hand. There are always more than enough of those. What Everett ensured was that we were always considering what was to come next.

Under Zia Rizvi's overall supervision, my deputy, Glen Dunkley and I were directly responsible for the planning and programming of the operation. We also dealt directly with the concerned Thai government departments, other United Nations organizations, the ICRC, and the voluntary agencies. This was for us a natural decision, and ensured that we played a pivotal role between the field officers and all the other significant operational actors. There is a temptation to appoint liaison officers to deal with one or another group of participants. In my view this is a mistake, since the people being dealt with by a liaison officer are well aware that that person does not play a part in decision making. The people taking responsibility also need to be directly exposed to the views of all the key actors on how the operation is being run.

As the program developed, we gradually amended the basic structure we had established. Inevitably, it never satisfied everyone. An unprecedented number of staff were employed, backed up by a corps of volunteers and voluntary agency personnel, yet there were always calls for more.

THE EARLY DAYS OF SA KAEO: A NURSE'S EXPERIENCE

Ann Grosvenor-Rosenblatt

The day that Sa Kaeo opened—October 24, 1979—we stood about waiting for the 100 buses to arrive and unload so that we could scan the refugees and direct the ill to the hospital. They were coming from their original refuge sites in Khlong Kai Thuen and Khlong Wa. They wore black trousers and shirts, and rubber-tire sandals, as well as cloth pakamas wrapped around their heads or waists and often sheltered babies among other things. Thai military officials were also waiting for the buses in order to direct the Khmers to the encampment area and to ensure orderliness. The refugees disembarked and fell into a line that headed for the designated area.

We inspected each child, woman, and man who passed and sent them to the hospital if we thought it necessary. The men and women carried babies and their few cooking pots. Some of the men and small boys wore necklaces of precious rice grains packed in thin, cloth tubules. No other worldly goods were evident.

Ann Grosvenor-Rosenblatt worked with the International Rescue Committee in Thailand from September 1979 to June 1981 as a Pediatric Ward Nurse and Head Pediatric Ward Nurse, and then as Hospital Coordinator and Medical Coordinator at Khao I Dang. She is currently a student of French language in Quebec City, Quebec, Canada.

I looked under one woman's pakama and saw the most emaciated baby I had yet seen. I told her to go to the hospital, but she was reluctant to do so, wanting to follow her husband to the encampment area. I and others told her she must go because of the baby's condition, and eventually she went. When I myself later went to the hospital, I was upset to find the baby there without the mother. Patients told me that she had left to join her husband and that one of them had agreed to look after the little one—the quintessential malnourished, old-man-appearing baby.

In retrospect, maybe the mother's behavior was understandable. The baby was so sick. Probably she had known or seen quite a few babies in that condition die. So one can imagine, that being in a brand new location, she was perhaps more concerned about finding and being with her husband than staying with her baby whom she expected to die anyway. After all, besides death, another common experience for the Khmer in Kampuchea since 1975 was the separation of families—husbands from wives, children from parents.

Although 60,000 refugees had been expected, it turned out that half that number had elected to return to Cambodia rather than be settled in Sa Kaeo. Nevertheless, the four bamboo field-hospital wards minus beds were full of what we assumed were the most ill of the Khmer population. Unfortunately, we were mistaken. For several weeks substantial numbers died daily outside the hospital—refugees who had never been designated hospitalized or had not reported on their own for hospitalization.

The first few weeks at Sa Kaeo were especially chaotic, and 15 French, Filipino, Canadian, and American medical staffers from two voluntary agencies were able only to focus our attention on those admitted to the hospital, where patients lay or sat on the ground in the four wards in no particular order. Such a situation complicated nursing and medical care and could have been avoided to some degree by the presence of beds and blankets that had been promised but had not arrived by the time the camp hurriedly opened. Beds and blankets would have provided elevation and warmth and might have prevented some of the deaths that occurred during, and possibly because of, the monsoons.

The monsoon season could not have flared up at a worse time. There is nothing soft about a monsoon rain, and the rains, fell relentlessly on the flimsy hospital wards of bamboo crowned with tarpaulin that were open on all sides. Some time had to be spent ridding the tarpaulin tops of pools of water to prevent their collapse on the patients, and moving the patients who were most exposed to the rain. This was accomplished efficiently during daylight, but not during the night when there was no light and few workers were present.

I saw the problem at first hand one night when I was on duty with the French doctor and nurse. The day had begun as had the other few days in Sa Kaeo: the French volag team attending to the patients in two of the wards; the American volag team on the other two. When time permitted, everybody organized the supplies. These included a small supply of blood that Roy Dexter—the lab technician—had collected after exhorting non-medical personnel, such as photographers, to donate. A sense of order was gradually developing, but it was temporarily set back when word went around that more ill Khmers were expected later in the day. Unfortunately, there was no more room for them in the wards, so long pup tents were set up and somebody thought to get us head lamps, such as miners wear, in case they arrived after sunset. Indeed, the ill refugees did show up late, though fortunately none of the volunteers had left the scene. We settled them in the tents as the rain began and started IVs on our hands and knees—even on one little boy, who in his desperate condition, called out what seemed to be a name over and over. There was nobody to succor and cuddle him, and within the hour he was dead. It was the type of incident that hindsight made me ask myself if I might not have better spent my time by finding someone to hold him than by repeatedly trying to insert an IV.

There were still more refugees and no room left in the pup tents, so as best we could, we sheltered them from the torrential rains with straw mats and blue plastic. In fact it was a sorry job but as there were no other resources on hand, there was nothing more to be done but go home. All did except the French doctor and nurse, me, and two colleagues who had kindly offered to keep me company during night duty.

The French doctor and nurse turned their attention to a French film crew while Gary, Moshe, and I decided to check the tarpaulins for water loads. We spent the next few hours ridding the hospital tarps of water and were horrified to find a few dead patients lying partially in shallow pools of water.

As there was nothing else we could do in the dark, we started looking for a place to spend the night and settled, with many Khmer, in the unfinished kitchen. The kitchen's attraction for us was a small charcoal-brazier fire, for we were very wet and cold. We huddled around it and talked briefly about how difficult it was going to be ever to interpret our experiences to our families and friends. Finally it was time to sleep, but sleep did not come quickly. Everybody was coughing; a cough we called "the Kampuchean cough" pervaded the kitchen all night. It persisted for months in Sa Kaeo.

I got up after a few hours to check on the patients. Walking from the kitchen to the wards in the early morning hours, I heard Pierre, the French doctor, calling my name and found him delivering a baby. He needed something with which to tie the umbilical cord, and, as no obstetrical unit had yet been established, the only material I could find was the string that had been tied to the joists in the wards from which to hang the IVs. I tied the nonsterile string around the newborn's cord, and we were happy to see mother and baby doing well. Normally a birth brings happiness and hope to the mother. Could even this mother entertain such feelings after her experience of whatever hell she had endured in Kampuchea?

It took six months, but eventually signs of well-being—among the children anyway—did sprout from the soil of Sa Kaeo: smiles and laughter, children playing with incredibly inventive home-made toys and flying kites that soared high above the confines of the camp.

THE EARLY DAYS OF SA KAEO:
A VOLUNTEER WORKER'S EXPERIENCE

Angela M. Berry

In early 1978, I had a dream that I was walking down a dirt road that was lined with the small coffins of children. It was a powerful dream, the kind that remains stored in one's memory for a long time. When in late October 1979, I was driven in a crowded bus down a very similar dirt road to the Sa Kaeo refugee camp, I remembered that dream very well.

I had interrupted my tour of Thailand, and early one morning had boarded a volunteer bus headed for the "tragedy" I had read about in the newspaper. When I stepped off that bus in the heat of midmorning, I could think of nothing but how differently I would imagine the look of a war zone. There

Angela M. Berry is a nutritionist who worked from October 1979 to January 1981 as a volunteer relief worker with the International Rescue Committee supervising feeding programs, and from February 1981 to April 1983 as UNHCR Nutritionist serving all camps in Thailand. She originally went to Thailand as a tourist intending to stay no more than one month, and worked there for more than three years. This chapter covers the last three days of October 1979, 10 days after the emergency began. She is currently UNHCR Nutrition Coordinator in the Sudan (Eastern Emergency).

were no gates, fences, or signs—just mud and bodies in an empty rice field, army tents and Red Cross flags, and the fierce sun. What would later be called "tent city" was pieces of blue plastic (covering 31,000 Cambodians) hung on anything available, stretched out, for covering as far as you could see. It was one week after the emergency at Sa Kaeo had begun.

I was immediately brought to what was called the "baby tent," where I found a tense Australian woman with a terrible cold who was madly mixing formulas. She introduced herself as the wife of a diplomat, and asked if I could stay a few days as she had to return to Bangkok. As she continued to talk in her panic-stricken voice, I noticed the child. Separated from five small babies—"orphaned infants," she called them—lying in the corner, was an extremely emaciated two- or three-year-old. It was difficult to recognize the form as human, the child looked like a ghost of half-alive bones, reminding me of some nightmare on world greed. A small sign of life could be detected by the slight movement of the yellow skin, stretched to near puncture over the ribs. I tried to nod, to smile, as the woman explained the mixing of formulas, or electrolytes, and where to get water. But the child absorbed my attention. Ten minutes after I arrived, the child died. We covered it with a towel donated by some Bangkok hotel, and it lay there in the corner for three hours before someone had enough time to carry it away to the crowded "death tent." Forty-three people died that day, the most recorded for any single day at any camp during the relief operation. Even now, this would register in my mind as mere numbers if the face of one child dying from starvation did not still haunt me.

After one hour of mixing formulas and feeding infants, I naively asked the Australian woman where the toilets were located. She laughed and pointed toward the mud surrounding the tent. There was not even a hole in the ground. A baby arrived for admission, the baby's mother had just died of malaria. A prescription was written in indelible ink on his protruding belly. There was no paper and no time to keep records. There was no time to reflect, to question, or indulge in mourning. There was no time even to attend the many dying.

I worked until 6:00 p.m., when the volunteer bus left for Bangkok. Sitting and staring numbly out the window, someone handed me an orange. I had difficulty peeling it as my hands were badly shaking. I had eaten no food all day, and had drunk just one glass of the precious water. That night in the city I could not sleep. Images of the day and a strange feeling that my consciousness had been somehow altered kept me awake.

The next morning I packed enough clothes for one week, and once again made the three-hour journey to the camp. When I arrived at the baby tent, I found that the infants were all severely dehydrated, and concluded that the one Khmer helper had not fed them as instructed throughout the night. As most of the infants were marasmic, and only constant feeding could ensure their survival, I decided to spend the next few nights in the camp.

It was an odd feeling that evening, sitting in my little tent, the only foreigner in a camp of 31,000 Khmers and numerous Thai soldiers. I had been instructed by the UNHCR field officer not to leave the tent, for the Thai guards had been told to shoot anyone moving about the hospital area.

It was almost midnight when I heard the soft wailing of a woman coming from the next tent. After a half hour of listening to this sad sound, I nervously made my way to the tent. I found a woman holding a child, about ten years of age, who was extremely malnourished and, judging by his color, severely anemic. Throughout the night I checked on the boy, having instructed the mother to keep him upright. In the morning I was surprised to find the child still alive, and hurriedly found a doctor who could give a blood transfusion. But two hours later, I discovered that the boy had still not received the blood.

When I went to see the doctor again, thinking he had forgotten the child, he looked at me angrily and said, "I have a very small supply of blood and that boy has probably already suffered brain damage. Now, do you want me to waste my supply on that child or save the life of another normal one?" Stunned, I made my way back to the baby tent. It was no wonder that most of the doctors present during those first few weeks of Sa Kaeo did not stay for more than a month. The stress of such decisions must have been tremendous.

During that day I was without a Khmer helper and by midmorning had discovered that I was out of water. I asked many passing refugees to bring me water by pointing to an empty bucket and saying *duk*—the first Khmer word I learned—but they all passed by, uninterested. I began to feel frustrated when finally a French volunteer offered to help. I later learned that the majority of refugees during that time would only lend assistance if it would directly aid a family member. For survival, they only took care of their own kin. This presented obvious difficulties for the understaffed volunteers at the time.

That evening I again stayed in the baby tent. The next morning, before the medical teams arrived, a refugee rushed in exclaiming in French that his wife was about to have a baby. I explained that I was not a nurse, but he was panicked and insisted that I help. I followed him into the next tent and found a woman there, lying on a table, in labor. Panicked myself, I asked him to go to the kitchen and fetch clean water. Before he ran out, I pleaded that he also locate a doctor. Standing there, helpless, the situation seemed unreal. Just as the woman was starting a heavy contraction and I could see the tiny head crowning, a doctor rushed in the door. Within one minute he was carefully cutting the umbilical cord. Both of our hands were still shaking as we smiled and introduced ourselves.

Later that same day, one of the infants started to run a fever. I called a doctor, who said it was probably malaria and started an IV. Within two hours the baby had died. I carried it myself to the death tent, wondering if I could have done more, if in some way I was to blame for this loss of life. As I walked past the obstetrics tent, I was suddenly reminded of that morning; the cycle of birth and death I had witnessed in one day struck me. Once again there was no time for grief.

That night I slept a few hours while the Khmer helper did one round of feedings. During that time I had vivid dreams about volunteers who were becoming sick and helpless and turning into refugees. The next day when my exhaustion finally hit me, I understood the message. I had slept very little in the past four days, I had a case of diarrhea from eating the camp rations, and an infestation of lice from my Khmer helper. I realized it was time for me also to find refuge.

The volunteers with whom I stayed that night consisted of a team of one doctor and three nurses. They had comprised the only medical team present in the first two days of the operation. They described how two thousand refugees were unable to walk during those first few days and how half of them had recovered after receiving water and food. They told how some people had died because they lacked the strength to raise their heads out of the mud. In all this talk there was an odd kind of humor and much laughing. Anyone listening would have thought we were either sadistic or mad. Yet what was occurring was an easing of the tension, a stress from observing a human circumstance that was tragic beyond description. We had the choice to submit to the pain of our observations through either tears or laughter. We chose laughter.

ONE INDIVIDUAL'S CONTRIBUTION

Paola Polacco Sandersley

If anyone ever got involved in a relief operation through the back door, it was me. I had never before dealt with, or even encountered, a crisis such as the one in which I eventually got involved. Indeed, before following my husband in early 1977 on a British government posting to Thailand, I had devoted my undivided energies for a number of years to the most conventional activity in the world: the bringing-up of my two small daughters. I also now had an interesting job with the cultural services of the French Embassy, served on several committees, played tennis, prepared to qualify as a scuba diver, and was once again into everything—and loving it.

On the positive side, in the light of what was to come, I suspected rather than knew that I had some organizational ability; I spoke Thai quite fluently—this was to prove immensely

Paola Polacco Sandersley was a volunteer relief worker in Thailand from September 1979 to April 1980. She ran the Bureau Pedagogique of the French Cultural Services there. She lives in London, and recently resigned her job as Director of the Stillbirth and Neonatal Death Society to mother her 3-month-old son.

useful—and I knew for a fact that I possessed above average energy and drive, having been told over the years by family and friends that keeping up with my pace was an exhausting business!

Kampuchea had been in the news for quite some time at the start of this story, which begins early in October 1979, but it probably was not until August that the front page of every newspaper in Thailand carried detailed stories of starvation and death and horrifyingly vivid pictures of refugees massed along the Thai-Cambodian border. My heart was heavy for them, but my life was, I thought, already too full of commitments and I remained in a state of unhappy noninvolvement.

Early in September, I was asked by a friend who was an official at the Israeli Embassy if I would care to join an Israeli convoy that was going to a northeastern border camp and help to distribute food to the refugees. I accepted at once, and though I tried to brace myself for what I expected to be the reality with which I would be confronted, I was by the end of that exhausting, sweaty, and ever-thirsty day, in a state of near shock.

Looking back, I think it was the word *camp* that most misled me. I had visualized tents, drinking water, emergency medical facilities, latrines. What I found was a far cry. Thousands upon thousands of people, in the particular area we visited, were squatting apathetically in the scorching sun, some dying, most in appalling conditions, all skeletal. Worst of all was the eerie silence. No one talked; the fetal-looking babies did not cry. There was no communication among these people too ill, too hungry and thirsty, too desperate, to react in any way whatsoever. A whole group of us volunteers started the distribution, first of plastic bowls and then of a bowlful of rice and a small can of sardines in papaya sauce. We ran from the distribution points—three large trucks stacked to the very top—up the line, stretched even farther, and back for more.

At the end of our supply food—untold thousands still patiently waiting ahead—we were a few miles from our base of supplies and into Cambodia. Although I saw one tank trunk distributing water on the site, the main source seemed to be a muddy brew from a hole dug in the ground—which people drank from and washed in, wading in with their filthy tattered clothes.

The drive back to Bangkok was a silent affair. We tried to digest an experience we were all unprepared for and gulped down gallons of hot water (stored in car trunks) to quench our raging thirst. The bright lights of the city, the luxury hotels, the well-stocked supermarkets, and fashionable shops, only four hours from the border hell we had just left behind, were another world. I was physically nauseated and knew my days of noninvolvement were over.

The idea of organizing a fund-raising evening came to me practically at once: I had many contacts at both the French and the Israeli embassies. An active member of the small Jewish community, I had many good friends there too, who were to lend their active support, both with the fund raising and throughout the subsequent relief activities. Furthermore, I had a much-admired ally in the American Embassy, Sheppie Abramowitz, the ambassador's wife, whose indefatigable work for the refugee cause is well known to all those who took any part in it.

I had a large house and garden, and if I was going to give, I was certainly going to make sure that I squeezed all my friends and acquaintances in the process! A friend, Jeff Farrell, and I drew up lengthy lists of major foreign companies operating in Bangkok, aiming more specifically at pharmaceutical companies, milk producers—both powdered and canned—and rice dealers. I spent long hours poring over the equivalent of an A-to-Z pharmaceutical index, selecting products that I considered would be safe to order and of immediate use. Many of the refugee diseases and disorders were fairly common knowledge: malaria, typhus, parasitic infestations, festering wounds, dehydration. I have always had a strong—if lay—interest in the field of medicine, and I knew what to look for. I also knew I could not go wrong with such staples as antiseptics, sedatives, analgesics, sterile dressings of all kinds, saline drips, thermometers, rubber gloves, disposable syringes, hypodermic needles, scissors, and so on. I was therefore able to compile a fairly wide-ranging and comprehensive list, entering next to each selected item the name of the manufacturer, or where necessary, that of the company's representatives in Thailand.

Jeff and I divided this list between us and contacted people at the highest level we could to ask for help. The response we got from these firms is something that will keep me a staunch optimist for the rest of my days. We had crates upon crates delivered to our gates, the appeal successful far beyond our expectations. We asked as individuals, with no agency or association to back up up. We were warned by the inevitable cynics that we would have doors slammed in our faces, but all we ever found was kindness and an extraordinary generosity. We sent out over 300 invitations, enclosing photocopies of articles and photographs taken from the local press, and reminded everyone to bring their checkbooks.

The urgency of the mounting crisis was compounded only three days before our fund-raising effort by the opening, on October 24, of the Thai border to Kampuchean refugees who had until then been refused entry. From one day to the next, more than 30,000 refugees were transported in truckloads to what was to become the first Cambodian refugee camp: Sa Kaeo. UNHCR, which was in charge of the organization of this camp under the direct authority of the Thai military, sent out immediate appeals to all embassies for volunteers to go out and help ease the desperate situation.

The much-prepared-for evening finally arrived on October

27—and it was a big success! We raised $20,000. We knew we could support a relief operation of sorts.

Having slept only a couple of hours, my husband Peter and I got down to the job of packing a first sample of goods and medicine in cardboard boxes and, just after six o'clock in the morning, with both our car and Jeff's packed solid, the three of us set off in convoy for Sa Kaeo. We found eager recipients for our goods at a variety of relief organizations. As we distributed our wares, we asked for and were enthusiastically given lists of needed emergency supplies. This was a pattern we were to follow for several weeks, expanding our selection of goods to include surgical equipment, fetoscopes and forceps, crutches, vast quantities of sarongs, baby clothes, and fresh fruit and vegetables.

There was a sea of sick people all over the place that first Sunday morning crouching, squatting, or lying on the ground. Only a few basic hospital tents were up, and there were few helping hands. The three of us were quickly farmed out on a variety of assignments—everything from washing the sick and cleaning up after diarrhea and vomit to fetching drinking water, from installing more vitally needed water tanks to digging latrines and helping on food-distribution lines.

I found I had no time for tears—there was too much work to be done. I remember that day vividly. There were refugees everywhere—emaciated brown living carcasses, all limbs and eyes and folds of skin. Some, whom I was told had malaria, walked around like zombies with glazed, expressionless eyes. Just previously, there had been fierce rainstorms—quite uncharacteristic of Thailand at that time of year—to aggravate the situation. The ground, when you stepped on it, if you did not sink in over your ankles, was "elastic" and bounced. I saw a wheelbarrow loaded with corpses over which a pitifully small cover had been thrown; I watched mesmerized all those heads, young and old, bobbing up and down as the wheelbarrow moved ahead over the uneven surface. My eyes ran instinctively to the barbed wire that surrounded the camp and—in the 120-degree heat—I shivered.

Back in Bangkok, I opened an account in the name of Khmer Refugee Relief (KRR), and for several weeks, working full-time Monday through Friday in our respective jobs—or perhaps more honestly, letting the papers pile up on our respective desks—Jeff and I spent many of our working hours and every spare moment of what we called our leisure time, collecting the long lists of requested items, keeping up a constant barrage of demands on friendly companies and organizations. Doors opened everywhere, and we went about thanking, collecting, crating, and then returning over the weekend back to the camp to face new emergencies.

After the first weeks of great confusion and high death tolls, the international organizations—their size making them initially slow-moving unlike the simple volunteer with a few "ready bucks" in pocket—began to get matters under control. On November 21, a second camp, Khao I Dang, was established only 5 km from the border. Jeff had left Thailand and I felt my energies would best be expended at Khao I Dang. Sa Kaeo was getting on its feet. The improvement from one week to the next was visible and comforting.

WHEN THE STATISTICS BECOME HUMAN BEINGS

Rosalynn Carter

How fortunate we are in the United States, and how little we realize the suffering, distress, and grief that surround us in the world. Those were my thoughts as I stood in the Sa Kaeo refugee camp in Thailand and witnessed the starving, homeless, and ill men, women, and children from Cambodia fleeing across the border from their homeland. It was a scene I shall never forget.

I had been familiar with the statistics about refugees in our world—several million in Asia, Central America, and Africa. The worldwide problem was so urgent that the United Nations had convened a special conference in Geneva to which Jimmy (President Carter) had sent Vice-President Mondale. Our government was working with the international relief

---

Rosalynn Carter is the wife of the former **President** of the United States, Jimmy Carter. She visited the Cambodian refugee camps in Thailand in November 1979 and returned with President Carter in June 1985. Mrs. Carter's autobiography, *First Lady from Plains,* was published in May 1984, and she continues to be actively involved in many issues, with special emphasis on mental health.

agencies, such as the ICRC, UNICEF, World Food Program, Catholic Relief Services, CARE, and others, and we had agreed to double the quota of refugees we could accept. Jimmy was also working to induce other countries to share the responsibility.

But then, in the fall of 1979, our whole country was shocked by the stark and terrible pictures of a new wave of refugees—the Cambodians—who were flashed on our television screens every day and every night. With all resources already strained to the limit by the sheer numbers of refugees around the globe, what would happen to these new hapless human beings? How could they possibly be helped? What could we do to alleviate the situation? What was the responsibility of our country to those so much less fortunate than we?

One thing for sure was that we could not sit idly by while a whole race of people faced extinction. As Jimmy and I discussed the options, we realized that the government alone could never do enough to ease the situation. We needed input and assistance from people all over the country. From my mail and the telephone calls coming into the White House, I knew people were eager to help but they didn't know how. I didn't know how either, but I felt an overwhelming responsibility.

I called my staff together to discuss what I might do, and Jimmy asked the National Security Council for advice on an effective way for me to contribute. There was no time for studies or contingency plans. We needed immediate information on the scope of the problem and an effective strategy for getting food to the hungry people and providing for shelter and medical care as soon as possible. Once a plan of action was developed, I, as First Lady, could publicize the problem and let people know what they could do.

Two days later, plans were underway for me to lead a fact-finding delegation on an emergency trip to the refugee camps in Thailand near the Cambodian border.

After intensive briefings by the State Department and the National Security Council, I met with officials of international relief agencies. From them I learned more about the proportions of the crisis and some of the problems in coordinating the activities of the various relief organizations. But coordination of efforts was crucial, and I wanted to do everything I could to foster good working relationships among the groups trying to help.

On November 9, 1979, five days after deciding to "do something," I was on my way to Thailand with a group of highly qualified advisers, each with a special area of concern. The 22-hour trip seemed like one long briefing, as I listened to them discuss what they knew about the refugee situation we were going to see firsthand, and what they wanted to find out while we were there.

Dr. Julius Richmond, the United States Surgeon General, would provide expert judgment on the extent of medical needs, along with Dr. William Foege, Director of the Centers for Disease Control. Jean Young, United States Chairperson of the International Year of the Child, would focus on the needs of children in the camps. Bob Maddox, from Jimmy's staff, would coordinate with religious groups on our return. Lieutenant General Joseph Heiser, United States Army retired, was a logistics expert who could give us advice on transportation of supplies and other related problems. Others in the delegation included State and Defense Department officials.

Our delegation arrived in Bangkok in the evening and were met by the young Crown Prince of Thailand, the Prime Minister, and United States Ambassador Morton Abramowitz and Mrs. Abramowitz. The Thai government hoped for additional assistance from the United States, as well as the rest of the international community, in dealing with the massive problem the refugees presented to Thailand. Their own small country was not equipped to deal with thousands of starving people, and there was a great deal of pressure on the Prime Minister simply to refuse to allow the fleeing Cambodians entry into the country. Thailand had already accepted many refugees from other parts of Indochina and believed that other countries should help in the current crisis.

Shortly after our arrival, Jimmy called to tell me that there had been a mortar attack on a refugee camp about 50 kilometers from the one I would be visiting the next day. He wanted me to focus public attention on the refugee crisis, but not by getting hurt in the process. "Be careful," he said.

We were up early the next morning and off to Sa Kaeo camp, which had sprung up only days before our arrival to try to accommodate the new wave of refugees pouring in. As we circled over the camp in a small airplane, we could see a vast area of bright blue and another area close by that was being cleared. The blue turned out to be huge sheets of plastic, crudely stretched across sticks to make shelters, and so close together that from the air it seemed to be one large sheet. There were a few substantial tents put up by the relief organizations, which were proud of what they had been able to do in such a short time.

Once in the camp, we discovered a virtual sea of humanity, men and women, young and old. In the tents they were lying on the ground, on mats or dirty blankets or rags. All were ill and in various stages of starvation: some, all bones and no flesh; and others with cracked feet and swollen as though to burst. All with serious diseases, such as malaria, dysentery, and tuberculosis. All wretching, feverish, and silent. When I tried to talk to them, most continued staring into space with blank looks on their faces—some frightened, some too weak to respond.

One woman who looked like a child told me through an interpreter that she was 35 years old. She was wrapped in blankets, although the temperature was 85 to 90 degrees, and she was softly crying, a sign that she was better off than most. She said that her husband and seven children had all been killed.

Another woman had come into the camp just the night before with her husband and three small children, one a baby 12 days old who had been born on the way out of Cambodia. The family had lived on bark from trees while they wandered searching for the border, and had brought the baby to the camp to give him away. The woman was too weak to eat yet, but she appeared to be very agitated. She managed to tell a Protestant missionary that she was frightened for herself and her baby because she had not built a fire under her bed to frighten away evil spirits when the baby was born. The missionary hurried to find some sticks for a fire.

Seeing the children was the most difficult part of all. I picked up a baby boy, four months old, who weighed four pounds and looked like a tiny monkey. And a little girl whose limbs fell limp. Standing in the middle of the tent, cuddling a baby girl who had not the strength to even hold up her little arms, and looking at the poverty and disease and suffering around me, I felt tears well up in my eyes. The statistics had become human beings, and I thought about our country and how blessed we were at home and how much we were doing to help refugees all over the world, and how insignificant that seemed now. But we could do more. I knew we could.

I kept thinking to myself, as the television cameras followed me through the camp, one thing our people have at home is caring. If they could see and know what I see and know, and if I could let them understand, they would respond. My crying would not do one thing to help. I had to do something tangible. I was ready to go home and get started. I had had enough. The needs were urgent, and there was no time to waste.

We continued the tour hurriedly. We came to the hospital,

a shack made of woven palm fronds waist-high for walls, open at the top, with a thatched roof and mats on the floor. The people here were supposed to be the ones in the worst condition, but they looked the same as all the others. In a corner, marked off by more palm fronds, a French doctor had set up a delivery room. Thriteen or fourteen babies had been born.

Under the low shelters made from the blue plastic that stretched for acres and acres, the rest of the people huddled together, without enough room even to stand. Every inch of ground was covered with them, and every time more ground was cleared, more people appeared to cover it.

We left the camp with a great sense of urgency and continued on through the remainder of the schedule, which included a visit to a refugee center for Laotians. There conditions were much better than at Sa Kaeo, but many people here had waited three or four years inside these confines for approval to resettle abroad.

Then hot and dirty from tramping in the mud of the camps all day under a broiling sun, I flew to the mountains of Thailand. After a necessary stop at the guest house to change clothes, I called on the king and queen of Thailand at their summer palace. It was quite a contrast to the conditions I had witnessed earlier in the day, but a very important visit. Their support of the relief effort was essential, and our conversation was frustrating to me. While the king and queen were obviously concerned about the refugees, they were even more concerned about the "burden" the crisis was placing on their own country. The king did not react to my urgent requests that additional camps be provided, nor did he respond to my compliments for all that Thailand was already doing for the refugees. My visit with the prime minister, who had seen the camps for himself, was more productive, but it was clear that his policy of opening the Thai borders to all newcomers was a great political burden to him.

A subsequent meeting with officials of the international relief agencies and voluntary organizations was uplifting to me. Prior to the prime minister's decision to open the borders, these agencies and organizations had been working independently, each trying to get supplies into Cambodia, with little or no contact among themselves. But when the refugees poured into Thailand, they had to work together in the emergency. They had been cooperating in an unprecedented way for the past week and were justifiably proud of their progress.

The tone of the meeting was frank and open, focusing on practical problems and specific solutions. The group agreed that the greatest need was for one overall coordinator, someone who could bring order to all the efforts. This agreement was a tremendous step forward and a great acknowledgment among the very independent, self-motivated groups present, one that indicated the urgency of the situation and the determination among the organizations to meet the needs they all knew were more pressing each day.

One other stop in Bangkok was the Lumpini Transit Center, a filthy place, but one where people were more hopeful. They were fortunate enough to have been selected for emigration and were awaiting final processing. (After my protests and those of many others, including the United States senators who visited Thailand, this center was cleaned up.)

Then it was time to go home and to initiate the next steps in helping. We had seen the grief and starvation firsthand and left with determination that we would not forget. As we flew back to Washington, the delegation worked feverishly to prepare a report for the President that would stress the urgency of the need and specify immediate recommendations based on what we had learned in the camps.

We had learned that there was a sufficient supply of food and medicine for those refugees now in the camps. The United Nations had supplied medicine from stockpiles held in Stockholm for emergencies. And there were doctors from several countries who had volunteered their services. But plans had to be made immediately for the expected influx of 300,000 new refugees in the next few weeks.

General Heiser reported a serious lack of coordination in logistics. Water-hauling trucks and sanitation provisions were nonexistent. One group, among the relief organizations with which he talked, requested trucks for carrying supplies. Another group reported that it had 370 trucks en route to the camps and did not know how they would use them all. In addition, the general's scouting indicated that inside Cambodia, whether or not there were trucks, there were no bridges, no barges for use in river transportation, and no unloading equipment. Even if ships got into port in Cambodia the people were so weak from starvation that they could not unload them. An overall coordinator was the first priority in order to ensure that needs were accurately assessed and met as efficiently as possible.

Dr. William Foege had discovered that there were few children in the camps between the ages of one and five, an indication that a whole generation of children was in danger of being lost to malnutrition and disease. He had found more people dying in the low shelter outside the hospital in Sa Kaeo than inside, just as it had appeared to me. The emergency treatment for malnutrition, malaria, and dysentery had to be followed up with specialized treatment and preventive measures, which would require many more doctors and nurses than were available.

We were emotionally drained by our experience, but we also came away with great admiration for our American officials and for those agencies and organizations who were struggling so valiantly with such an enormous tragedy. I was especially proud of Ambassador Morton Abramowitz and his wife, Sheppie, who had labored day and night in the border camps helping to save lives.

After returning home, I tried to do everything at once. I called Kurt Waldheim, then the Secretary-General of the United Nations, to urge him to name a coordinator for the Cambodian relief effort, the most pressing need. I talked with Jimmy about ways in which our government could help. Then two days after our return, representatives of more than 40 voluntary agencies in the United States met at the White House to hear reports of our trip and of the steps our government was taking, and to talk about their specific roles in the relief effort. I was able to report that the United States government had granted UNICEF an additional $2 million for the immediate purchase of rice. We had also authorized the United Nations High Commissioner for Refugees to use $4 million of United States-allocated funds for immediate support of refugee programs in Thailand. Working with international agencies, Jimmy saw to it that our government airlifted special foods for infants and children, as well as desperately needed communications and water-supply equipment.

Jimmy also directed the State Department to work with the Thai government and the international agencies in Thailand to prepare for the new refugees expected and to continue efforts to move food directly into Cambodia. United States refugee quotas from Thailand were eased to help that country cope with the huge burden the influx would present, and the process of resettlement was streamlined. The Peace Corps was directed to accelerate its support of the United Nations efforts in behalf of refugees, and the Surgeon General helped to establish a clearinghouse for volunteers in the health field who were willing to lend a hand in Indochina [see the chapter, "Coordinating the United States Volunteer Response" by Margaret R. Cronyn and Russell E. Morgan, Jr.].

I was proud of the immediate response of our government to the crisis, but I was even more proud of the response of the private voluntary agencies and of the American people. Their response was overwhelming. The contributions they made in the next four months exceeded more than we could ever have expected or anticipated, and it made me feel proud to be part of a country like ours. The horror I had witnessed in the refugee camps was far removed from the life most Americans live, but the concern and caring that poured out was proof to me that human suffering touches us all, and that we can respond with the best that is in us.

THE UNITED STATES RESPONSE

Robert C. Porter, Jr.

The response of the United States Embassy was formed in large part by Ambassador Abramowitz and people on his staff like Refugee Section Chief Lionel Rosenblatt.* Their two major concerns were that the Khmer population seemed to be headed for extinction and that the stability and security of Thailand, an ally, was threatened.

The United States had long had emotional ties with the countries of Indochina. Many Americans still had a strong personal involvement with and commitment to the Khmer. For some, the image of United States Ambassador Dean evacuating Phnom Penh with the American flag folded under his arm would not go away. The nearly total absence of hard news on Cambodia since the Pol Pot takeover and the stories of tremendous suffering and millions of deaths under the Khmer Rouge were also factors. Americans are self-critical; some felt that although the

---

*Lionel Rosenblatt, in a quietly persistent and persuasive way, fought the political battles with the Thai government, the United Nations, and the United States government, giving up career advancement at the State Department many times over the years in order to help the refugees. He had great empathy for them and real understanding of their suffering. His hours were seven days a week from six in the morning until twelve at night, and longer when necessary. He was also personally involved in searching for refugees who had been pushed back. To him, every individual mattered. —Editors.

United States fought to prevent a Khmer Rouge takeover, its policies may have contributed to their coming to power, and that the United States shared indirectly in the responsibility for what happened under the Khmer Rouge. In the minds of many at the United States Embassy in Thailand was the forced pushback of the Khmer at Preah Vihear in June 1979 and the feeling that the United States was somehow responsible because it had not been able to forestall the repatriation.

Ambassador Abramowitz and others on his staff played an important role in persuading Thailand to take a more benevolent attitude toward the Khmer on its borders. This enabled international donors to send emergency relief to the Khmer and allowed the Khmer, during a critical period, to seek refuge on the Thai side of the border and eventually in UNHCR camps well inside the country.

On the border, the international response to events both north and south of Aran in the fall of 1979 was characterized by a spirit of dedication and close cooperation and an atmosphere of informality. A person's nationality or affiliation was irrelevant; it mattered only that he or she was willing to work. There was little concern about empire building or bureaucratic and operational turf; it mattered only that the job got done.

The voluntary agencies and their staffs played a crucial role during the first few weeks. While the larger international organizations (in part because of their huge bureaucracies and regulations) "studied" the problem or attempted to procure emergency supplies through regular channels, the smaller voluntary agencies were able to react almost immediately to meet the need for doctors, personnel, supplies, shelter, and food. Their staffs in many cases worked from 18 to 24 hours a day.

Although they viewed their role primarily as that of a catalyst, United States Embassy personnel continued to play a significant operational role in planning, organizing, and delivering emergency humanitarian aid. They worked closely with other international, *non*governmental personnel. A few other foreign embassies in Bangkok—particularly the French, Swedish, Canadian, and Australian—were seized with the enormity and severity of the situation, but only the United States Embassy sent personnel to work on emergency relief matters on the border.

American, Thai, and Khmer staff members of the United States Embassy who could speak the Thai and Khmer languages or provided a needed skill were loaned for weeks at a time to the international organizations. United States Embassy personnel assisted in a major way in organizing and carrying out the movement of refugees from the border camps at Non Mak Mun and Nong Samet to the UNHCR holding center at Khao I Dang. Its personnel accompanied international medical personnel treating the sick in dangerous border areas. Its aid experts assisted in the planning and construction of Sa Kaeo and Khao I Dang holding centers. Its interpreters greatly assisted the UNHCR in bringing order out of the chaos among the newly arrived Khmer residents at Sa Kaeo and Khao I Dang. Its communications equipment provided the link among UNHCR facilities until the UNHCR was able to procure equipment through its own channels. Ironically, the early assistance given by the United States Embassy to the international organizations was viewed later by some as an attempt to control and/or spy on the activities of these organizations, rather than as a cooperative gesture designed to assist them in providing urgently needed emergency relief to the Khmer.

In early 1980, at a time when its relations with ICRC in Bangkok had deteriorated, the United States Embassy's relations with several of the other international organizations continued to be characterized by the spirit of informality, close cooperation, and dedication that had been prevalent during the fall of 1979, and important new projects were able to be carried out quickly and efficiently. In February 1980, for example, UNICEF officials became convinced that there was a critical shortage of rice seed in western Cambodia and that seed must reach the farmers there in time for planting. Over a quickly arranged lunch in Bangkok, a United States Embassy official promised UNICEF several thousand dollars on the spot from Embassy contingency funds and within 36 hours had transferred $2 million to UNICEF for its land-bridge program at Nong Chan. The land-bridge program was coordinated by Robert Ashe, who had spent many years in Thailand with Christian voluntary agencies. Sponsored by ICRC, this program brought food, seed, and farm implements into western Cambodia, where little of the relief supplies that had entered the country via Phnom Penh had reached. By the end of 1980, about 149,000 tons of rice had reached northwestern Cambodia by this route. Many observers believe that the land-bridge program constituted the single most important and effective element in the rapid and critically important restoration of Cambodian agriculture.

KHAO I DANG: THE EARLY DAYS

Esmeralda Luciolli

I had just come back from Mairut camp when the MSF [Médecins Sans Frontières] coordinator notified me that I had been selected to be the representative of Dr. John Naponick, who was the medical coordinator of the UNHCR (specifically, of its Regional Office Kampuchea Unit, or ROKU) at Khao I Dang. With volags acting under the cover of UNHCR, and in this case of ROKU, my assignment seemed quite clear—at least, in theory. I was to try both to coordinate the work of the volags and to ensure good communications with Bangkok. In practice, it was more complicated. My task had not been clearly defined either to me or to the principal parties involved, the ICRC and the volags; and ICRC, which had taken control of the operations at Sa Kaeo and along the border, intended to do the same at Khao I Dang.

Esmeralda Luciolli is a physician who served from May 1979 to February 1981 as a medical coordinator with Médecins Sans Frontières at Surin Camp and then as Volag Coordinator and assistant to Dr. John Naponick at Khao I Dang. She is now affiliated with the Public Health Department, Faculty of Medicine, Paris, performing teaching and research.

In Sa Kaeo, the arrival of the refugees had preceded the setting up of the camp. At Khao I Dang, the first refugees arrived four days after the bulldozers—which was a major improvement. An extraordinary effort was accomplished during those days: out of the bushy and uneven ground, a place fit to receive tens of thousands of refugees was created. All those who participated will remember the intense "race against the clock" of those first days. Bulldozers leveled the ground while hundreds of workers built the hospital and administration buildings. Many trucks arrived, carrying water, food, and raw materials.

In the meantime, those who were responsible were planning the construction of the camp and the arrival of the first refugees. The field officer of UNHCR and his assistants were in charge of the administration of the camp, and the coordinator of the ICRC—Magnus Grabe—and myself were in charge of the medical activities. Due to misunderstandings that had occurred in other camps between ICRC and the volags, Magnus was slightly suspicious of me when I first arrived, but he was soon reassured, for we had the same approach to the problems, and instead of being opposed to each other, we worked in close cooperation and in a complementary way.

While Magnus attended to all questions relating to ICRC—relations with the border, the building of the hospital, and the installation of equipment—I was in charge of the volags. For a better comprehension of the difficulties raised by this task, one needs to understand the atmosphere then prevailing at Khao I Dang. We were obsessed with the thought that while the whole world was fixing its eyes on this area, Khao I Dang must not become a second Sa Kaeo. This obsession overlooked the facts that the refugees who were about to arrive would be in far better health than the "skeletons" of Sa Kaeo, and that they would not arrive en masse as they had at Sa Kaeo but came on buses in smaller groups over a period of several weeks. In addition, we had enough time to set up the medical assistance that would be needed when they entered the camp. All the volags, both those who had been in Thailand for some time and those who had recently arrived, struggled to be present at Khao I Dang with a maximum number of teams. Medical care was established for emergency cases, hospital inpatients, and clinic outpatients. A "screening" system for the refugees upon their arrival had been established in order to detect the emergency cases immediately, especially cases of malnutrition, dehydration, and serious disease in children. They were then taken to the emergency ward along with the injured and seriously ill patients, who had been driven there directly from the border in ICRC vans.

All the refugees were given a curative dose of Fansidar because of malaria at the border—a practice later abandoned. They also were registered so the necessary daily statistics could be obtained.

The hospital, situated at the camp's entrance, was composed of 11 buildings erected during the first days of the camp. It included an emergency ward (where those who were to be admitted were first examined by a physician and then sent to the appropriate inpatient ward), an operating room, a surgical ward, and nine other wards—three for pediatrics, one for obstetrics, and five for adult medicine. Each section, with about ten thousand people, included an outpatient department (OPD) or clinic where consultations could take place, a maternal and child health center, and a supplementary-feeding center for children, pregnant and lactating women, and malnourished people of any age.

Coordination among the various relief organizations was difficult for many reasons, the main one being their number. Because of the tremendous international effort launched for the Khmer refugees, representatives of numerous agencies had flocked to Thailand. The warmth and sincerity of everyone cannot be denied, but difficulties arose from the sheer multiplicity of organizations. It is, of course, easier to coordinate the action of two or three volags than that of 20 or 30, especially in an emergency.

Thus, in Khao I Dang one of the first requisites was to ensure liaison among the volags. For this purpose, all had to inform and to be informed: two daily meetings were accordingly scheduled to take place: one consisting of those persons in charge of the camp (UNHCR) and the two medical coordinators (for ICRC and the volags), the other of the medical coordinators and the persons in charge of each volag, who in turn were supposed to convey information to their own teams.

This "pyramidal" organization was rather complex, but it was the only way to be efficient and accurately update many people on many activities. While the first meeting was regularly held on time, the second one, with more and more participants, was always late and increasingly fell short of satisfying everyone's need for information.

For this reason, reassignment of the volags to different camps gradually came about. This reduced the number of volags in the camps, with each agency concentrating its staff in one or two camps and each camp having one "lead volag." The problem consisted of finding a democratic means of coordination to prevent anarchy and inefficiency while respecting the individual characteristics of each volag. Related to this was the fact that the doctors were not inclined to any self-discipline and often demonstrated extreme individualism. The Israeli team in Sa Kaeo, for example, which was admired by everyone for its efficiency, had been trained in military medicine and was so organized.

Another reason that coordination among the different relief organizations was difficult was competition. It was quite normal and justifiable that each team was devoted to doing the best work possible. Relief for the refugees was the purpose and the ultimate motive of each endeavor, but sometimes purely ambitious, political, evangelistic, or other aims took precedence. Competition among the volags was sometimes evident, such as during the allocation of wards at Khao I Dang when each organization vied to get the biggest share of the "cake."

Competence was another matter that affected coordination. In the fall of 1979, many medical missions arrived from different countries. Their members had been recruited overnight, and were faced with a strange situation for which few were adequately prepared. Most of them adapted remarkably well and were devoted to their duty. However, due to the emergency, some staff members were recruited who despite their goodwill had had no previous experience and were not at all equipped to deal with such an emergency. The tremendous need for training and management was clearly demonstrated.

Although the screening process was far from perfect, triage was highly important in order not to "overlook" those patients who needed immediate care and overcrowd the medical services with patients who could wait for treatment–thus not wasting time and energy on them when others were really in need. We, therefore, tried to insist that screening be done by the most competent and experienced members of each team, but many considered the process boring and unimportant. In addition, the volags did not care to use their staffs for this since they were more anxious to acquire the maximum number of wards and OPDs. Therefore, the less skilled staff members were often sent to do it. Screenings were despised by the doctors who sent the nurses, who often were not familiar with the anticipated pathology.

Badly understood and badly performed, the screening became inefficient and absurd. The situation went from one extreme to the other: On the first day, every "sick" person was sent to the hospital without taking into account the seriousness of the case; in some wards, most of the beds were occupied after only a small fraction of the refugees expected to arrive had come, even though the wards had been cleared of most of the sick people admitted earlier. On subsequent days, however, emergency patients, such as dehydrated children, were not admitted to the hospital and were later found in the camp in a wretched state.

Another problem was the short length of the tours of duty of many relief workers. While certain agencies provided teams for a long period–six months to a year–others did so for very short periods—four weeks or less. Even though long-term contracts were not required, the presence of teams with short-term contracts became a problem, considering the fact that when they arrived, the staff members were usually unaccustomed to this kind of work. As good as adaptation may be, it still involves a period during which new workers are not operating at full efficiency. That was the case with volunteers hired on the spot: more problems were created than solved. In fact, some skilled staff had to be assigned to training these volunteers, rather than being utilized for other activities; to make matters worse, once the training was completed, the volunteers sometimes left.

The continuous turnover in team members did not facilitate coordination, which was based mostly on the bonds established among the relief workers and the refugees. Eventually UNHCR requested the volags to provide relief workers who would stay for a minimum of six months. The diversity of relief workers was also a barrier to coordination. The gathering of volags coming from every part of the world, with totally different motives, aims, and methods, constituted both a strength—due to the diversity of the people represented and the exchanges it allowed —and a weakness—due to the diversity of approaches, especially in medical practice.

At the beginning, each new team had its own medications, its own therapeutic protocols, and so forth. It became essential to create a central pharmacy, to have only one list of medications likely to be ordered and to establish standard protocols in order to ensure a certain uniformity and continuity. Although everyone agreed in theory on the merits of these principles, in practice it was more difficult: each team was attached to its own methods and anxious that these be recognized. It was essential, however, to standardize treatment, to have it provided by the most competent staff, and to keep the number of medications to an absolute minimum in order to minimize logistic problems, enable teams to become accustomed to medications different from those used in their own countries, and enable "the medics" to formulate, administer, and even prescribe them.

As a result, some basic principles of relief work have emerged from our experience at Khao I Dang: (1) limit agencies to a reasonable number; (2) determine common aims, leaving aside as much as possible the individual interests of each agency; (3) insist upon a minimum of skill, or at least of training and management, in the medical teams; and (4) meet the standards required for sound medical practice.

IMPRESSIONS OF A MEDICAL COORDINATOR AT KHAO I DANG

Daniel C. Susott

Khao I Dang's opening days were an incredible time. From the border were brought first the most ill and starving, as well as the orphans. I was part of the screening teams which greeted each truck and bus as it arrived; we unloaded the people. I called in Khmer, "Hello! Welcome!" as the people handed me their babies and their grandmothers off the backs of the trucks; they each carried all their worldly possessions in two buckets and a bag, tied on the ends of a pole. They were herded into fenced-off areas where they squatted in the dust under the glaring sun while the "screeners" moved among them looking for any indication that a person might need intensive medical care or feeding. The new arrivals were counted, pregnant

Daniel C. Susott, co-editor of this book, is a physician and an international health and preventive medicine specialist who served from October 1979 to December 1980 in Thailand with the American Refugee Committee, first as PVO medical coordinator at Khao I Dang and then as medical coordinator of the Committee for Coordination of Services to Displaced Persons in Thailand. In the summer of 1982, he also served briefly as medical coordinator for the United Nations Border Relief Operation. He is currently an international health and preventive medicine consultant and film maker in Honolulu and New York.

women were brought in out of the sun and spared the Fansidar (malaria treatment/prophylaxis) which was given to everyone else; some of the children were immunized—though not enough of them. It was hot, dusty, exhausting—yet joyous!—work. In October 1979, weeks before I reached Thailand under the aegis of the American Refugee Committee (ARC), word had come of the first medical workers to arrive at the Thai-Cambodian border being devastated by the death surrounding them: babies dying daily in their arms; skeletal, black-clad Khmer people dying under trees, and a few expiring in the mud of their new "home" at Sa Kaeo. A pair of American doctors had fled in despair. The world was responding, but not fast enough for many.

I was privileged to work first at the border near Aranyaprathet, where 500,000 Khmer had congregated, already zealously triaged and intensively rehydrated by Soforthilfe, which had preceded us, and less enthusiastically by the ICRC. The Khmer people, who had known no medical care for five years, must have been glad to see us, but all I remember is the crush of the seriously ill, starving refugees flooding our clinics—and the gentle, anxious Khmer doctor—"Dr. Sam"—who welcomed us so gratefully, and sent us home each night with, "I'll see you tomorrow—early!" In that border no-man's-land, even a day trip was a danger; no foreigners stayed overnight.

In those days, when I was newly arrived and naive, it seemed to me that the ICRC was offering only a token, Band-Aid approach to the problem. I remember that their supplies of milk and other foodstuffs would run out quite early in the day and mothers with starving babies would be told, "Sorry, no more today. Come back tomorrow." Perhaps it only seemed that the members of the staff were unconcerned and only too happy to be on their way in the early afternoon. I just remember wondering why they were there at all, and why they were not allowing the other eager and able groups access to the border and the most needy people.

With what relief we learned that the United Nations was imminently to open a new camp safely within Thailand, in which up to 300,000 of these tortured souls could find temporary respite. I did not then understand the political ramifications of such a major move; I only understood that this meant safety and life for the small orphan I had seen so briefly in the clinic: a 12-year-old looking as if he were seven—a somber little man, so polite, saying that he shivered alone in the cold night with no one to care for him and now there was his fever and no food.

There were hundreds like him. I had nothing to offer him. I pinned a few vitamin pills in a tiny plastic bag inside his tattered shirt, and wrapped a fresh towel around his feeble frame. He thanked me silently with his hands held together before his face as if praying.

When he had gone, I sobbed uncontrollably for a few moments while the tearful nurse kept back the flood of people at the door of our hut. What more could we do? Treat him for malaria? Tell him to come back every day for a checkup and whatever food we could bring in for him? Anything seemed better than to lose him in that sea of suffering people.

This was the first of several times I wept during those early days, sometimes for the overwhelming misery I saw or learned of, and sometimes for the joy and relief of experiencing the liberation of persons who had been kept in hell during the previous years. So I shared the euphoria which greeted the opening of Khao I Dang, a safe haven just inside Thailand, but far enough away from the agonies and uncertainties of the border zone and Cambodia. In those opening days, after my hospital work was finished in Khao I Dang, I would go to the orphanage and watch for the solemn little man, not feeling that I could rest until I was assured that he was safe and well.

In those first days, a few Khmer refugees came forward who spoke better English or French—and even Japanese!—and who volunteered to be our interpreters. I remember, in particular, two young men, both of whom had lost their entire families. They helped us with the screening and later became permanent members of the American Refugee Committee. Living in the adult medical ward and working around the clock, they sometimes would sleep exhausted in the small hours of the morning, huddled like puppies on a bare board bed.

Early in the process of screening, after a particularly long hot day, just as we were saying good-bye to the last of the day's arrivals marching off in a line with bamboo and plastic into the empty fields to set up their dwellings, a truck rolled up as if it had just emerged from hell itself. Of the 30 or so people on board, half were in such terrible condition that they had to be immediately rushed to the hospital. A woman apathetically presented the little bundle she was carrying; it was her baby, who had died on the way to the camp. (No time to mourn for that one then, so I do it now.) As the dust was settling in the golden glow of sunset, out of the group of a dozen remaining refugees stepped a small boy of about ten and his grandfather, who set down in the dust a flat box he had been carrying on his shoulders. They opened it to reveal a stringed instrument shaped like a hammer dulcimer, and the boy proceeded to make the most marvelous music any of us had ever heard. There, in the golden sunset, exhausted relief workers and refugees gathered around and shared this miracle: we could feel the fatigue being washed from us, and our spirits soared. To think that somehow, in·the horrible years of the Khmer Rouge world—a world with no laughter or music—somehow this had survived! A young child playing so wondrously his people's music. Perhaps there was, indeed, hope for the Cambodian people.

As the screening became more routine, I devoted more time to working in the hospital ward. While there were mostly encouraging recoveries (What miracles can be wrought with food, clean water, rest, and a few antibiotics!), a few people stand out in my memory as being all the more tragic for having come so close to liberation, only to die when just in sight of relief. There was a young woman, age 27, with a liver tumor that filled her abdomen; her lovely face, stoic except for the tears of pain, seemed as if it could not belong to the horribly swollen abdomen and tortuous blood vessels snaking across her breasts and belly; her husband and infant daughter stayed silently by her bedside as she wasted away and died. And there were the two little boys who sat by their mother, Sem, as she became progressively weaker and thinner from her intestinal tuberculosis; I was on duty the night I found them sobbing silently by her bedside, her breathing stilled and her suffering ended. I had told her through an interpreter only hours before that we would guarantee that her children would be cared for, that their future would be assured. She could leave with that small comfort.

As the months passed and the short-term emergency volunteers came and went, I attained some seniority, based—rather than on any special talents—on my having been able to stay longer than many voluntary agency (volag) personnel. In the early days, there were two hospitals, each with a 1,000-bed capacity, and at the height of the new arrivals during the opening days, the census attained a peak of some 1,500 inpatients. This eventually declined enough so that much of Hospital B could be closed and its former wards used for other purposes: the school of nursing [see the chapter, "Medical Training Programs for Refugees," by Barbara Bayers], the sewing center, administration, etc. Rehabilitation and tuberculosis wards remained in Hospital B while the wards for more acute illnesses were located in Hospital A near the admissions (emergency) ward.

Khao I Dang experienced the mixed blessing of a glut of medical personnel. At one point, there were more than 20 volags involved in some aspect or another of medical care, with the number of expatriate volag personnel approaching 450. There were almost 100 doctors, a ratio of one doctor to each 1,500 refugees. This was ludicrous since another camp was being served by a single physician who was also responsible for training, public health, and care of the 100,000 Thai villagers in the vicinity. I wonder how he did it. My only clue is that when I visited his rather humble lodgings, we were attended by servants who served us on their knees lest their heads be higher than ours, a Thai custom which indicated to me that he was used to being treated very respectfully and was probably able to delegate a lot of his work with the dignity appropriate to the region.

One problem with the "physician glut" was that it made the level of medical care obviously of a different—rather than better —standard from that available to the local Thai people and contributed to the rivalry in which the volags engaged. A major justification for having so many extra people on hand was that one honestly did not know if the population of Khao I Dang would climb to 300,000 (as in the original plan) or shrink, or if new service sites would open up, requiring personnel on rather short notice. The medical coordinator was therefore left to act as mediator in the rivalry and to participate in the planning as best he or she could.*

I began dividing my time between working on the ARC ward and coordinating Hospital A. This put me in a unique position because the medical problems I experienced on the ward could be translated into effective administrative action. It also severely strained my time, but in those early days we all worked harder than we were accustomed.

I remember one haunting lesson: the first surgery performed in the camp. A young man whose appendix had ruptured was taken to the new "operating room," and his abdomen was opened. His belly was full of feces. The Scandinavian surgeon closed the hole in his intestines very artfully. He neglected, however, either to wash the bowels thoroughly before closing the abdomen or to leave a rubber drain inside, so that the infection that one might expect to devleop in such a situation in the tropics could freely drain, and not cause the horrendous problems of an abscess forming. The worst happened, and a few days later the young man's condition deteriorated, and a second operation had to be performed. This time the poor fellow's abdomen was a soup of pus and draining fistulas. We cleaned up this (preventable) mess as well as possible, but in the post-op ward, fluid (and undigested food) seeped freely from his intestines through his abdominal wall. He began to waste away—while his wife and five children helplessly watched—because the overworked post-op nurses could not keep the flow of food into his system high enough to make up for the losses through his many fistulas.

A temporary improvement came in surgical care when, in my new position as hospital coordinator, I was able to shift staff around to give the post-op staff some extra support and relief. It was a temporary victory, and I still lament the fact that skilled surgeons (and other medical people) because of

*One of the Cambodian physicians working with Dr. Susott and the American Refugee Committee was Dr. Haing S. Ngor, who later received an Academy Award for his best supporting actor role in *The Killing Fields*.

ignorance of basic differences in practice in their own countries and the underdeveloped tropics, have the capacity for
doing more harm than good.

I continued to take night duty, which at first was made
memorable and poignant by the presence of the Cambodian
medical students who assisted us on our wards; between bedside visits (which they would usually handle) we had long discussions in the quiet nights which more than once deeply
moved me. They told me the stories of their lives, these young-
sters who turned out to be so similar to myself in background
and aspirations. To think that these educated city kids had
been forced to live under such appalling conditions for years,
to have lost so many of their family and friends under the
worst imaginable conditions. (When I returned briefly to the
United States after eight months in Khao I Dang, I saw a friend
whose mother had just died of breast cancer, and I remember
thinking, "What a luxury it is to have your mother die in bed,
at a relatively advanced age, surrounded by all the medical
attention necessary and an adoring family, rather than to be
hacked to death tied to a tree!" Observations like this were
difficult to share with those who had not experienced what
we had.)

At night there were babies to deliver (if the midwives needed
assistance) and medications to administer; the background
symphony was the "Khmer cough" (or "Kampuchean crud"
or "Khao I Dung lung") which afflicted almost everyone at
"Khao I Dust"—and on the border. There were deaths at night,
and sometimes humorous moments, such as the exasperation
and triumph of a young Cambodian medical student, who had
not held a scalpel since Phnom Penh fell in April 1975: she
removed a bullet from the thigh of a wounded man while
the whole ward full of patients jeered and cheered and the pair
of Khmer doctors and nurses gave too much advice. (I still have
the bullet.) Months later, walking through the camp, I would be
hugged by a joyful healthy person over whom I had labored
many nights for months, such as the terribly anemic young
women who kept going into heart failure, or whole families
who had resided for indeterminate periods in the ward while
various members fell ill as others were being cured.

I found many occasions to be grateful for the presence of "the Holistics" [see the chapter, "Holistic Health Care," by Virginia Veach]. After I was "promoted" to camp medical coordinator—a job in which I represented the volags in conjunction with the ICRC medical coordinator, who was being phased out as the "emergency" calmed down, I spent what then seemed an inordinate amount of time defending the "family practice" team which ran Ward B6. Rumors were rife that they were treating measles with massage, and malnutrition with acupuncture. (The latter embarrassingly almost seemed to be the case as I took the then CCSDPT medical coordinator, Dr. John Naponick, on ward rounds. We discovered a woman with obvious beriberi whose chart—a dusty card clipped to the foot of her bed—indicated that she was receiving daily acupuncture therapy, but there was no indication of vitamin therapy. After my initial consternation, it was clarified that *all* such patients received appropriate levels of vitamin pills and injections, though it was yet to be marked clearly on the card. For a moment there I felt that my months of standing up on behalf of "the Holistics" would be washed down the drain.)

I thank Heaven and all the Buddhas that Ward B6 was there the day of the border flare-up that sent us truckloads of dying and wounded; in one truck was a bewildered elderly woman with short white hair, desperately and gently cradling the body of her dead son in her arms. All alone now, where were we to take her? I took her myself to Ward B6, knowing that there above all places she would receive the caring and nurturing she needed at this horrible time. They received her with such care and love that my eyes burned with tears. I will never forget how, upon my visit a few days later, I encountered a transformed person. No longer the mute, paralyzed, grief-stricken woman of a few days earlier, but a poised and animated lady whose first actions were gestures and words of thanks for having brought her to this wonderful healing place. She had been able, with the help of the resident monk, to mourn for her son, and the ward staff had even been able to facilitate the tracing of other family members (all of whom we had thought were lost).

The issue of the appropriate level of care (medical care consistent with that available to the local population) came to a head one day in Aranyaprathet when a Khmer man in his forties became so paralyzed by Guillan-Barré syndrome that he was unable to breathe unaided. In Western countries, such a person can be maintained on a respirator until the disease resolves itself enough for the patient to be able to breathe unaided. But in Khao I Dang, the best that could be hoped for was for someone to stay at the bedside around the clock, pumping by hand a small Ambu bag to "breathe" for him. It might have taken weeks for the man to recover, and it was obviously impracticable to expect such hand ventilation to continue on for so long a time. Furthermore, there was no facility for artificial respiration at the hospital in Aranyaprathet. Thus, one of my last acts as medical coordinator of Khao I Dang was to authorize the use of an ICRC ambulance to take the man on the four-hour ride to Bangkok for hospitalization. He was the head of a family with several children, and it made sense for all concerned that he should be given a fighting chance for survival. Cambodia did not need more widows and orphans.

We had previously had difficulty convincing the director of the local hospital to allow patients with special medical problems to pass through his hospital to more sophisticated care in Bangkok; we had to obtain the needed permission and passes from him. This was especially sad in the cases of the young people needing heart surgery, where timely intervention could give a youngster a better-functioning heart and perhaps 60 more years of life. When delayed too long—as tragically happened on several occasions—the heart could deteriorate to such a degree that it was beyond saving. We railed against the incredible political red tape that we often were unable to cut through in time to save a person's life.

On this occasion, the ill man was blessed with the presence of a strong-willed American nurse who volunteered patiently to pump the football-sized bag all the way to Bangkok. Her determination to keep the patient alive was severely tested when they arrived at the hospital in Aranyaprathet. The director refused to give them the needed permission to take the ill man to Bangkok, and when the nurse ordered the pickup-truck ambulance to drive on, the director chased them in his car 20 kilometers down the road, finally stopping them for a roadside argument, the nurse pleading as she continued to pump the bag. Eventually compassion and good sense prevailed, and the patient arrived in Bangkok, where after a time on the respirator, he fully recovered and was safely returned to his family.

Would the same care have been available for a Thai villager in similar dire straits? Perhaps not. But in this instance, the life of a man was saved at the risk of permanently damaging relations with the local authorities. It was an unfortunate trade, but one that no one at the time regretted.

KHAO I DANG:
A REFUGEE'S PERSPECTIVE

Siphana Sok

On December 30, 1979, I arrived at Khao I Dang with the help of a French Red Cross team. My first impression of Khao I Dang was a feeling of security that was quite unknown to me for the previous five years. I stood there in the middle of the crowd, staring at faces full of hope. I was confused about my feelings, so much they have crossed my mind, and on many a night at Khao I Dang, I dreamed of thousands of things.

After five years where brutalities and tortures were common, I experienced compassion, affection, and love. Uusally late at night I sat by myself and thought about everything that came into life in this refugee camp. Here people smiled; they found again the notion of living, and they showed in their faces new rays of hope. The rations of food were not excellent, but they were enough. At least, we refugees could eat with peace with our families without any fear. The presence of foreign relief workers from all over the world brought our morale up and strengthened our sense of security. All along the dusty roads, the appearance of any of them—a medical volunteer, a journalist, or simply a visitor—generated a strong stream of enthusiasm

---

Siphana Sok, a Cambodian, was a radio operator and a translator with the ICRC and then the United States Embassy in Thailand from January to October 1980. He was at Khao I Dang from December 1979 to July 1980. He is now Assistant Marketing Director, Pennsylvania Branch, General Development Corporation, Bensalem, Pennsylvania.

and a warm welcome. Understanding the different language might be a barrier, but the deep expression of sincerity in their faces filled up the wide gap. For me, every day was a new day, full of hope and value. What else could I do to respond to this great noble act toward my people but to help in any way I could? So far, I had nothing to sacrifice but my spirit, my willingness to help, my physical strength, my compassion, and my love.

On breaks at work during the daytime or in the evening, I liked to go from one ward to another, making more friends, and when circumstances allowed, I liked to help the relief workers translate or do whatever needed to be done. I paid many visits to the French-speaking MSF team, not primarily to practice my French but to observe their medical practice. They specialized in obstetrics, and it made me feel so relieved to see newborn babies being delivered under safe and proper conditions and pregnant women being taken care of meticulously by nurses. I just couldn't imagine the anxiety and fear they would have been experiencing if they were still in the jungle, somewhere on the border. Here, besides feeling safe and secure, they received good treatment from people who cared.

Two other wards were also the focus of my visits—the admissions ward and the surgery ward—mainly because of their feverish activities. The atmosphere of the admissions ward was always tense since every patient that had to be hospitalized had to check in there. From general cases to the wounded, they came unceasingly; after initial treatment they were admitted to hospital wards. Despite the intense influx of patients, many relief workers still volunteered to conduct a medical training session for the Cambodian helpers. Their determination to help us was strong and deep, and the personal energy expended was tremendous.

COORDINATING THE UNITED STATES VOLUNTEER RESPONSE

Margaret R. Cronyn and Russell E. Morgan, Jr.

To address the overwhelming need of the Khmer refugees and to respond to the outpouring of volunteer assistance from the American medical community, President Carter directed in November 1979 that a clearinghouse be established to match up medical personnel wishing to volunteer in the relief operation in Thailand with those agencies that needed them. This was in response to a request by Thailand that PVO volunteers be used, rather than employees of foreign governments. Because of Phnom Penh's sensitivity to the numbers of international relief personnel admitted into Kampuchea, initially the great majority of medical volunteers were to be assigned to the voluntary agencies working with Khmer refugees. In fact, Phnom Penh did not authorize international medical volunteers to enter Kampuchea until mid-1980 and then, with few exceptions, only ICRC volunteers from Eastern-bloc nations.

The National Council for International Health (NCIH)—a nongovernmental consortium of health professional associations, governmental agencies, universities, and PVOs involved in the improvement of world health—was mandated and funded by

Margaret R. Cronyn was Coordinator of the Cambodian Refugee Health Clearinghouse at the National Council for International Health, Washington, DC, from November 1979 to August 1980. She is currently Contract Manager, Maryland Office of Refugee Affairs, Baltimore, Maryland. Russell E. Morgan, Jr., has been Executive Director of the National Council for International Health since September 1979.

the State Department to establish the clearinghouse. The Cambodian Refugee Health Clearinghouse began in late November 1979, staffed by a coordinator, two assistants, and 30 volunteers. Staff expertise included backgrounds in Third World development, refugee work, primary health care, public health, and Asian studies. The clearinghouse was to be a telephone information service, a volunteer health-personnel data bank, a voluntary-agency data-bank search service, and a public-information and training support group. Because it was substantially funded under a grant from the State Department, all services were provided to PVOs free of charge.

As a telephone information service, the clearinghouse was a central point for all those needing information about the refugee situation in Thailand. Because of its staff members' broad knowledge of activities in Khmer refugee relief, it was able to link groups in mutually beneficial alliances, forestall the provision of unneeded goods and services, channel donated medical supplies to those PVOs needing such supplies, and handle referrals from PVOs, governmental agencies, and the United States Congress.

The volunteer health-personnel data bank attracted over 3,000 health professional volunteers during the nine-month "emergency" phase of clearinghouse operations, and the PVOs came to rely increasingly on the clearinghouse as they exhausted their own files in search of volunteers. Included in the data bank were physicians, registered nurses, dentists, and other health professionals, such as optometrists, paramedics, laboratory technicians, nutritionists, public-health administrators, educators, epidemiologists, and teachers, social workers, and other nonmedical personnel.

The voluntary-agency data-bank search service was highly effective. Usually within 24 hours of having received from a PVO a request for specialized medical assistance, the clearinghouse would locate and refer several candidates to fill that particular need. Also, at the request of the ICRC and the State Department, the clearinghouse assembled a standby surgical team of five surgeons and two anesthesiologists ready to go to Thailand should the border fighting intensify. A formal liaison with

American medical schools and various health professional associations facilitated identification and deployment of specialized medical personnel. The public-information and training-support component was a very satisfying and useful tool in educating the public and the departing volunteers bound for Thailand. The clearinghouse developed informational materials describing its services and the health situation among the Khmer refugees and distributed this information to all the American PVOs, the health-professional associations, members of Congress, and interested members of private industry. It also published a monthly newsletter to keep its constituent groups and the data-bank volunteers informed about developments in the refugee situation. It sponsored a briefing for all interested groups given by John H. Bryant, M.D., director of the Office of International Health, Department of Health and Human Services, shortly after his inspection trip to the refugee camps in December 1979. Technical training in the identification and treatment of xerophthalmia (nutritional blindness) was given by NCIH in conjunction with Helen Keller International, the American Council of Voluntary Agencies for Foreign Service, and IRC in February 1980. In June 1980, the clearinghouse hosted a two-day workshop entitled, "Cambodian Refugee Relief: Lessons Learned and Future Directions," which was attended by 60 people representing PVOs, universities, professional associations, international organizations, the United States government, and various other interests. A transcript of certain presentations and summaries of the workshops was compiled and given wide distribution among those involved in refugee relief efforts.

The clearinghouse developed orientation packets addressing various aspects of tropical medicine, Thai and Khmer cultural traits, epidemiological studies of the refugee camps, and treatments being employed to combat the various health problems encountered among the refugees. The 300 orientation packets were then donated to PVOs for use by departing medical volunteers.

Thirty-nine United States PVOs raised an unprecedented $62 million from October 1979 to September 1980.

The clearinghouse experience with the PVO community was, for the most part, quite successful. Each PVO felt that protecting its own autonomy was important, and clearinghouse staff members were careful to respect that need and work within the framework offered. The PVO community had rarely demonstrated the cohesiveness evident in the Cambodian relief situation.

The Cambodian relief operation attracted many people, and several new PVOs were formed to meet the emergency needs. The newer PVOs, by their very nature, had little experience in dealing with foreign governments and international organizations; and the information which the clearinghouse was able to provide them, or direct them toward, was as beneficial to them as it was to the overall efficiency of the relief operation.

To obtain the best possible medical information concerning the Khmer refugees in Thailand and along the border area, members of the clearinghouse staff interviewed many experts in the field of refugee relief and tropical medicine who had visited Thailand during the emergency. A very important contact was a weekly telephone conversation with John Naponick, M.D., the medical coordinator for the CCSDPT. He advised the clearinghouse of the present situation in the camps, what PVOs were assigned to particular tasks (assignments changed frequently and so therefore did the volunteer needs of the PVOs), which medical and sanitation needs he felt were not being adequately met, and what medical specialists that were not then being sent out by the PVOs were needed. At the same time, the staff was able to advise him of the kinds of specialists the clearinghouse had available. With the information furnished us by John Naponick, the clearinghouse was able to contact the American offices of PVOs and offer the specialists requested. Additionally, he mailed us the timely reports issued by the UNHCR concerning the needs and treatment of the Khmer refugees.

When the Khmer refugee situation stabilized in August 1980, a group of PVOs encouraged NCIH to continue the operations of the clearinghouse. These PVOs recommended that the clearinghouse set up a permanent, continually updated data bank of volunteer health personnel that would enable PVOs and United States government agencies to respond to international and domestic health needs in refugee and disaster situations. The clearinghouse, renamed the NCIH Volunteer Health Clearinghouse (VHC), began operation in 1981. In addition to referring health volunteers, the VHC has a mandate to inform public and private sector organizations about humanitarian needs generated by international emergencies and to promote regular training programs for American health personnel to improve their skills and capabilities in international relief situations.

COORDINATING MEDICAL
PVO ACTIVITIES IN THAILAND

John J. Naponick

Private voluntary organizations (PVOs) play a significant role in international relief and development work. In Thailand, the majority of the medical workers caring for Cambodian refugees came from the PVO sector. PVOs had from 400 to 600 workers, while the ICRC had 200 to 250 and the Thai Red Cross about 100. Thirty-five PVOs contributed $42.2 million to the cause. Because of the numerous organizations involved, coordination of PVO activity was of paramount importance. PVOs had to coordinate among themselves, as well as with the international organizations (UNHCR and ICRC) and the Thai government.

The importance of such coordination had been recognized and practiced in Thailand since 1975, when the first refugees from Laos, Vietnam, and Cambodia began to arrive. The PVOs formed the Committee for Coordination of Services to Displaced Persons in Thailand (CCSDPT). The head of each PVO attended a monthly CCSDPT meeting to discuss common problems, share information, distribute resources, and coordinate activities. A subcommittee was formed to deal exclusively with

John J. Naponick served in the Cambodian relief operation in Thailand first from January to July 1979 as Health Officer for patient care and public health with the International Rescue Committee. He then served from October 1979 to July 1980 as Medical Director of the Committee for Coordination of Services for Displaced Persons in Thailand. He is now a Public Health Physician and Medican Advisor to the United States Agency for International Development Mission in Rangoon, Burma.

medical problems. Initially coordination took the form of division of responsibility. The camps were divided among the PVOs. One PVO assumed the role of "lead PVO" for each camp and essentially controlled the input into that camp. This form of coordination worked very well until October 1979, given the small number of PVOs involved, the limited resources, and the enormity of the refugee problem—approximately 150,000 refugees in 15 camps. The situation changed dramatically with the influx of Cambodian refugees into Sa Kaeo in October 1979 and the massive influx of aid that followed. Each PVO representative of the CCSDPT then became so occupied with his or her individual PVO programs that little time could be devoted to coordination.

The CCSDPT then decided to appoint an executive secretary and a medical coordinator. These appointments did not come to pass easily. The concept of coordinator was first introduced in the summer of 1979 and again in October 1979, and both times motions to create such a position were defeated. In order to fully understand these developments, one must understand the PVOs more completely.

PVOs exist in all corners of the world, but most come from the developed nations. The common denominator is humanitarian assistance, motivated by strong religious, moral, political, or social beliefs. PVOs have a long history of very valuable humanitarian work. Each agency represents a well-defined constituency of people sharing common beliefs. Funding is usually provided through private donations. Home-office and field staff members generally share similar beliefs. As a consequence of their organization and funding, most PVOs are independent and very highly motivated. Money is raised for a specific cause, and the PVO feels obligated to spend it on that specific cause. This policy causes several problems.

First, there is need for visibility. Donors want to see concrete results from their contributions. Most PVOs try to keep administrative costs below 10 percent of their budget so as to assure donors that their money reaches the purpose for which it was given. Although this is a good principle, it sometimes leads to inefficient practices. The need for visibility also causes concentration on programs that are visible and easily understandable to the donors, such as a hospital ward with the PVO's name on it. Some PVOs encounter such problems as having the money to buy a vehicle (on which it is easy to place the PVO's name), but no funds for gasoline with which to run it.

The second problem relates to programming. Certain situations carry much emotional appeal. In the Cambodian situation, the starving children caused a great outpouring of emotions and contributions. Many PVOs came to Thailand determined to spend this money on the children. But not all groups can work with children. A major problem in the camps was sanitation. A pile of human feces does not generate the same outpouring of sympathy or money, so consequently very few groups were willing to deal with the sanitation problem.

Programming is very closely tied to the perception of need as well as the type of individual volunteer sent. In the Cambodian situation, the need was perceived to be a need for acute-care medical personnel. PVOs sent out traditional curative doctors and nurses. The need for this type of medical input was a correct perception from October to December 1979. In 1980, death rates had fallen to prewar (1975) Cambodian levels. In spite of changing conditions, the PVOs continued to send curative medical personnel, whom I found to be very inflexible in their ability to change roles in response to a changing situation.

PVOs, then, are groups supported by donors who give money to do specific programs carried out by people who believe in these programs. PVOs are strongly motivated, and it is difficult to change their direction. Now it becomes clear why the PVOs were not anxious to have a medical coordinator appointed. To the PVOs—and the international organizations—coordination is defined as "my PVO doing what it wants to do and the other PVOs doing whatever is left to do."

I had at least 40 PVOs in the field with another 40 trying to get into the action. The problem was that most of them were willing to send out medical teams composed of curative medical personnel. All PVOs and donors wanted to run a hospital or staff an OPD. All were expecting to bring food and medical care to starving children. This was their perception of the problem. My perception of the problem in the refugee camps was very different. What is needed in a refugee camp is not just curative medical services, but emphasis on community health—that is, interaction of health and nonhealth components, such as food supplies on a regular basis, improvement of hygiene practices and sanitation facilities, adequate housing, health education, programs for self-sufficiency, and *finally* appropriate medical services. These concepts are not new, they are tantamount to reinventing the wheel, but they are necessary for newcomers.

The ICRC guidelines for a general medical policy concerning Cambodian refugees in Thailand stated: Give priority to basic public health, sanitation, nutrition, and hygiene; give autonomy in as many medical fields as possible; provide the same level of medical aid which is normally provided by the Thai government to their population; and avoid overmedication. This approach was very difficult for curative medical personnel from the developed countries to believe in. They had been trained to do everything possible to cure each individual patient, regardless of cost, with little understanding of community health. The structure of the PVOs would allow medical teams to treat patients with diarrhea in the hospital forever, without solving the basic sanitation problem that initially caused the diarrhea.

Whenever there is a disaster, people flock to the scene to aid the victims. Most of the workers are substantial professionals in their own countries who sacrifice their time to come and assist. They arrive on the scene, work hard, do their job, and return home. I do not wish to address my remarks to these hardworking, upstanding people. But it seems to me that the relief effort in Thailand attracted many more of these whom I would call the "lunatic fringe": people who described themselves as journalists, paramedics, and just plain do-gooders. They have, at best, only a very limited medical background, and even those with a good background tend to be very venturesome. They come to the relief effort with highly unrealistic expectations of what they can do, of what contributions they can possibly make. They demand full-scale support, without realizing that any contribution which they have to make may well be minimal.

There were many others who for humanitarian or whatever other reasons tended to ignore their own personal safety and rushed into combat zones in order to give assistance. This was a continuing source of embarrassment to me. ICRC was given the responsibility of patrolling the border areas, which they did with help from the Thai military. Radio contact was established and daily briefings were given, so that ICRC could go into the safe areas without risking their personnel. Many people, however, with no regard for organization and coordination rushed into areas that were unsafe, risking their lives and limbs in the effort to provide service.

The relief effort also attracted many persons who held unorthodox medical beliefs. For example, several groups came to give relief immersion—hot and cold therapy. From my medical perspective, I do not think that these groups contributed very much. One doctor, for example, who believed in charcoal for his own prophylactic treatment for malaria, found out that it did not work, by ending up with cerebral malaria and almost dying.

There are others, like some of those who attended the Civil Rights marches of the 1960s—who flock to relief efforts because they view them as social happenings. Such people caused the entire Cambodian relief effort a lot of embarrassment. They seemed to enjoy nude sunbathing and communal showers, which the Thais considered quite bizarre. Throughout the entire relief effort, the Thai people exhibited a remarkable amount of restraint and understanding of the odd ways of foreigners.

To me, one of the major problems was the lack of sensitivity on the part of the workers. One would have thought that they would have realized that they were in a foreign land, where they should observe the customs and beliefs of the local population. This, however, was not the case. Most workers felt that they were in Thailand on a mercy mission and were therefore immune to local customs and practices. They seemed to take very few precautions regarding their own safety; I know of two incidents in which young women were raped and stabbed. Workers did not seem to take proper health precautions. I often made rounds on volunteers who had developed a tropical disease that could easily have been prevented.

Another source of chronic irritation for me was the shipment of relief supplies. Whereas some supplies are needed in a relief operation, others have no value whatsoever. Many hours were wasted sorting through drugs that were outdated, used for only the most rare indications, or had no use in a refugee situation. The various and sundry goods that I was offered included frozen orange juice in an area were there was no refrigeration. I was offered breast milk in the form of breast-feeding mothers from the United States. While breast milk is obviously the best source of nourishment for babies, and while this was a remarkably kind offer, the logistics of trying to care for American women providing American breast milk under these adverse situations caused me to refuse the offer. ICRC has published guidelines on what equipment, supplies, and medicines are needed during a relief effort. This list should be consulted before collections are taken, donations spent, and valuable money and valuable time wasted.

Given the multiplicity of problems with the PVOs, their organizations, funding, program goals, personnel, and materials, the challenge was how to coordinate their activities. I was involved with two distinct phases of coordination: the organization of ongoing activity and the planning for future directions. Initially the refugees were in two large camps: Sa Kaeo and Khao I Dang. Through meetings with the PVOs, their roles were defined and their scope broadened to encompass the ideal set out by UNHCR and ICRC. During this phase, coordination was achieved by consensus of opinion. The PVOs would agree on what they wanted to do. As long as each PVO had a defined function, they were willing to participate in coordination.

In the camps, the PVO, ICRC, and Thai Red Cross volunteers worked side by side, doing a marvelous job caring for the refugees. Along the border, where ICRC was in charge of coordination, the situation was different. To ICRC, this meant being in total control of the situation; in essence, ICRC blocked any PVO participation on the border. From the PVO point of view, this was unacceptable and represented control, not coordination. During this phase a few "pirate" PVOs became active along the border, working on their own, outside of either PVO or ICRC coordination. This uncoordinated activity could have been deleterious to the entire effort—not to mention the safety problems created.

The most important endpoint of coordination was good health care for the refugees, resulting from the PVOs and international organizations working together in a harmonious fashion. In the second phase of these coordination activities, the Thai government and UNHCR announced a shifting of the refugees from the two large camps, Sa Kaeo and Khao I Dang, to smaller camps at Kab Cherng, Mai Rut, Kamput, Chonburi, and Sa Kaeo II. This shift in the refugee population gave the PVOs a wonderful chance to regroup, reorganize, and rethink their involvement in the relief operation.

By this time, the UNHCR had made the very wise decision to sign contracts with the PVOs to provide services in the camps. This announcement was welcomed by the PVOs as it gave them legal documents that protected their own positions.

In close consultation with the UNHCR, the CCSDPT drew up a list of services that needed to be provided. Listed were not only acute medical services but also the full range of community and public-health services, with a view toward creating self-sufficient development programs. Now that we had a list of services for each new camp, the CCSDPT held a meeting with all the PVOs working in Thailand. At this meeting, the various agencies discussed where they wanted to work and what they wanted to do. This meeting was an excellent opportunity for each PVO to reevaluate its goals, consolidate its programs, and make plans for the future. The meeting produced many important concepts. First, all agreed that the number of PVOs working in any one camp should be minimized. Each PVO should try to consolidate its programs into one camp instead of having many programs in many camps. (This concept of a "lead volag" in each camp proved to be a great success.) Those PVOs who knew they could work well with other PVOs should plan to work together.

The meeting was highly fruitful. Afterward, separate meetings were held for each camp to decide on responsibilities. Package programs were offered so that responsibility was delegated to provide total curative medicine and public-health services. For example, a group could do children's feeding only if they also agreed to do health education and provide sanitarians.

Agreement was quickly reached in five of the six camps, and private discussion between the CCSDPT and UNHCR worked out details for the one remaining camp. Of all the more than 40 PVOs participating in these meetings, only one was unable to work where it wanted, but an acceptable alternative was found. The UNHCR was very impressed by this process and decided to use it for new programs in education, cultural activities, and vocational projects. The PVOs demonstrated that they could work together and coordinate their activities. All were pleased.

In this planning, the role of the medical coordinator was critical. Never before, to my knowledge, had an overall medical coordinator been appointed. As already mentioned, to establish such a position was difficult. Each PVO was suspicious that other PVOs would get preferential treatment. I had no power except the power of friendly persuasion. I had to have an over-all view of the situation, and take on a sense of fairness in dealing with the groups. I had to keep in mind what I was receiving were offers of curative medical services, but what I wanted was a balance of curative and preventive, public-health/sanitation, and community services. I did manage to establish good public-health teams in the field and find them financial support from various sources.

My other contribution was being a person to whom all could make inquiries. Individuals and groups who wanted to volunteer, make donations, or receive information came to me for suggestions and referrals. Perhaps this was my major achievement: I could channel resources.

Ideally, the role of the PVO medical coordinator should have included:

1. *Representing the PVOs in discussion with the Thai government and international organizations:* The various groups that deal with the PVOs do not want to have discussion with 40 different people. They prefer to have one representative.

2. *Coordinating the activities of the PVOs among themselves:* The PVO medical coordinator should be in a position to

mediate disputes between agencies, thus "keeping it in the family" and avoiding escalation of disputes to higher levels.

3. *Defining, solving, and evaluating problem areas:* Here is where I believe that the CDC or the PVOs could assign a public-health team composed of an epidemiologist, public-health nurses, and public-health technicians to survey refugee camps and define problem areas, such as epidemics, poor sanitation, or an inappropriately low level of medical care. Once the problems are defined, programs can be initiated to correct them. Finally, such a team would be invaluable in evaluation of ongoing projects. Evaluation is an area that is usually totally rejected in refugee work. Programs are done because PVOs have good intentions. PVO projects are rarely evaluated, and I believe this should be changed. Evaluation is essential, even in humanitarian programs.

4. *Setting guidelines and policies acceptable to PVOs, international organizations, and local governments:* This is an informative process that is essential to cooperation between the local authorities and the volunteers. For example, the Thai TB program found it could control the TB problem in Thailand very well with inexpensive drugs alone. On the other hand, many expatriate physicians felt that they had to use the newer, more expensive medicines. The PVO must work toward mutual understanding on these issues.

5. *Acting as a resource person to direct new PVOs into appropriate areas of work, to channel new donations in the proper direction, and to answer individual queries:* All through the crisis, people were eager to donate money or supplies. If the PVO medical coordinator can meet these people, he or she can channel more of their donations into needed areas, such as buying vaccines rather than antibiotics.

6. *Educating the volunteer workers:* This approach requires both helping volunteers recognize and treat exotic diseases and—I think this is the most important point—educating the volunteers that they were in *Thailand* taking care of *Cambodian* refugees. A sensitivity to the culture of the Thai and Cambodian people must be explained and indelibly impressed on the volunteers.

If I were to advise someone who was about to become PVO medical coordinator—or, indeed, any relief volunteer going to work overseas—I would recommend the following: Learn about the host country and its culture. Try to realize the problems that the refugees are causing by the very fact of their being there. Consult with the local health officials. Learn about the refugees—their culture, their capabilities, and their perceptions of their problems. Learn about the PVOs. Realize that they are independent but very capable, that they can work together and cooperate. Realize what they want to do and try to figure out how you can get them to do what is needed. Avoid high-cost technology and sophisticated methods. Rely on low-cost, labor-intensive local solutions that involve the refugees themselves. Be wary of traveling experts, especially those who go to the tropics when it is wintertime at home. Experts, I found, generally only write reports. The problems are rarely complex; they are simple. The only problem is finding someone willing to do the work. Develop a sense of humor—and, finally, be patient.

A THAI PERSPECTIVE ON REFUGEE RELIEF

Wongkulpat Snidvongs

Refugees are no strangers to Thailand, which borders five other countries. The Thai Red Cross Society was founded over 80 years ago as a result of armed conflict over territorial disputes with one of the major powers in Indochina at that time. It is therefore ironic that we should now be tested by such a large influx of refugees fleeing from similar conflicts in one of the Indochinese countries. We have strived to fulfill our humanitarian obligations while maintaining friendly cooperation with the Royal Thai Government authorities and the tide of expatriate relief workers.

The 1979–1982 period was not an easy time, but we tried to be both a self-reliant Red Cross society and a dependable partner in the world Red Cross movement. With such a massive relief operation involving hundreds of thousands of refugees and thousands of relief workers, both Thai and expatriate, there were bound to be both good and bad experiences. Mistakes have been made but we have no wish to condemn anyone, merely to share our experiences.

In May 1979, more than 40,000 Kampucheans fled into southeastern Thailand at Kao Larn, 450 kilometers southeast of Bangkok. We were then alone in our humanitarian endeavors,

Wongkulpat Snidvongs is a Thai physician who has been, from September 1979 to the present, Liaison Officer for the Red Cross Task Force for Kampuchean Relief Operations of the Thai Red Cross, Bangkok, Thailand.

doing the best we could for the starving, sick, and dying refugees at Kao Larn. Under the direct supervision of Her Majesty the Queen and our President, a camp to care for those people was established using our own budget, Her Majesty's own private fund, and domestic donations. Four months after their arrival in Thailand, the refugees, many of whom were unaccompanied minors, were regaining their health, hope, and self-respect. School classes were organized for children, adults were given vocational training, and all were registered so that tracing work could begin and families could be reunited. Three years after the camp came into being, only 176 refugees remained, the rest had been reunited with their families and repatriated or resettled in third countries.

For illegal immigrants in holding centers, we have done what we can for them out of compassion and for humanitarian reasons. We have not been alone in this, with the ICRC rapidly joining us at our side in August 1979, and still with us today. The ICRC, the LRCS, the United Nations organizations (notably UNHCR, UNICEF, and the WFP), international organizations, voluntary agencies, and the Thai authorities helped avert, for the time being, the death of a nation. Since the beginning of the relief operation, we have had medical teams, each composed of one doctor, four female nurses, one male nurse, two helpers, and one driver, working in holding centers and also on the border. At the height of the action in August 1980, we had up to 14 teams deployed, with a total of 112 workers, in addition to support personnel in Bangkok. In addition, emergency surgical teams were equipped and on standby in Bangkok, with the cooperation of the Faculty of Medicine, Chulalongkorn University. Surgical services were available in the holding center at Kamput, approximately 300 kilometers southeast of Bangkok, and throughout have been available at our health station in Aranyaprathet, approximately 300 kilometers east of Bangkok. These services were given by personnel from our relief division and specialists from the Faculty of Medicine, Chulalongkorn University. By 1982, at the health station in Aranyaprathet alone, 7,600 refugees and

6,000 Thais had received medical or surgical treatment for their eye, ear, nose, or throat conditions by our weekend surgical teams.

Since 1979, our relief division has been responsible for the provision of drugs and medical supplies to 18 refugee camps and six holding centers, with financial assistance from the UNHCR. A liaison office was established in November 1979 to coordinate relief activities of the Red Cross and to make available assistance or cooperation to international organizations and voluntary agencies. In May 1980, Thai Red Cross established its own tracing and mailing service center for refugees with the financial and initial technical support of the ICRC. By 1982, over 4,700 requests had been received and over 4,300 family files had been opened; of these, over 2,200 had been successfully closed with reunion of families, but sadly about 2,100 files had to be closed because of unsuccessful family tracing. By 1982, we had almost 120,000 index cards of Laotian refugees and Vietnamese boat people illegal immigrants at our tracing office.

From 1979, the Thai Red Cross Society gave paramedical training to over 300 Laotian refugees in the camps under the supervision of the Ministry of Interior and with the support of LRCS. Instructors were personnel from our relief division and our College of Nursing. In early 1980, when we were experiencing an influx of expatriate relief volunteers, orientation courses were organized for the new arrivals, with the cooperation of the Faculty of Tropical Medicine, Mahidol University. Later these courses were discontinued, possibly because many volunteers felt that they had become "veterans" and the newly arrived were better prepared to cope with conditions and diseases of the tropics. We still, however, maintain our academic advisory committee, established in 1980, and our contacts with the Faculty of Tropical Medicine in order to cope with medical crises that occur from time to time.

From 1979 to 1982, we fielded almost 500 teams, with rotations every ten days. Our relief division only has six doctors and 40 nurses full-time, but we have been reinforced by volunteers from the medical and nursing professions and have not had any problem whatsoever in fulfilling our obligations. By July 1982, we were still fielding nine teams, with emergency surgical teams on standby in Bangkok, and two ophthalmic and ENT (ear, nose, and throat) surgical teams giving weekend services at our Aranyaprathet health station. We would not have been able to sustain this scale of involvement for long without the financial assistance from ICRC's central appeal fund, and donations from sister societies and numerous benefactors both domestic and from abroad. We are proud to have been involved in the present action, and can summarize our involvement by mentioning that since 1979 we have given medical assistance to refugees on over 1,000,000 occasions and to Thai border people on over 630,000. Over 5,000 Thai Red Cross personnel and volunteers have been involved in this operation.

Since late 1980, medical problems in holding centers have been those that lie within the scope of community health. Overcrowding and poor sanitation encourage infectious diseases, including tuberculosis and malaria, which have been medical thorns in our sides throughout. This was worsened by different treatments given to refugees and to Thai people in the area, which encouraged the emergence of resistant strains of bacteria and parasites. Thailand has a national program dealing with both of these diseases. Unfortunately, expensive drugs given to refugees have had adverse effects on this program. Lack of accepted standardized treatments for each of these two diseases has continually been a cause for concern.

In November 1980, the Thai Red Cross Society, the ICRC, and LRCS established a task force to coordinate all Red Cross relief actions for Kampuchean refugees. It has been chaired jointly by our secretary general and the ICRC's chief delegate in Thailand. Earlier the voluntary agencies came under the coordination of the CCSDPT. Both bodies hold regular meetings, and the Thai Red Cross Society is represented in all the CCSDPT meetings. The Ministry of Public Health also has a subcommittee dealing with medical assistance to refugees, where again all concerned are represented.

In theory, this should ensure a smoothly coordinated operation for both refugees and the affected Thai border people.

In reality, the situation is far from satisfactory. Most of the difficulties are not realized at committee levels but at the field level. In our opinion, frictions and difficulties arise out of misunderstanding and the failure of relief workers to understand the security aspect of this operation. Professional differences among relief workers are other causes of the difficulties that can lead to grudges or mutual losses in confidence. These include doctors criticizing other doctors, expatriates insisting on standards of care common in their affluent countries, and Thais greatly concerned with the disparity between standards of treatment given to refugees and to Thais. At one time, we calculated that the cost of drugs and medical supplies to refugees was, on a per capita basis, 16 times the *total* budget of the Ministry of Public Health.

We feel very strongly that the medical aspect of relief must be jointly agreed upon by the government sector, the relief agencies including the Red Cross, and the academic sector of the medical profession in Thailand. Management of common diseases in this country should be agreed upon and standardized. In addition, expatriate medical relief workers should familiarize themselves with such standardized regimens. An advisory committee should also be set up to help solve occasional disputes and deal with crises. This committee might be composed of experts from the Ministry of Public Health, the medical faculties, the Red Cross, and the voluntary agencies.

Our solution, with standardized treatment regimens and an advisory medical committee, would result in appropriate medical care for refugees, with little disparity to that given to Thais. It would drastically reduce frictions among relief workers, reduce the enormous expense of medical care, and, most importantly of all, prepare the refugees for the health situation that they will face when they are repatriated.

To achieve this solution, we encourage the presentation of medical workshops, attended by representatives of relief agencies, Ministry of Public Health, and medical faculties for the development of standardized-treatment regimens and their eventual distribution and use by all relief workers. Our commitment to the refugee problem is therefore to reach this standardized level of medical care, acceptable to all concerned. When this happens, we can revert to our role of emergency relief and leave the long-term care of refugees to relief agencies, both domestic and expatriate.

PART 2

MEDICAL ACTIVITIES

WORKING AT KHAO I DANG:
A PHYSICIAN'S EXPERIENCE

Barry S. Levy

For six weeks in February and March 1980, I served as a physician at Khao I Dang, the largest of the camps for Cambodian refugees in Thailand. It was the most moving, sobering, and gratifying experience of my life, and in many ways the most real.

My experience and that of many other relief workers probably do not conform to most readers' expectations about what it must be like to work in a refugee camp. My overwhelming sense there was not of death but of life; not of the Cambodians' ability merely to survive but of their vitality; not of their grief for the past but of their hope for the future; not of our superficial differences but of our shared humanity; and not of the hopelessness of the situation but of the difference we and they were making.

I chose to participate in the relief effort in November 1979, and my wife, Nancy, chose to support me in doing so. For several weeks, we had read and listened to reports on Cambodia

Barry S. Levy, co-editor of this book, is an internist and public health specialist who served in the Cambodian relief operation in February and March 1980 with the Cornell Medical Team of the International Rescue Committee. He is currently Professor of Family and Community Medicine and Director of the Occupational Health Program at the University of Massachusetts Medical School in Worcester, Massachusetts. This chapter is adapted with permission from Levy, B.S., "Working in a Camp for Cambodian Refugees," *New England Journal of Medicine,* 304:1440-1444 (June 4), 1981. Copyright, 1981, by the Massachusetts Medical Society.

with horror and disbelief. We had contributed money to relief organizations, but somehow that did not seem enough. I soon joined the Cornell Medical Team, which was created by Ted Li and other medical residents at New York Hospital and by Courtney Pastorfield, a visiting nurse. They had convinced the medical school and the hospital to make a one-year commitment with the International Rescue Committee to send to Thailand teams of about 18 physicians, nurses, and medical students, each of whom would serve for overlapping periods of from six weeks to three months. The teams would staff the admissions ward (emergency room) of the 1000-bed field hospital at Khao I Dang.

During the two months before I left, I read everything I could about Cambodia and its people and about the medical and public-health needs of refugees. I was immunized against eight diseases—probably overimmunized—and I began taking two antimalarial medications. I recognized, however, that the most important preparation was not intellectual or immunologic, but emotional: getting beyond my "Be careful" approach to life to do something I wanted to do. My wife, family, friends, and colleagues were extremely supportive.

In early February 1980, members of our team from New York, Washington, D.C., and Boston flew to San Francisco, where some of us met for the first time. Although we had different backgrounds, previous experiences, and various areas of interest and expertise, our sense of common purpose enabled us to coalesce quickly. The following day we left in a chartered jet for Bangkok, and when we landed 23 hours later, Southeast Asia suddenly became very real for all of us. . . .

By the time we arrived, Khao I Dang's population had grown to more than 120,000, and no more Cambodians were legally permitted entry. On this former rice paddy, a few square kilometers in area, was the second largest aggregation of Cambodians in the world and the second largest "city" in Thailand. Although the people lived crowded together in huts of bamboo and thatch, the overall organization of the camp was miraculous. It contained ten sections, each of which was subdivided into about 100 groups. It had an organized political system with section and group leaders; and each section had facilities and services, including food and water distribution, an out-patient clinic, a supplementary-feeding center, a police station, and usually a school and an orphanage.

The United Nations, the Thai government, the International Committee of the Red Cross, and two dozen private agencies and their volunteer workers deserved much credit for this organization and the relatively smooth functioning of the camp. But so did the Cambodian people. It is easy to overlook the fact that the success of any relief effort is closely tied to the willingness of the affected people to help themselves.

The strength, courage, and spirit of the Cambodian people were extraordinary. They were determined not only to survive but to be fully alive and to ensure that their culture and their traditions continue.

Many of the Cambodians at the camp worked long hours in the heat—not merely for the wage of 50 cents a day, but largely out of pride and a desire to contribute to their community. Cambodian construction workers built huts and hospital wards and dug latrines. Cambodian public-health workers gave thousands of immunizations for polio, measles, and other diseases to children who were susceptible to them. Cambodian technicians performed microscopical examinations in the clinical laboratory. Cambodian craftpersons—including one woman who was almost blind—made bamboo baskets, mugs, and fish traps and sold them at the crafts center to relief workers for one or two dollars each. A Cambodian artist—Bun Heang Ung—drew chillingly graphic scenes of torture that he had witnessed under the Pol Pot regime.

Wind Song, the most remarkable Cambodian whom I met at Khao I Dang, reflects in many ways the strength and spirit of his people. He worked as an assistant by day and a translator by night in the camp hospital; he taught an English class for adults hoping to emigrate to the West, translated for other courses, and recruited blood donors—more than 300 by the time I left in mid-March. Why? He once explained to me, "I love so much helping people."

I was moved by the Cambodian teachers at Khao I Dang, who

operated the first schools available for their children in five years; some children could not attend, for there was a teacher shortage. Mr. Heng, a school principal, explained: "Most teachers were invited to a 're-education' weekend in 1977 and brought to the forests and slaughtered."

I was also moved by the young girls and boys who each day performed traditional Cambodian dances at the cultural center in the camp, accompanied by men playing traditional instruments. One day shortly after I arrived, Kong Loeup, an assistant director of the dance troupe, spotted me deep in a crowd of about 300 Cambodians watching a performance. He ushered me to a front-row seat on a straw mat, explained to me the symbolism of the dance, and afterward introduced me to Mrs. Mom Kamel, director of the troupe. (She had taught and performed internationally with the Classical Royal Ballet of Cambodia for almost 20 years.) They expressed their thanks to me and to all the relief workers. I told them that they were contributing much more to my life than I was to theirs.

A striking characteristic of the Cambodians at Khao I Dang was their spirit, most clearly manifested by the happiness of the children. By February 1980, only about 1 percent of the children were severely malnourished (down from 15 percent three months before), and there were few outward signs as I walked through the camp that they had lived through a holocaust. When not in school, they were jumping rope, tossing Frisbees, kicking soccer balls, and most often, playing makeshift games—pebbles and bottle caps served as checkers on a cross-hatched piece of cardboard—or dutifully toting pails of water hanging from bamboo poles balanced on their shoulders. They willingly posed for my camera, taught me to count in Khmer as we chanted numbers back and forth, and sold me much outdated Cambodian currency for 10 to 15 cents a bill.

Not all the children, however, were so outgoing and happy. There were more than 1,200 children living in camp orphanages, and many more orphans were being raised by relatives or friends. I met several orphans whom I shall never forget: An 11-year-old boy who had witnessed the torture and murder of his parents three years before and had been unable to see since then; an eight-year-old boy whose left arm had been paralyzed by a gunshot wound and whose five-year-old brother had been shot to death as they tried to cross a battlefield at night to get into Khao I Dang; a two-month-old orphan boy from a border camp who was left at our ward one afternoon and who was adopted by a woman who miraculously showed up a half hour later. (She said that she had no children; we did not ask whether she had had children who had died during the Pol Pot years.)

Many of the patients who came to the admissions ward were referred by physicians at outpatient clinics, who were often overwhelmed with patients and sent to us the ones who appeared most seriously ill for further evaluation and treatment. Others were brought in by medical teams who worked at the border about eight kilometers away. In the late afternoon and at night, after the clinics had closed, anyone who needed to see a doctor came directly to our ward. Although we worked six days a week on shifts about 12 hours long, we felt tired infrequently. We were assisted by a dozen Cambodian translators, some of whom were among the most sincere, brightest, and most ingenious people I have ever met. They anticipated our questions to patients and often obtained much information before we started. Hong Gau, for example, often said to me something like, "High fever every other day for five days. No cough. No diarrhea. Temperature 39 C. Chest clear. Probably malaria. Here is the blood smear. Do you want to examine it with me?" We were also assisted by a dozen Cambodian "helpers," who escorted patients to other wards, brought specimens to the laboratory, and assisted in other ways. In addition, Chu Pheng, one of about 50 surviving Cambodian physicians out of approximately 500 who were alive in 1975, worked with us. He had been about to graduate from medical school when Pol Pot took over; he had forgotten much of what he had once known and was relearning medicine as he saw patients under our supervision.

The admissions ward did not have the trappings of a modern emergency room in the United States. The bamboo-and-thatch structure with its gravel floor was a far cry from the facilities in which we had practiced back home. Medical records were kept on index cards that were carried—and rarely lost—by the patients. We had only a marginally adequate supply of drugs: plenty of antibiotics, but almost no strong pain-killers. We had a limited number of laboratory tests and x-ray procedures available; there were no controversies over base-line chemistry profiles or CAT scanners. But we seemed to manage well, so well, in fact, that some people complained that the quality of medical care at Khao I Dang was too high. It was much higher than what the Cambodians had been accustomed to before Pol Pot or what they could expect to provide for themselves after the medical relief effort ended, and it was higher than the quality of medical care in much of Thailand. This realization, added to the existing irritation among some Thais, had led some relief agencies to operate mobile clinics and public-health programs in nearby Thai villages [see the chapter, "Thai Village Program," by Richard W. Steketee].

In the admissions ward we saw from 80 to 100 patients a day. Their median age was 15, and many of us needed to relearn some basic pediatric knowledge and skills. Over three-fourths of the patients whom we saw had infectious diseases, respiratory and gastrointestinal infections being the most common. We saw many complicated cases of measles; more than 500 children were hospitalized during a huge outbreak of this disease. In just over a month we saw 40 cases of meningococcal meningitis; on some days we did more lumbar punctures than venipunctures. We saw an average of two new cases of tuberculosis a day; we often made presumptive diagnoses by obtaining a classic history of chronic cough, bloody sputum, weight loss, and night sweats even before we examined the sputum or obtained a chest film. We saw many cases of malaria, virtually all of which were relapses of inadequately treated earlier infections (it was the mosquito-free dry season). We saw numerous children with intestinal worms; one survey of asymptomatic children revealed that almost three-fourths had hookworm, roundworm, or other intestinal parasites.

Although most of the acute effects of malnutrition had been markedly reduced during the first few weeks of the existence of the camp, we still saw some children with kwashiorkor and many people with long-term effects of chronic undernutrition.

One day I saw a seven-year-old girl who weighed only 12 kilograms—about the same weight as my nine-month-old son. We saw numerous teenagers and young adults who looked five to eight years younger than their actual age as a result of stunted growth. Many women continued to have amenorrhea. We also saw a few tragic cases of blindness due to vitamin-A deficiency in children.

The rest of the hospital consisted of about a dozen wards, which were similar to ours in structure and located nearby. In the obstetrical ward about 12 babies were delivered each day, mostly by European nurse-midwives. Although they weighed on average one kilogram less than American-born babies, they generally did well. On four pediatric wards with about 80 patients each, mothers and sometimes other family members stayed with their children to assist in their care and also to keep their families intact lest the camp suddenly be dispersed (a large border camp was dispersed during fighting shortly after I left).

In a ward adjacent to ours, surgeons mainly treated patients who had been wounded at the border, often in clashes among competing Cambodian factions. Some were innocent bystanders, like one man who had stepped on a land mine and had shrapnel wounds all over his body. In the family medicine ward, physicians and nurses dealt largely with psychosocial problems and developed working relations with monks and shamans—folk doctors whose traditional practices, like rubbing or burning a coin on the skin, were sought by many Cambodians.

There were two small rehabilitation centers, where patients crippled by traumatic injuries or by cases of chronic arthritis that had gone untreated during the Pol Pot years received physical therapy. There was one boy with juvenile rheumatoid arthritis whose crippling deformities might have been avoided if simple arthritis medication had been available under the Pol Pot regime. There was also an eye clinic, where many Cambodians put on glasses for the first time in five years; one old man cried when he donned his new glasses, saying that he had forgotten how beautiful the world was.

All in all, the medical-care system at Khao I Dang—staffed

by about 80 physicians and 200 nurses from more than a dozen countries and working for a similar number of relief organizations—functioned surprisingly well. To be sure, there were administrative and other problems, but the hospital and clinics seemed to function better than the dozen or so United States medical centers where I have worked or trained. Part of it, no doubt, was due to the group's tremendous esprit de corps, and part was due to the challenge of making things work against incredible odds.

The most dramatic result was the sharp decline in the death rate at Khao I Dang, most of which occurred in the first few weeks of the camp's existence. We were gratified when some of our patients who were almost moribund pulled through. One fourth-year medical student in our group saved the life of a young Vietnamese man who had walked across Cambodia and had a severe case of pneumonia. Yet two or three patients—mostly children—died each day, usually of pneumonia, malaria, severe diarrhea, or other infectious diseases that are theoretically preventable.

Much preventive medicine, of course, was practiced at Khao I Dang. The measures were usually less dramatic than those of curative medicine, but they were probably of equal benefit. Adequate amounts of food and uncontaminated water are crucial to public health. The distribution of basic daily food rations by the United Nations seemed to be adequate, although most Americans would probably consider the diet marginal at best: 500 g of rice and small amounts of fish, beans, and other vegetables for adults and even less for children Supplemental-feeding centers in each section distributed additional nutrients to malnourished children and pregnant and lactating women. A few Cambodians were able to buy chickens, vegetables, and other food items in the camp market. There was no ground water at Khao I Dang in the dry season; the United Nations had to truck in about two million liters a day at a considerable cost.

Another set of public-health activities consisted of a three-pronged epidemiologic approach: surveillance, investigation of outbreaks of disease and other problems, and institution of control measures. Such measures included measles and polio immunization programs (implemented mainly by Cambodian health workers), spraying with insecticides, and education about personal hygiene and sanitation. Another public-health measure was family planning, primarily with a long-acting, injectable contraceptive that has been shown to be relatively safe and effective in many developing countries. Although most of the Cambodians welcomed this program, a few criticized it as yet another attempt to reduce their number.

As time went on, we recognized that perhaps our greatest impact would be in educational activities, upgrading the knowledge and skills of the Cambodian people. Many of us participated in ongoing in-service training for Cambodian physicians, translators, and "helpers," a three-month nursing program, and a course in communicable-disease control for 60 Cambodian public-health workers. We were continually amazed by the eagerness of the Cambodians to learn. Ironically, the Cambodians who were most likely to profit from such educational programs were those most likely to emigrate to the United States or to other countries, causing a brain drain of the people who will be most needed if the opportunity to rebuild a neutral Cambodia arises. But they had no other viable options. . . .

In many ways, the Cambodian people contributed more to me, during my six weeks at Khao I Dang and since, than I did to them. They brought me much personal and professional gratification. They taught me to be even more grateful for all that I have, especially my freedom. By sharing themselves, they enabled me to see who I am and to realize how similar we are to them. Despite superficial differences of diet, language, and custom, the Cambodian people are motivated by the same things that motivate us: the desire to contribute to their communities and their nation, the desire to love and be loved, and the desire to create a better life for their children.

IMPRESSIONS OF AN INTERNIST
AT KHAO I DANG

Ivan P. Howie

My first impressions have remained. A coarse-gravel-floored bamboo barn, waterproofed with blue plastic and palm-leaf thatching, held together by wire over low plywood beds of blue tubular-steel folding framework, and supporting thin bodies on thinner woven mats. Round smiling brown faces of all ages and both sexes in a hive of activity. Steaming rice and dried fish from the hospital kitchen are being doled out from a large pot into plastic bowls. Water from the central yellow plastic bucket—tied down to prevent theft of such a useful utensil— is being scooped into thirty green plastic cups. Dressings and drugs are being distributed from a red plastic basket hauled about by willing Cambodian assistants who are also translators. People, not quite so plastic, in all postures are lying dozing beneath festoons of medical record cards and x-ray plates clipped together on the overhanging wires. One man hobbles to the toilet trenches outside—upwind today I fear. Children

---

Ivan P. Howie, a physician, worked as a generalist in an outpatient clinic, an inpatient ward, and in public health activities with World Vision from February to April 1980. He is now in general practice on Great Barrier Island, New Zealand.

116

splash with delight outside under water spilled during the filling of the square metal water tank from the tanker truck. A blind boy, aged 12, is singing Cambodian songs, banging his rhythm out on an old tin can. It seems dark inside at first, out of the glare. Dust drifts in through the gaps coating all with yellow powder. In the distance, a generator chugs without pause or pity.

Ours was a general medical ward of about 100 beds, but sometimes with many more than 100 patients. The number of patients depended upon the flow through the emergency surgical units, for we also took postoperative cases waiting for fractures to knit and wounds to heal. Everyone was amazed at the fortitude of the middle-aged Chinese lady with a fractured femur, due to a land-mine blast, tethered to one spot for weeks in makeshift traction (several large stones in a plastic bag). We watched—discreetly—how she kept herself clean and comfortable and used the commode, preserving her modesty behind a few towels. No privacy here. How quickly the Khmer "apprentices" learned to change dressings and remove sutures. We probed for and extracted several sharp twisted jags of shrapnel as they surfaced in the remaining leg of a cheerful young lad. The other members of his family had been less lucky. . . .

Western medicine and procedures, especially injections, enjoyed great prestige among the Cambodians. The dramatic effect of an epinephrine injection on a man with severe asthma impressed onlookers in the OPD very much. Intravenous fluids so often needed in the treatment of dehydration were the very acme of "injections." (From the used plastic tubing, enterprising Cambodians made all sorts of interesting souvenirs.) We saw a teenage girl with severe aplastic anemia. We wondered if she had taken chloramphenicol, perhaps bought on the black market with the diamonds dug out a few weeks ago from under the the skin of her arm. In the OPD we used to give two days' supply of drugs at a time. How much was taken at once, shared among the family, or sold, in spite of careful instructions via the interpreter, was anybody's guess. Another example of Western relief workers' expectations was that we often had ambulance vans to rush people the few hundred yards from the

OPD to the hospital when many of them had been carried in serious condition over hills and through forests for weeks on the backs of relatives.

There were more than enough cases to keep all the wards busy without a sense of competition. There was no threat of discipline or litigation if something went wrong; but no opportunity either, however, to check our diagnosis in a fatal case by means of a postmortem. I was surprised that we saw no proven cases of cholera or typhoid while I was there. Like the tinderbox risk of fire through the dry thatching, so this debilitated group of people in poor sanitary circumstances seemed to be a time bomb for such epidemics. Diarrheal diseases were all about, however. An angelic ten-year-old girl was brought in dead one morning to the busy clinic. The sketchy history was of many loose bowel movements during the night. I carried her body in my arms to hospital and then to the mortuary tent as if she was just very sick, but the hush meant they all knew. . . .

I was astonished at how little diagnostic gear beyond the stethoscope, otoscope, and blood-pressure cuff was really needed to practice medicine at Khao I Dang. I was glad that I had brought with me a few instruments, such as scissors, forceps, and probes, especially useful in exploring wounds and clearing ears of pus and debris. The Red Cross provided a good supply of standard drugs, intravenous fluids, bandages, and other supplies. I think we all resorted too much to pills in treatment; the placebo value was very great.

The relief operation communicated care and hope from the rest of the world to a disillusioned and despairing people. It was a special delight to hear the ward ring with Cambodian music when the small group of musicians began playing on traditional instruments made in the camp. The happy laughter of children flying kites over the disorder, dust, and disease of Khao I Dang seemed to make it all worthwhile, and celebrated the indomitable courage and vitality of the human spirit.

A CAMBODIAN PHYSICIAN'S PERSPECTIVE

Chhoeunly So

The Khmer doctors, dentists, and nurses were very happy to work with our foreign colleagues. Thus, we took advantage of the advice and opportunity for improvement of our knowledge and skills that we had abandoned for years. The only handicap we faced was language. There was also, however, the regrettable situation of certain Khmers, who had previously been emergency aides, sanitary agents, and salesmen for pharmaceutical products, misrepresenting themselves as Khmer medical personnel. Because of this, the camp medical coordinator named me, as the oldest and most experienced Khmer doctor, as coordinator of the Khmer medical corps.

Some aides abused the trust of the foreign personnel and committed regrettable acts, such as stealing medicine or caring for people only in exchange for money. This brought dishonor to the honest workers and forced us to create the Khmer Medical Corps Association. This association, supported by the camp director and medical coordinator succeeded in combating the abuses, the impostors, and theft and waste of medicines. Advice and education were provided to all medical corps members and aides to increase their responsibilities and their honor and to improve their medical skills and knowledge.

Chhoeunly So is a Cambodian physician who lived and worked at Khao I Dang from November 1979 to July 1980, during which time he was Chief of the Cambodian Medical Team, President of the Association of Refugees from Kampuchea, and a provider of medical care at Outpatient Department II. He is now President of the Cambodian Survivors Association in Washington, D.C., and is awaiting acceptance into a medical residency training program.

In the association were 21 medical doctors, 6 pharmacists, 8 dentists, 120 nurses and nurses' aides, 46 midwives, 15 medical students, 37 pharmacy students, and 3 student midwives. Our activities with the ICRC were helping qualify and certify Cambodians who actually were doctors, pharmacists, dentists, nurses, midwives, and other health workers; equitably distributing personnel to each OPD or building of the two hospitals according to needs; and instituting work discipline and good professional conscience in order to have a harmonious collaboration with our foreign colleagues. Other activities of the members of the association included choosing nursing-school students from among the aides who had worked in the different OPDs and hospital wards; supporting courses for sanitary agents and other public-health workers; and sponsoring courses for training midwives.

The Khmer Medical Corps Association opposed the practice of traditional medicine. Under the reign of the Khmer Rouge, the whole population received only the blind care of people employing this traditional medicine—based upon using bark, roots, and tree leaves—and thousands died because of this medicine. We accepted that an experimental traditional medicine center was set up at Khao I Dang and that only well-known, nontoxic materials were used there; however, allowing traditional doctors to use our products remained a cause for concern. Perhaps new arguments are now available which prove that this traditional medicine is useful and effective.

We congratulate those who have husbanded all their energy and their time to help the refugees, whether it be in Thailand or in any other part of the world.

A PEDIATRICIAN'S PERSPECTIVE
AT KAMPUT

Edwin A. Sumpter

Kamput was formerly a small marine outpost in southeastern Thailand, 12 kilometers from the Cambodian border. Refugees making their way out of the dense jungle across the border from Kamput were provided with housing in sturdy, permanent structures with raised floors and metal roofs, buildings that had formerly been used as barracks by the marines. With only a trickle of refugees coming across the border, there was time to prepare an enlarged facility, so Kamput was designated as an eventual transfer site, designed to relieve the serious over-crowding and water shortages of the other camps. The refugee population of 2,500 was expected to swell to at least ten times that number "at any time" during our tenure. New hospital structures, outpatient facilities, latrines, and water supplies had already been constructed, and housing was being built. Medical resources were being geared toward this expected influx. There was even an overconcentration of medical personnel for a time, a contrast to the desperate shortage of a few months earlier.

At this time, the refugees in Kamput were all Khmer Rouge, an uneducated peasant population, identified with the horrible excesses of Pol Pot over the previous five years, and brutalized

Edwin A. Sumpter is a pediatrician who, during January and February 1980, provided clinical pediatric services at Kamput and in nearby Thai villages with the
American Baptist Convention. He is currently providing clinical pediatric services at
the Roanoke-Amaranth Community Health Center in Weldon, North Carolina.

both as victims and as perpetrators of the atrocities. Warfare, starvation, disease, and the long and arduous wanderings through the jungles had taken an awesome toll. Only the more physically robust survived. Accordings to the refugees' own accounts, children who were too heavy to carry and too young to manage on their own were unlikely to survive. Also vulnerable were the elderly and those with chronic debilitating illnesses. The age distribution of the camp population testifies to the accuracy of these accounts. Only 4 percent of the refugees were under 12 years of age (for comparison, almost 15 percent of the United States population is in this age group), and very few were more than 35.

With most of the camp residents being adolescents and young adults, many had been exposed to little but Khmer Rouge guerrilla life and values since childhood. Not surprisingly, they were often suspicious and hostile when they first entered the camp and confronted both the Thais and the Westerners whom they had been taught to despise. As the weeks passed, the more trusting side of charm and warmth, historically characteristic of the ethnic Khmer, began to emerge. With most, one felt a sense of friendship and an eagerness to help. Our Khmer translators often lingered after clinic hours to talk with the Westerners, a few even expressing an interest in moving to the United States.

Some were reticent to talk of their past experiences while others seemed eager to do so. One exuberant and likable translator had been an executioner for the Khmer Rouge and was personally responsible for the beheading of countless of "the enemy." Another, unusual in being educated and multilingual, had been an engineering student in Yugoslavia, having won this opportunity as the outstanding scholar of his village. He was summoned home "to rebuild your country" when the Khmer Rouge came to power, only to be put into one of the notorious labor camps. He escaped into Thailand, but was forcibly returned to Cambodia. Even more in jeopardy now, he took a fictitious name, masqueraded as a peasant, and again escaped into Thailand—this time to Kamput.

Even though these refugees were members of the Khmer

Rouge, virtually all could tell of the murder and scattering of the members of their own families. A tiny five-year-old girl, obviously the darling of the camp as she charged about shouting "OK!" to white faces and peeling all the bananas in the kitchen, had been found in a border village, the only living person among the grotesquely strewn corpses. An affectionate seven-year-old boy, victim of an exploding land mine, had suffered a mutilated hand and lost an eye. Because of inadequate medical care, sympathetic ophthalmia had set in and was destroying the other eye. Two other young men were suffering the same fate. One can only speculate on the future of these and other seriously handicapped and homeless individuals—tragically disrupted lives in a tragically disrupted society, their future further complicated by being identified with one of the most brutal regimes in history.

The refugees were actively involved in many support areas of camp life, such as helping to distribute food, constructing new buildings, scouting the housing with stretchers to look for those too sick to get to the outpatient clinic on their own. For these efforts, a system of extra-food rewards was inaugurated, since no payment in wages was possible. Gardens sprang up everywhere, sometimes closer than acceptable to latrine runoffs. Exquisite basket weaving from bamboo strips and improvised fashioning of musical instruments were among the traditional skills that began to be exhibited as camp life became more familiar and relaxed.

There was still much idle time, however, as health improved and survival became less of an immediate issue. Debates arose between the Thai and Western authorities over the institution of any kind of educational programs that might better prepare the refugees for life outside Cambodia. This could have the effect of encouraging the refugees to stay in Thailand—not a welcome prospect to the Thai.

The hostility of the Thai military toward the refugees was apparent, and reflected the feeling of many of their compatriots. There is an ancient animosity between the Thai and the Khmer. Humanitarian considerations and world opinion placed

Thailand in the position of having more than 200,000 refugees within its borders, and none of the massive influx of materials and personnel from all over the world was to be used to benefit Thailand's own needy population. The Thai authorities were therefore quite understandably not eager to have the Cambodians provided with more than the basic human needs.

A dramatic change had occurred in the health status of the refugees after the fall of 1979. Because there were adequate supplies of food in Thailand, those victims of acute starvation depicted so graphically in the mass media were no longer seen; they either had died or were on the way to recovery. Malnutrition was therefore no longer the major problem. For those of questionable nutritional status, a supplementary-feeding program was established.

There was much more acute illness than one would have expected, given the size of the population. But except for malaria, which usually presented itself in its acute manifestations, there was little chronic organic illness.

The outpatient clinic consisted of a thatched-roof shed attached to a small building which contained a pharmacy and facilities for minor surgery. Patients were seen as they came, with a Khmer translator usually working between two clinicians, one of whom was sometimes a physician's assistant or nurse practitioner. There being no examination tables, patients were examined sitting upright or lying on a bench. Prescriptions were written according to the inventory of the pharmacy, which was run by Thai Red Cross nurses who rotated every ten days through their tour of duty. Their command of Khmer, like their commitment to the Cambodian patients, was far from consistent, and we were often concerned about the directions given for the use of medications. One need only reflect upon the poor record of compliance among the middle-class American population to feel less than confident that our prescribed treatment was being carried out.

Working with lay translators with very recently acquired English proved to be a real challenge. It is difficult to work through interpreters even when they are medically experienced and have a comprehensive language facility. Only the most concrete and obvious issues are addressed, with little likelihood of exploring symptomatic subtleties. After several patients in a row presented precisely the same complaints, I realized that, far from being an epidemic, the translator was asking only what he knew, and in such an irresistably directive manner that he was able to get precisely the answers he could translate: "Runny nose, white 'spootum,' diarrhea three times a day for three days." He was nevertheless doing far better with his English than I was doing with my Khmer.

The age distribution of those visiting the outpatient clinic was consistent with that in the camp at large—very few below the age of 12 or as old as 40. Upper-respiratory infection was the leading primary diagnosis in the outpatient clinic, accounting for about one-third of 656 patient visits. Many cases were mild and required little medical attention.

Patients with malaria, mostly due to *Plasmodium falciparum,* were often very ill, several a day arriving by stretcher with very high fevers, delirium, markedly enlarged spleens, and dehydration. As might be expected, malaria was the most frequent reason for hospitalization, and continued to be troublesome diagnostically and therapeutically. We were a few months into the dry season and mosquitoes were relatively few, but the frequency of the acute cases was hard to explain entirely on the basis of relapsing chronic disease. The standard outpatient treatment with pyrimethamine-sulfadoxine (Fansidar) and primaquine was often unsuccessful, and patients returned more acutely ill than before, requiring hospitalization and quinine therapy. A high percentage of new refugees had positive smears for malaria, and a program of routine prophylaxis on entering camp had been instituted almost from the outset. Resistance of falciparum malaria to Fansidar was suspected and has since been confirmed.

Gastroenteritis and intestinal parasites were the next most frequent primary diagnoses, and were exceedingly common as secondary diagnoses. Bronchitis and pneumonia, anemia (presumably due to iron deficiency), scabies, impetigo, and complaints related to old trauma, such as shrapnel wounds, accounted for the remainder. The high frequency of scabies among these dark-skinned people is interesting, considering its rarity among black persons of African origin. Exotic "tropical" diseases were virtually nonexistent!

Accounting for a significant number of outpatient visits, but not classifiable among "primary diagnoses," were patients with symptoms very familiar to Western primary-care physicians: complaints of being weak, nervous, easily fatigued, and subject to headaches and/or vague abdominal pains. Physical examination was unlikely to produce an explanation. Depression and anxiety take a psychosomatic toll in Southeast Asian jungles even as they do in Western society, but we were in no position to respond effectively, either diagnostically or therapeutically. Some causative factors have already been suggested in this chapter—the destruction of families and their way of life, the ever-present threat of death, an uncertain future, a life without meaning—surely no people ever had better reasons for situational depression, but this may well have been only part of the story. As ignorant as we were of their culture and of the refugees as individuals, we had no way of really understanding their emotional reactions to their situation. They needed healers and counselors from among their own people. An effort to seek out Khmer herbal doctors was underway when we left [see the chapter, "Traditional Medicine," by J.P. Hiegel].

In the meantime, we stumbled into an increasingly counterproductive pattern of response. In *our* need to respond to the complaints of these people, we did what is so often done in many doctors' offices in the United States—we gave the patient a prescription for some mild medication and a semiapologetic "Here, try these." As we acknowledged the polite bow of thank you, we had to wonder how this was translated. Then in a few days we would see the return of the same person with the same or another complaint. The expectation was that we could cure anything, and we had reinforced this idea. We were treating a symptom instead of a patient and did not really know what to do about it.

Medical records were very spare. A single card attached to a patient's bed was used to record the few lines that were written on admission and the even fewer noting progress. More comprehensive notes were discouraged, again in keeping with the policy of an ad hoc response. To a degree this was also reflected in the care provided. Conditions that were life-threatening, likely to produce significant morbidity, or of epidemiological importance were usually treated reasonably well, but at that time, little effort was made to seek out problems of a more insidious nature or to undertake preventive and health educational programs. This was difficult to reconcile with our medical "habits." Though time and personnel were available to do more, it was considered inappropriate and even unethical to provide comprehensive care to people unlikely to have continued access to Western medicine. The patients, the medical personnel, the hospital, the situation itself, were all seen as transient. There was a "fire," and we were among the "firemen."

Follow-up care after discharge was a concern. Many patients were young people who were orphans with no one to look after their needs during convalescence. One building near the hospital was designated for those no longer requiring hospitalization but not yet fully capable of looking after their own needs. Regular rounds were made by a physician and nurse, and medications were given. Patients could also be referred to this building from the outpatient clinic if their illness did not really warrant hospitalization.

Nurse and physician night coverage was on a rotating schedule, of course. Nurses on duty had a doctor sleeping nearby, on whom they called in the event of an emergency or an admission. On one particular night, there were several medical emergencies, and the generator had ceased to function, leaving the hospital with only lantern light. The combination of a darkened hospital with the noises of a large number of patients coughing and vomiting, the occasional sound of artillery fire in the distance, and the startling cries of night jungle birds created an eerie and memorable atmosphere.

It was through contacts with the Thai military that we learned of the dire medical needs of the people in the Thai villages in the vicinity of the camp and along the border. Living in poverty themselves, the village peasants were understandably resentful of the massive concentration of international resources on these uninvited and unwelcome "guests" in their country. With the Thai military making the arrangements and escorting us, a few medical and nursing personnel from Kamput took a mobile clinic to each of some dozen villages on a rotating basis. The medical care delivered was obviously limited and lacking in continuity, in that we visited for one half a day a village of several hundred persons, to return again a few weeks later for another abbreviated visit. It was, nevertheless, an important expression of concern for these villagers and was greatly appreciated by the military and the Thai Red Cross doctors who sometimes accompanied us. We were also warmly welcomed by the village people themselves, particularly on our return visits. The question, however, must again be raised about the problem of gestural encounters with Western medicine when its availability is only transient at best.

The frequency of malaria varied strikingly from one village to another, even though they were only a few miles apart. In one village, virtually every child examined had significant spleen enlargement, even if not acutely ill at the time. In another, very few were seen with enlarged spleens. Though there are other reasons for an enlarged spleen, its occurrence in such large numbers seemed to indicate malaria as the cause. In these villages, children were often seen with neat circular scars on the upper abdomen, arranged in a triangular or diamond-shaped pattern; these scars were the result of small burns inflicted by incense or a cigarette—a traditional treatment for fever with enlarged spleen.

We could not confirm the presence of tuberculosis since our diagnostic capabilities were limited to what we could carry with us, but there were many patients with symptoms highly suggestive of the disease. Pneumonia, parasites, malnutrition, and vitamin deficiency, probable anemia, probable malignancies, goiter, and various arthritic and skeletal symptoms were among the many diagnoses. Only one case of a possible "tropical disease" (cutaneous leishmaniasis) was recognized. In general, there was a much broader spectrum of both acute and chronic illness in the villages than there was in Kamput.

There was also a more normal age distribution in the village population. We saw mostly children and the elderly.

With the help of the Thai Red Cross, a referral system was eventually set up, utilizing facilities in Chantaburi, about 25 miles away, and providing transportation in selected problem cases; but this was woefully inadequate to the needs.

In conclusion, we initially found the situation at Kamput at variance with our expectations: we expected to be very busy treating the Khmers, but medical needs were relatively limited because the camp population never reached the projected numbers. We had come halfway around the world for a limited time at others' expense and sacrifice, and we did not want to spend our time idly. As it developed, particularly because of the Thai village program, our experience proved to be brisk medically and gratifying in the unforgettable personal encounters with the Khmer and the Thai—extraordinary people, indeed.

SURGERY IN A BORDER CAMP

James C. Cobey

The type and level of surgery in an acute refugee crisis depends on the stability and politics of the situation as well as the availability of surgical personnel and supplies. Obviously the presence or absence of war directly affects the type of intervention needed.

Because of the political limitations, many extensive war wounds were treated in the three larger border camps or settlements, where surgical facilities were of necessity limited. All long-term plans changed every 24 hours. No one knew if a camp of close to 100,000 refugees might become part of a demilitarized zone or might disappear or be overrun at any time. There was gun and mortar fire daily. This uncertainty was exemplified by the fact that Mak Mun, the camp that in March 1980 appeared to be the largest and most stable, was completely destroyed six weeks later.

In the middle of what appeared mass confusion, the international volunteers had to function. Few of them had had any prior war experience. At Mak Mun, at the start of the operation, only the camp administrator and one other volunteer had had

James C. Cobey, a surgeon, was Medical Coordinator of Camp 204, from December 1979 to March 1980, as an American Red Cross Volunteer to the International Committee of the Red Cross. He is currently an orthopedic surgeon in private practice in Washington, D.C., and Secretary and Program Chairman for Bangladesh, Nepal, and China of Orthopedics Overseas, Inc.

public health training and previous Third World experience. Each volunteer was desperately trying to find his or her own role while coping with the frustrations of the action. Initially they were all appropriately frightened by the shelling and the small-arms fire that landed in the camp. At times, bullets even penetrated the bamboo huts or clinics. The first order of business was to dig deep, covered shelters in the dense earth next to each makeshift clinic for protection from the shelling.

Because of this instability, a concerted effort was made by the international voluntary-agency leaders to limit treatment to the wounded and those sick people who could be moved by family members or friends if an attack came. Inasmuch as for reasons of safety, no international volunteers were permitted to stay in the camp at night, it was felt not to be ethical or appropriate to provide a high level of care that would require intensive medical attention in the evening.

As the volunteers became acclimatized to the action, many became cavalier—dangerously so—about the fighting. Some wanted to explore east of the camp into Kampuchea, while others wanted to remain overnight in order to provide more care. The administrator had to ensure strict discipline. If volunteers failed to follow the rules, the whole action would be jeopardized. Everyone had to be accounted for every day. This made many independent nurses and doctors frustrated at times until they were brought back to reality by nearby shelling, forcing the evacuation of all the expatriates for a few days.

By the end of December 1979, there were fewer offensives and the shelling seemed to decrease. We felt that Mak Mun appeared stable and therefore elected to construct a bamboo inpatient facility there. With the help of close to a hundred Thai workers, eight buildings were erected in four days. These consisted of three outpatient clinics, three supplementary-feeding centers, and a large two-ward hospital. The buildings were basically bamboo shells with roofs of thatch. The structures were spread throughout the camp, depending on where the camp was then being constructed or to where we felt it would eventually extend. The two-ward hospital was in the approximate center of the refugee huts with access to the road we had built a few weeks earlier. All the buildings were constructed in abandoned rice paddies—that was the only cleared land. We recognized that these structures might well be flooded in the monsoon season, then six months away. Due to the political instability, however, it did not seem practical at that point to spend the time or money to construct more substantial facilities. This decision, in hindsight, was correct since six weeks later, as already mentioned the camp was destroyed by fighting and had to be completely rebuilt.

The new buildings had floors with gravel to keep down the dust—a great improvement over the previous bare and dusty dirt floors. The camp environment was so dusty in the dry season that the Red Cross flag nailed to the top of the hospital had to be brushed off each day. Between the walls and the roof we left a space for air to circulate and light to enter. The hospital itself consisted of one adult ward and one pediatric ward. Inside the adult ward, we built a number of low walls of split bamboo to divide off some small rooms around the edges for the storage of drugs and supplies, for surgery, and for childbirth deliveries.

The pediatric unit was used for inpatient rehydration and outpatient intensive feeding. Other patients with infectious diseases, such as measles, were kept in a separate section of this ward. Though the ward could house more than 60 patients, usually only a dozen stayed overnight.

The beds, when we had some, were either canvas stretchers or light steel-frame structures supporting a plywood board. No mattresses existed in this type of setting. Often two or more patients would be placed on a bed. Intravenous infusions could be hung from the bamboo overhead rafters. Traction for fractures was also devised by tying ropes from the splints of the involved extremities to the bamboo supports of the roof.

The basic purpose of the hospital was to supply care to those who needed help, but refused to be evacuated to Thailand. We tried to make very clear to our patients what we medically could and could not do. Many patients, however, chose to stay in the camp against our professional advice rather than leave their families.

Penetrating abdominal wounds simply could not be treated in the hospital. We refused to set up in this unstable camp the extensive facilities needed to attempt a higher level of care. If patients were willing to be evacuated to a UNHCR holding center inside Thailand, we could offer only first aid for such wounds.

Most of our surgery was debridement of gunshot and land-mine explosion wounds. Next to malnutrition and malaria, our greatest public-health problem seemed to stem from people stepping on land mines. It became almost a law that we did not use sutures or close any wound. A few physicians tried to show their skill at cleaning and beautifully closing wounds only to have the patients end up with massive infections. Our instruments consisted of scalpels, scissors, and hemostats. The few surgical tools that we had were sterilized by boiling them in a large rice kettle over a wood fire outside. I once used the saw on my pocket knife, sterilized over a flame, to amputate part of a hand of a patient who refused to be transported to a safer camp. We used either local anesthesia with xylocaine or general anesthesia with intravenous ketamine.

The operating room was approximately 15 feet square. We covered the openings with mosquito netting to limit the number of flies in the room. Sterile paper wrappings from our surgical gloves protected our sterile field. We had a room for deliveries where one or two children were born each day. In hindsight, we should have insisted more strongly that the nurse-midwives not waste their time delivering babies, but get out into the camp and work with the indigenous women who were delivering many more children in this camp of close to 100,000 people.

In the operating room, we erected two sets of four bamboo posts on which we could place simple bamboo-canvas stretchers. We used these stretchers for transporting patients, as well as for operating tables. In this way, patients could be quickly brought in, treated, and then admitted to the ward, or stabilized for transport back to a holding center inside Thailand—all on the same stretcher. For patients with severe wounds and in obvious shock, we started a simple intravenous (IV) with a No. 18 needle and pumped in a liter or two of normal saline from a plastic bag. We then pulled the IV out. We found it was a waste of time to put an IV line in a patient and keep it going at a predetermined rate while trying to get the patient back to the better-equipped hospital in the holding center across the border. Plastic IV catheters were not available.

Our ambulances were either the backs of flatbed trucks or small pickup trucks. We found that we could accommodate three stretcher patients in a pickup truck by putting one patient on the floor and the other two above the first, balanced on the side seats in the back of the truck.

We had no electricity and therefore, no x-ray machines. We treated all fractures initially with bamboo splints. When plaster became available, we made sugar-tong-type splints which could easily be removed by the refugees. No circular plaster was used, since we had to be sure the refugees could remove their casts or splints themselves if they decided to return to the interior of Cambodia, as they often did.

We treated gunshot wounds, and compound fractures with debridement, irrigation with saline, and antibiotics. We found that high doses of IV penicillin in this environment were perfectly adequate. Most of the gunshots were of low velocity and therefore the wounds could be treated by through-and-through irrigation. All fractures were treated by splinting. Complicated nerve and arterial repairs were not appropriate in this setting, nor did we attempt them. All amputation stumps were left open.

No surgery was performed to correct chronic conditions such as club feet, malunion of old fractures, or TB abscesses. This concept was very hard for many physicians to accept. Many physicians felt that they could perform many more small procedures if they just were allowed a little more equipment. Some wanted to treat cataracts, while others felt that they could do simple reconstructive surgery. It was a continual challenge to the administrator or camp leader to keep the volunteers' efforts solely on the acute problems. The closest we came to treating a chronic condition was pulling hundreds of loose infected teeth.

During the entire relief operation, we never knew, of course, from day to day when more fighting or shelling would come. We would function for a week or so with no severe injuries and become very complacent. The next day shelling would occur and result in many injuries. The staffing of the hospital and clinics, therefore, often changed suddenly, depending on the acute immediate need. At times, due to expected fighting we allowed less than one quarter of the volunteer staff to go across the border and into the camp. On those days we closed down supplementary-feeding, health-education, vaccination, and sanitation programs. We only wanted enough volunteers on whom we could depend to handle evacuation procedures and to triage or simply treat acute injuries.

These precautions were necessary because of the need to account carefully for every volunteer in the event of shelling. Strict discipline had to be maintained. The volunteers were there to perform a humanitarian function for wounded and sick people—not to act as medics in a war. They were neutral, thereby pledged to treat all noncombatants. If the camp were to be overrun by opposing forces, they would treat them as well. This continual anticipation of war, coupled with weeks of only seeing land-mine wounds and intermittent shelling, challenged the camp administrators to keep up the morale of the volunteers.

Our major efforts were directed toward teaching the Khmer aides how to treat wounds by washing them and applying clean dressings. We went to great efforts to avoid administering antibiotic ointments and packings. We found that the Khmer aides inappropriately covered dirty wounds with these rather than letting them stay open and heal from the inside. We spent a lot of time removing gauze packing placed by refugee aides only to find grass and dirt deep in the wounds. At times, we found it easier to teach Khmers with previous nurse or nurse's aide training than the partially trained Khmer doctors, who were sometimes more interested in passing out drugs than in washing wounds.

Some important points were reemphasized by this relief action. One's goals were to compensate only for the changes due to the crisis and not to provide a level of care greater than the recipients had known before or could expect to have again, after the crisis. Although one may have the technical skill and even the tools, I believe that providing more than acute care does a disservice to the refugees for several reasons. First, it raises their expectations, making it harder to cut off care later. More importantly, it diverts one's precious time to treating a few rather than working on public-health projects and health education to prevent many deaths from ever-threatening epidemics, endemic and potentially lethal pediatric diarrhea, and malnutrition. Second, refugees will have already started some type of relief or first-aid action by themselves before outside relief arrives. All care should, therefore, fit into a plan of having the refugees help themselves and hopefully perform most of it themselves with advice and assistance. And finally, since no one knows at the time how long these operations will last, training of local paramedics and primary care workers should start the day outside help arrives.

The only thing an expatriate surgeon really leaves behind after a relief operation, besides the relatively few lives saved, is the knowledge imparted to those afflicted so that they can treat future wounds themselves.

A DAY AT 007 (NONG SAMET): JANUARY 4, 1980

Thomas S. Durant

9:00 A.M.: As we approach the road that leads to the camp, Thai troops are chasing a couple of hundred Khmers across the field back towards the camp. A group member asks, "Why are so many Khmer leaving the camp?" Another answers, "It's a sign—it could be a good sign or a bad sign." The group laughs and drives on.

9:30 A.M.: We arrive at the camp. There seems to be less activity than usual. Why are there no patients? The Khmer interpreter replies, "In this camp there are some group of bad soldiers. So the good ones in this camp invited the other camp soldiers to make the bad ones falling down."

10:00 A.M.: The first rounds of automatic fire begin and increase rapidly and appear to be not very far away.

10:15 A.M.: We huddle behind the German bus as small arms fire increases. Lisa, an American nurse with ARC has brought a two-year-old, who is convulsing with probable measles

---

Thomas S. Durant is a physician specialist in obstetrics and gynecology who worked in providing direct patient care in Cambodian refugee camps in Thailand with the American Refugee Committee from December 1979 to March 1980, June to September 1980, March to April 1982, May to July 1983, and June to July 1984. He is Assistant Director for Hospital Administration and Patient Care at the Massachusetts General Hospital in Boston.

encephalitis, and his mother to the huddled group. Walter a German pediatrician working with Soforthilfe, and Lisa try to suction the baby, and suddenly the gunfire increases and comes closer. Eric, a Dutch general practitioner, runs up and says that the ICRC bunker about 200 yards away has a radio—Lisa, Eric, and I head for it. The Khmer mother and her baby run in the opposite direction. Walter and several others head for a bunker that is 50 yards away—but with no radio!

10:30 A.M.: The bunker, approximately 20-by-30 feet by 8 feet deep, is jammed with approximately eighty Khmer—men, women, and children—and twenty expatriate doctors and nurses: Dutch, German, English, Irish, Swedes, Danes, Americans, Thais, Finns, and Khmer. It is roasting hot. It has to be the biggest international sauna ever.

11:00 A.M.: There is a lull in the firing. People begin to come out of the bunker for some fresh air. A wounded Khmer is brought in by two friends. Kate (an Irish nurse from Dublin) and John (an emergency-room nurse from California) and I take him 25 yards away to the surgical tent and dress the bullet wounds of his right arm and left leg; as we finish, the firing increases and we scurry back to the bunker. Kate says, "AAh' sure, isn't this just like Belfast?"

11:30 A.M.: Another lull, and Kate gets a Red Cross flag and a bamboo pole and plants the flag on top of the bunker.

12:00 NOON: Trish (a New Zealand ICRC nurse) is operating the radio: "Alpha One to Alpha Six, How many personnel are there? What is the status of firing?" Trish: "Alpha Six to Alpha One"—in classic clipped British tones—"There are 22 internationals and 80 Khmer—we are experiencing sporadic small-arms fire and occasional mortars." It is fiercely hot, and everyone is sweating profusely. Stimulated by Trish's accent, someone quips, "Never have so many sweated so much, and urinated so little!!!" "Alpha Two to Alpha One," the radio crackles. "We are surrounded by Khmer Rouge and unable to move." Again there is a lull in the firing and an impeccably dressed Swiss journalist casually saunters up to the entrance to the bunker, peers in, says, "Hello," and strolls on, exactly as if he were in Boston's Quincy Market. Just then the loudest bang of the morning takes place, and the concussion shakes the bunker. Who the hell is shooting what, with which, and at whom? Doubt that the Khmer Serei or the Khmer Rouge have that caliber mortar. Thai artillery? Vietnamese mortars?

12:15 P.M.: "Alpha One to Alpha Six. We are coming by to pick you up in five minutes. Do you have any vehicles?" Trish: "Yes, we have transport!" (a Datsun pickup truck in front of the bunker).

12:20 P.M.: An ICRC pickup truck races up to the bunker. Everyone piles out and into the two pickup trucks. Firing is minimal. We race to the edge of the camp to join eight other pickup trucks and other ICRC doctors and nurses. We start to treat several wounded Khmer in a bamboo hut near the edge of the camp.

12:30 P.M.: Suddenly the firing increases again and comes closer. Lisa, Kate, and I head for a pickup truck. Lisa does a diving belly flop over the tailgate. We barrel off to approximately two kilometers from the camp and regroup. Several wounded arrive, and Lisa, John, and a German doctor and I take three wounded Khmer (leg, abdomen, and shoulder bullet wounds) and one of the wounded's husband and daughter (five years old) back to Khao I Dang in a pickup truck. The wounded are silent, the husband stoic, and the daughter cries and vomits. (The German doctor holds her over the tailgate and comforts her.)

1:00 P.M.: We arrive at Khao I Dang and bring the wounded to the German Red Cross surgical ward.

2:00 P.M.: John, Walter and I head back to 007. We get to the edge of the camp and are again driven back by the heavy firing.

We drive two kilometers—here six or seven pickups and ten to twenty ICRC doctors and nurses are grouped, all asking, What is going on? Who's shooting at whom?

2:30 P.M.: Several wounded arrive—Walter, John, and I start IVs, and pack eight wounded Khmer in the back of a large Thai diesel truck. I head back to Khao I Dang with the wounded.

3:15 P.M.: A 30-year-old Khmer woman with a bullet wound in the chest dies in her mother's arms on the way back; the others all make it. When we arrive in Khao I Dang, there are ten thousand Khmer gathered around the entrance to the camp looking to see if their relatives are among the wounded.

4:15 P.M.: More wounded and refugees arrive. Everyone asks, What's happening? Is it the Vietnamese? The Khmer Rouge? Who? The Khmer Serei of 007 vs. the Khmer Serei of Mak Mun? I am reminded of the Churchill quote, "In war *truth* is the first victim!"

6:00 P.M.: Approximately fifty wounded have arrived and maybe two thousand refugees. There is a beautiful violet Thai sunset in the schizophrenic Shangri La. But there is no ending to this bad grade-B movie, and at the end of this episode of an eternal serial, as always, there are no real victors—only the dead, wounded, grieving, and the tired, dirty, confused observers.

PHYSICAL REHABILITATION

Joseph Julian

One of the most visible and graphic reminders of the tragedy that has befallen the Khmer is the presence among them of many who are maimed and seriously disabled. Among these victims of crippling illness and trauma, there is a shocking predominance of children and young adults. The long history of continuous armed conflict, deprivation, and the mass movements of Khmer refugees through or into inhospitable areas has resulted in the frequent occurrence of blunt trauma and serious wounds from bullets or larger projectiles. Perhaps unique to the Khmer situation are the many refugees who have lost one or both legs, usually by accidentally stepping on land mines, indiscriminately planted along the Thai-Kampuchean border.

Ynip and Sokhom are typical ten-year-old Khmer girls. They are quick to smile, and as the mood strikes them, they are alternately vivacious or mischievous or even petulant— but they are always quite charming. Both had lived in border camps. Now—late 1982—they are housed in the 30-bed inpatient rehabilitation ward at Khao I Dang.

Ynip had lived at Nong Samet until the day that she attempted to wash off her foot by dipping it into a depression filled with muddy water. The puddle hid a land mine. The explosion so

Joseph Julian is a physician who in the Cambodian relief operation was Coordinator of Rehabilitation Services with Catholic Rellief Services (one year) and with Operation Handicap International (six months) from April 1981 to October 1982. He is now a Fellow in Physical Medicine and Rehabilitation at the Mayo Clinic in Rochester, Minnesota.

badly mangled her left leg that the surgeons had to amputate it close to her hip. Sokhom had been playing with friends in the woods outside of Nong Chan camp when her brother stepped on a large mine, killing himself and three other children; Sokhom's right leg was severed below the knee.

Ynip and Sokhom have become great friends. Each morning they put on their simple bamboo "peg legs" and then, books under arms, head off with the other camp children to the Khmer school located near the hospital. In the afternoon, they visit the workshop where a newer, more "sophisticated" leg is being made for each of them. Ynip has never been very happy with the appearance of the temporary bamboo "training leg," but with its use she has acquired the skills necessary for her to walk safely and efficiently. Now she is ready for her new permanent leg with its movable knee and artificial foot.

Ynip's new leg is being made by Has Phan. He, too, is an amputee from Nong Samet. Six months ago he stepped on a land mine while gathering wood in the forest. He was brought to the Khao I Dang hospital, and his shattered right leg was amputated below the knee. Within three days of surgery, he was being seen by one of the ten Khmer physical-therapy workers assigned to the surgery wards. Within two months, he was transferred to the "rehab" ward. There he received further care for what was left of his leg and was given strengthening exercises. He was fitted for a new limb and then completed gait training with the artificial leg. Has Phan then volunteered to stay at Khao I Dang to learn in the workshop how to make artificial legs. His training program is almost completed, and he will soon return to his family at Nong Samet. There in a small workshop he will work making and repairing artificial limbs. It is one of five such workshops run by Khmer workers-trained at Khao I Dang. There he will continue to receive support, further training, and supplies from the rehab staff based at Khao I Dang.

Ho Chom is a double mid-thigh amputee. He once had the bed next to Has Phan in the rehab ward, but he has since moved out on his own. First, he went to a special halfway house for the seriously disabled. Later, when he felt more comfortable with his handicap and was able to take adequate care of his own needs, he moved into a regular house in the camp. He shares this house with four friends, two of whom are also physically disabled. In the morning Ho Chom studies typing. In the afternoon he usually visits his friends in the rehab ward or goes to one of the rehab workshops, where he watches Has Phan and the other Khmer craftsmen making artificial limbs. Sometimes he entertains the staff and patients by playing his flute or guitar; other times he tells them jokes and funny stories. Quite amazingly, he can even joke about the time in February 1981 when he found himself trapped inside the camp hospital as it burned to the ground. In those days he had no artificial legs and no wheelchair. By his own means there was no way for him to escape the fire, and he was only saved because two Khmer nursing aides picked up his bed, with him in it, and rushed it out the door. He laughs about this now and makes light of his predicament, but in his eyes the laughter fades and one can see the terror and utter helplessness of that moment.

In the uncertain and often dangerous world of the Khmer refugee the greatest handicap is the loss of mobility. Programs to maximize the mobility of disabled refugees therefore received the earliest and highest priority. These programs and the equipment and devices made to implement them were based on the principles that the aides to mobilization should be inexpensive to make and made exclusively from locally available materials. They should be simple in construction, durable, and easy to maintain and repair. They should be made by the refugee workers themselves. There should be no dependency on outside sources of high-technology, expensive, Western-style rehab equipment. Thus more than 600 amputees have been given artificial legs of bamboo, steel, wood, and leather. Scores of children crippled by polio have received simple braces and shoes. More than 100 sturdy wheelchairs constructed of wood and bicycle wheels have been provided to paraplegics and other severely disabled refugees. Hundreds of bamboo and wooden crutches, canes, and walkers have been given to patients with painful bone and joint injuries, and these patients have been instructed in their proper use.

Because of the very large number of patients requiring rehab services (200 to 250 seen daily), it would have been impossible to serve more than a fraction of those diabled if all the services had been performed solely by the expatriate staff. The primary work of the ten volunteer rehab professionals was to train Khmer counterparts and then provide them with guidance and support. Programs were created to train refugee workers as physical and occupational therapists, rehab nurses and counselors, makers of braces, shoes, artificial limbs, wheelchairs, and all the other various types of rehab equipment. These training programs were ongoing, not only to upgrade the skills of the Khmer workers but also because of the turnover of the Khmer staff, often severely depleted by sudden relocation moves to other camps. With little or no advance warning, the expatriate staff was frequently faced with training a whole new group of workers while simultaneously attempting to continue patient-care activities.

Chhoueth is a pretty young woman. She is very shy but captivates everyone with her disarming smile. When she was 27, she and her husband were accused of stealing some coconuts. They were beaten with steel rods. Her husband died, and Chhoueth's spinal column was crushed, leaving her legs paralyzed. For more than three years, she lay immobile in bed. When she was admitted to the rehab ward, her muscles were markedly wasted from lack of use. Her legs lay bent and lifeless. Her bladder was infected, and large deep bedsores had eaten away the flesh on her back.

Chhoueth's Khmer nurse is Seang Heng. He is a gentle young man, and he too, seems quite shy. His right arm is missing, and it is only now after working for a year with the severely disabled that he seems at ease with his own handicap. Under his care, Chhoueth's bedsores are slowly healing. Supervised by the expatriate rehabilitation nurse, he treats the bladder infection with antibiotics.

Yin Sotean, Chhoueth's physical therapist, is one of the most experienced and capable on the Khmer staff. He was trained with the original class of physical-therapy workers, more than two years ago. All the rest of the trainees in the first class—as well as scores of others trained since—have been relocated to other camps and then on to Europe, the United States, or other lands. But Yin Sotean was less fortunate; he was not re-settled. He remains at Khao I Dang, faithfully working six days a week without complaint and with no apparent bitterness for having been left behind. He is extremely dedicated and knows his job well. The expatriate physical therapist who supervises the ward has confidence in his evaluation of Chhoueth which allows him to devise and.institute for her an appropriate plan of therapy. Over several months, his daily efforts will slowly loosen her frozen joints and his exercises will help her to increase in strength and endurance.

Chhoueth will never again be able to run or dance but with the support of devices made for her by the Khmer rehab staff, she will learn to walk once again. Som Sari, a double amputee, makes her specially fitted shoes. Te Yo Hung, one of the brace-makers, measures her for stainless-steel and leather braces that will support her weakened legs from ankle to hip. One of the carpenters constructs a bamboo walker to give her added support when, for the first time in years, she stands upright and takes her first halting steps.

While Chhoueth is in the midst of her physical rehabilitation program, she is also being seen by Ngo Tieu Than, her rehab counselor. He, too, was once a patient in the rehab ward. An old paralytic illness has left him with diminished physical strength, but he is intelligent and articulate and good at problem-solving. He is adept at using his wheelchair to move around the hospital wards and to attend the various social, educational, and vocational programs in camp. He has enrolled Chhoueth in a Khmer literacy class, and he has also been able to find someone who is willing to teach her how to knit.

Another of Ngo Tieu Than's counseling patients is Vuthea. At the age of 24, he and a group of friends tried to sneak through the treacherous border area leading toward Thailand. He and 15 others were captured by soldiers and told to line up in single file. Then, one by one, without explanation or apparent reason, they were methodically disemboweled. Vuthea, who had been placed at the end of the line, escaped death only because he was able to flee during the confusion caused by a surprise shelling. He continued toward the border and was close to his destination when he was captured by a different band of soldiers. He was beaten with a rifle and left paralyzed in both legs. A year later, he was brought from the border to the rehab ward. He required treatment for the complications secondary to his paraplegia, and he needed to be fitted for a wheelchair. Unlike most patients, he was very uncooperative and moody, endlessly complaining about his physical pain, the food, and/or other patients. He would not socialize but preferred to sit alone, silently staring out the window. Ngo Tieu Than talked with him daily, and now after two months on the ward, Vuthea is finally beginning to be able to speak of his ordeal, his anger, and his fears about the uncertain future. For the first time, he has cried and grieved for his murdered friends and the senseless act that left him without the use of his legs. He has made some friends and has started a class in reading and writing Khmer.

The story of physical rehabilitation and the disabled Khmer refugees is essentially one of enormous needs being met with limited resources in professional staff, equipment, and other materials. That this large task is in some measure being accomplished is for the most part a tribute to the fantastic courage, ability, dignity, and compassion of the patients, their families, and above all, the dedicated Khmer staff.

EYE CARE

Paola Polacco Sandersley

At Khao I Dang in late 1979, although the overall medical care provided was satisfactory, there remained a whole area of "peripheral medicine" that was deficient, including the diagnosis and treatment of eye problems.

Virtually no Cambodian crossed the Thai border wearing glasses: for the five years of Pol Pot rule, eye glasses were considered the trappings of the intellectual who must be eliminated. Some people had had bad eyesight before that, and others developed eye problems during the Pol Pot regime as a result of disease, injury, and malnutrition.

We explored several alternatives with the camp coordinator and medical coordinator. They finally suggested that an eye clinic would be an appropriate project for us to undertake. The project was soon begun.

With the help of my husband and the ingenuity of Wolfgang Stutzel (managing director of the Thai branch of a Dutch dairy firm), who raised more money by appealing to the firm, I recruited the head of the ophthalmology department of a well-known Bangkok hospital to lead a team of specialist ophthalmologists and optometrists to Khao I Dang to conduct a preliminary survey. The purpose of this survey was roughly to assess how large a part of the camp's population was in need of eye care, what diseases were prevalent, where surgery might be required, and where glasses should be provided. A weekend survey of five hundred refugees confirmed the need for a regular eye clinic.

As no team of specialists—quite understandably—would risk putting their regular hospital jobs in jeopardy, it soon became

147

apparent that this would have to be a weekend operation. It eventually consisted of five specialists going to the camp and operating a clinic between 8 A.M. and 4 P.M. every Sunday. At the beginning, nothing was easy. In retrospect, I have come to believe that the enterprising volunteer—whose efforts can be seen at will as either complementary or disruptive—should not expect to be made welcome in any relief operation. Something of a fly in the ointment, his or her ability to operate effectively outside the relief establishment is viewed with skepticism—and often with some degree of resentment.

In our case, there were endless papers to be rubber-stamped, permissions to be sought, documents to be signed. Every relief organization has its internal bureaucracy, above each stood the UNHCR with its own separate set of rules and regulations, and at the top of the pyramid sat the Thai military with further requests for identification, purpose of involvement, etc.

There were two sides to our activities: (1) providing ordinary eye care and fitting eyeglasses, and (2) providing surgical eye care, limited to such urgent cases as double cataracts, done outside the camp (due to a lack of appropriate sterile facilities inside the camp).

The specialists we employed, in addition to their hospital positions, owned and ran a small private clinic on the outskirts of Bangkok. This, we decided, would be the obvious place to accommodate our refugee patients in need of surgery. They could be kept together in a quiet and somewhat suburban setting which—while reassuring the Thai military authorities who feared a breach of security—would on humanitarian grounds better enable them to comfort and sustain one another through the ordeal. Thus each week, four or five emergency cases were identified by our team in camp and transported to Bangkok for surgery.

Transport became something of a headache. Our Thai doctors, though we hired air-conditioned and chauffeur-driven vans for their comfort, categorically refused at all times to take part in the transport of the selected surgical patients. Their involvement was strictly business.

In addition to the accounting and management of the project, I now also had to drive the patients from camp and back, be available with an interpreter during the surgery—and the preparation beforehand—and visit them across town daily throughout their stay to check on their progress, boost their morale, and tend to any problems and needs.

Most of our eye patients were in poor health. We tried to use the week the Thai military authorities granted us to get them in better shape. All were subjected on admission to a chest x-ray and to a complete medical examination: skin infections, parasitic infestations, head lice, festering stumps, and once even pneumonia were treated in conjunction with the eye surgery. On one occasion, a boy of 12 was so weak that, risking the Thai military's wrath, we decided to keep him an extra week.

Early on Sundays, at the wheel of a battered, nonairconditioned van, I would pick up our interpreter, Nari Kol, go to the clinic, get the postoperative patients, drive them to camp, check them into the hospital, where they would receive postoperative care, and rush to the clinic to supervise "my" team.

By three o'clock, with surgical priorities established, I had to get the required authority to take the selected refugees out of camp. A list of names was drawn up, our medical team leader wrote a synopsis of each case stressing the urgency of the proposed operation; the Thai Red Cross then had to countersign this, and finally, it had to be approved by the military commander.

After three months, 50 operations had been successfully performed, and about 1,000 refugees had received eyeglasses.

With my time in Thailand drawing to a close, Russ Doreland, an American optometrist, then joined the clinic, and was soon flanked by John Dollar, an ophthalmologist who was sent out from the United States in answer to urgent and repeated pleas. Both worked for the American Refugee Committee (ARC). With these two men and two Cambodian ex-ophthalmological student recruits, ARC pioneered the first eye operations in the much-improved camp hospital and turned what until then had been a general ward into a predominantly ophthalmological one. The Thai specialists were dismissed, and the surgical back-up facility in Bangkok was no longer required.

It was with great relief and satisfaction that before leaving the country in April 1980, I witnessed the smooth takeover and the considerable expansion of the small project I had been fortunate enough to run.

DENTAL CARE AT KHAO I DANG

Keo Sambath

During the Pol Pot years, dentists were sent to the fields to work the land. Most of them were killed. Dental care consisted of traditional medicine treatment and simple tooth extraction. Whatever the cause of the disease, care was given by apprentices who had received a few weeks of "training." These boys and girls who knew neither how to read nor write believed themselves able to do what had taken us years to learn. I cannot imagine what they did! The Communists deprived us of everything, not only toothbrushes and toothpaste (which they considered luxury products of Western capitalists), but also adequate food. Malnutrition and lack of dental hygiene were the principal reasons for the bad dental condition of the people.

In late December 1979, a German team (from MHD), equipped only with forceps, dental syringes, and a few other instruments opened the first dental office at Khao I Dang. I was asked to come to help them because the number of patients was increasing daily. In response to growing demands, a new room was built in which four dentists could work. The Germans furnished medication and the French (from MSF) provided more necessary instruments. In February 1980, two

Keo Sambath, a Cambodian dentist, lived and worked as a volunteer for the United States Catholic Conference and Catholic Relief Services at Khao I Dang from November 1979 to August 1980. He was President of the Cambodian Medical Association there. He now lives in New York and is working as a dental technician while preparing for his dental licensure examinations.

young expatriate dentists from the Catholic Relief Service (CRS) came to see me about opening another dental office. Soon it opened, with the most simple equipment: chairs propped against a wall for the patients, dining tables for instruments and material, a bamboo cabinet for medicine, beds for resting, and a tank of water. Thanks to our two bright and friendly expatriates, we had the necessary instruments and materials. Three nurse's aides and two Khmer dentists were added to the staff.

Despite our lack of equipment and supplies, we saw an average of 175 patients daily at the two Khao I Dang dental clinics. Since there were so many patients, we distributed numbered tickets in the morning. We saw patients from 9:30 A.M. until 4:00 P.M., with a one-hour break at noon. Ninety percent of the cases were extractions—teeth had become decayed during the Pol Pot regime due to lack of hygiene, bad diet, and the unavailability of endodontic treatment. We also filled simple cavities and scaled teeth on two to four patients daily. Most of the afternoon was devoted to dental care of schoolchildren and orphans. With the help of CRS, we were able to distribute a toothbrush to each child. But we were not able to give them toothpaste; we advised them to use kitchen salt instead. We placed posters demonstrating how to brush teeth in several important locations, such as the OPDs.

We diagnosed cavities of all types, periodontal disease, decayed teeth, gums with no teeth, dental malformations and malpositionings, premature loss of temporary teeth, and absent or late dentition. Patients came for emergencies with unbearable pain, for infections, for aesthetic reasons, and to be able to chew food properly. Loss of teeth made girls appear older than they actually were. Rarely had anyone conserved all teeth in good condition. We could only alleviate pain by extraction and by trying to preserve as many teeth as possible. In some mouths, we could not find a single healthy tooth. What could be done?

THE MENTAL HEALTH OF REFUGEES AND RELIEF WORKERS

David N. Ratnavale

Refugees and relief workers alike run a high risk of developing mental-health problems. Throughout the Cambodian relief operation, psychiatric problems and severe manifestations of stress were reported. Yet by early 1983, although the camps remained nearly full and tensions were still running high, not even one camp had a facility set aside for the emotionally ill. In no camp was there a psychiatrist, psychiatric nurse, clinical social worker, or psychologist. In addition, there were almost no Cambodian health professionals left, because they had already been settled in distant lands. Major psychiatric disorders in the camps were managed by physicians unskilled for such work. Most psychiatric drugs were in short supply, except for Valium which was overprescribed. Patients who became too difficult to handle were sent to regional and district hospitals where they sometimes faced additional problems of a cultural nature.

Experts who have studied at first hand the conditions in refugee camps have all urged that mental-health services should be provided in every center, emphasizing prevention, early

Dr. Ratnavale, a psychiatrist, was a Distinguished Visiting Scientist at the National Institute of Mental Health (NIMH) and Head of the Alcohol, Drug Abuse, and Mental Health Administration/NIMH Task Force on Refugee Mental Health from October 1979 to October 1981. He is currently Director, Georgia Avenue Division, District of Columbia Institute of Mental Hygiene, and a psychiatrist in private practice in Washington, D.C. He is also Professor of Psychiatry and Behavioral Science at the Eastern Virginia Medical School.

detection, and a sensitivity to culture. A social-service coordinator, working in parallel with the medical coordinator and camp administrator, has been advocated, and a broad community perspective encouraged. Some experts, however, impressed with the resilience of the refugees ask, "If they can smile, how can they have mental problems?"

The mental-health needs of refugees reflect the problems of uprooted persons and the unique traumatic experiences encountered during their refuge-seeking course. At a minimum, these include the following: (1) the conditions causing the person to flee from his or her homeland; (2) vicissitudes during flight; (3) adjustments in the country of first asylum, which could mean being shunted from one camp to another, and (4) problems arising in the land of final resettlement, which could indeed mean repatriation. If unrelieved, psychological problems occurring in one phase are added on to those that emerge in subsequent phases. Hence, the need for early detection and resolution. This chapter will focus on the third of these phases.

Flux is the norm in refugee camps similar to Khao I Dang. Although the camp initially symbolizes a safe haven to the refugees, it is nevertheless an alien place in which they are restricted, fenced in, and under the control of foreigners. It is a place in which to rest but not to stay. Because of their past experience of chaos and lack of direction, the refugees hunger for permanency. Besides this, their extreme sensitivity to change renders them easily threatened by the slightest variation —creating an inner restlessness and hypervigilant state that can be contagious.

Just two days after my arrival in Thailand, a military coup d'etat was attempted, bringing civilian movements to a complete halt. It aroused fear in the foreign relief workers. Communication between the camps and with Bangkok was cut, which led to fears of internal turmoil and of foreign incursions. Although brief, it illustrates how easily refugees and relief workers alike can find themselves in the same boat. Other examples of stress-generating events that further illustrate this phenomenon were rumors of new incursions across the border; plans for forced repatriation en masse; an epidemic of suicides—six in a row; a sudden policy shift requiring close search of personnel entering the camps; the robbing and murder of a foreign volunteer physician; a sudden resignation of senior staff, an unannounced change in the leadership of UNHCR, the volags, and the Thai military command; the rape of a volunteer nurse; a sudden increase in neonatal deaths; the drowning of six children in an unprotected well; the distribution of a questionnaire to all refugees by UNHCR without clarifying the objective; and the departure from the camp of a truck filled with refugees, its destination unknown (heading for Bangkok en route to a third country or to the border for repatriation?). The camp community was extremely sensitized to separation and loss. Refugees and refugee-relief workers in all the camps spoke of the silence that hovered over the camp following every mass separation: "As if the whole camp becomes depressed." Preventive approaches would be effective in reducing such tensions, but at present no mechanism or authority is available to attend to such issues.

The diagnosis of mental disorder by general physicians and even psychiatrists unfamiliar with the cultural norms of their patients is never easy. The delusions and hallucinations of schizophrenia may be difficult to distinguish from certain organic states, or in the absence of physical disease, a patient's beliefs in spirits or in ancestor worship may sound very confusing to the average Western physician. Knowing what we know about post-traumatic stress disorders—reactions to victimization and stress that may occur immediately or as much as 20 years after the trauma—must make us wonder why this diagnosis was relatively rare in refugee health statistics. Was it because of poor data collection or the difficulty in distinguishing emotional disorder from the array of confusing signs and symptoms presented to the physician? Is the same mistake that was made with the United States veterans of the Vietnam War being repeated? Could it be that in the refugee context, because of ethnic variations in perception and experience, manifestations of stress and their diagnosis and treatment were delayed?

Obvious anxiety states were diagnosed without difficulty and in the Western-type OPDs minor tranquilizers, mainly

Valium, were prescribed—in one camp, as many as 6,000 capsules per week. On the other hand, major psychiatric disorders were not readily identified. During the early crisis, most of the psychological symptoms were related to cases with severe fluid and electrolyte imbalance. Toxic psychotic states appeared as complications of severe malnutrition, cerebral malaria, and typhoid. Some cases of hysteria (hyperventilation syndrome) were reported, as well as some cases of gastrointestinal psychosomatic reaction—a diagnosis that is hard to confirm in the presence of vitamin deficiency and intestinal parasites. Asthma and pneumonia were very common, as were allergic reactions, but there was difficulty in determining the extent of the emotional component. Children suffered from the deficiency syndromes, but psychological reactions akin to hospitalism and deprivation syndrome were noted. Sleep disturbances affected every age,with nightmares being prominent.

During the crisis period, health workers noted many puzzling conditions. Some witnessed what seemed to them to be "indifference" by refugee mothers toward their infants and small children. These mothers were seen to be "insensitive" to the cries and whimpers of their offspring, causing volunteers in some instances to feel outraged. Little did they know of the inner mental state of these women or their past experiences, which had primed them psychologically for adapting to yet another loss. Such beahvior has to be understood as an anticipatory grief reaction as well as a signal for handing over to the relief worker the child and the responsibility for aggressive lifesaving action.

Nor is it difficult now to understand why persons severely starved, injured, or diseased may not have the mental wherewithal to register or signal their inner mental state or need. Emaciated children, likewise, lying motionless, half dead, affectless, unable to cry, suck, or swallow, were consequently incapable of transmitting to caretakers the nurture-evoking cues shown by normal children. When such victims, especially older children and adults, are finally able to begin to gain some physical stamina, regain their minds (so to speak), and come alive to reality, they can remember who they are, realize who else is present, and even perhaps comprehend why they are there. It is possibly at this moment that they are confronted with their enormous losses.

Health workers have reported feeling helpless to deal with such situations. Overwhelmed, they tended to move away to care for other victims for whom a standard medical or nursing procedure was simpler to apply. When disorganizing grief reactions occurred, they further choked the victims' will to live and blocked efforts already being made to revive them—a response that left relief workers extremely frustrated and puzzled.

In times of crisis, people revert to those traditional and cultural supports that previously gave them a sense of identity and security. Individuals may turn to religious leaders for solace and guidance, to traditional healers for mental and physical ills, and to those traditional rituals and customs that helped to anchor people's lives.

The popularity of the traditional medicine centers attests to the value of providing health services appropriate and familiar to the indigenous population. After a period of skepticism and resistance, Western health workers came around to acknowledging the effectiveness of such unfamiliar practices. There seems little doubt that a significant proportion of emotion-laden ills was being appropriately managed by the Krou Khmer traditional healers [see the chapter, "Traditional Medicine," by J.P. Hiegel]. Likewise, newly erected temples and houses of worship—however makeshift—provided the refugees with yet another anchor, a place for meditation and rest, and for the mental accounting of losses and assets. The religious and spiritual dimension in relief assistance is now well understood. Indeed, during the height of the emergency, relief workers conceded that healing the psyche was their biggest problem. Inherent in these processes, persons in distress can find enormous psychological support and restoration. This may well account for the seemingly sparse reporting of psychiatric disorders in camp statistics.

In any event, transient or even serious mental problems could well go undetected in a refugee camp setting. Once basic life-sustaining resources have provided some stability, families may not only deny their emotional problems but also seek to conceal them. This was particularly true in the case of families being processed for sponsorship abroad, whose eligibility would be compromised if one member was found to have suffered from "previous attacks of insanity"—one of the "excludable conditions," according to out-of-date immigration guidelines. Responsible staff members were reported to have joined in such deceptions out of humanitarian concern or antagonism to the United States Immigration and Naturalization Service policy. Others were known to have conveniently underdiagnosed, because of an aversion towards labeling individuals as schizophrenic or being suicidally depressed, which may have delayed detection and treatment.

Another argument that might be offered to explain the seemingly low incidence of psychiatric disorders among refugees is that those reaching the camp represented the healthiest among the population—the most fit being the ones who survived. This is quite likely the case. (Elders among the refugees conceded that psychotic and retarded individuals had either been abandoned in the scurrying for shelter or perished during the trials of escape.) If this is true, refugees are individuals who possess remarkable coping skills They deserve warm care and have many lessons to teach and share.

The relief workers also had their own mental-health needs. They had a life with the refugees within the barricaded confines of the camp and a life outside among Thai neighbors, where the barriers were less apparent to see. They also had a life they had left behind, one to which they could return in a hurry if need be. On completion of their terms of service, following a brief but distinct "reentry" process, they would finally go home considerably enlightened by the whole refugee experience.

Relief workers arriving in Thailand had, at least initially, to contend with disaster shock as well as culture shock. The majority had been inadequately prepared, some receiving their briefings at the airport just hours before boarding the plane. Transported rather suddenly to an alien environment, they experienced initial stress, having to adapt to new sounds, sights, temperatures, and smells. In the camps, they were exposed to the victims of human carnage and a variety of stimuli hard to integrate.

In the very early acute stages of the operation, personnel had no choice but to assume a variety of roles. Many were straddled with the heavy responsibility for triage—never being certain about who had a chance to survive and who was doomed. Totally new situations had to be tackled, Western health workers inexperienced in caring for the severely undernourished needed much guidance in the early crisis period. In dealing with those starved, panic-generated efforts at forced feeding caused even greater damage.

Mental health becomes a critical issue under such circumstances and must be considered from a very broad perspective. It must not be viewed in terms of diagnosable mental illness, requiring traditional hospital, community, and outpatient services. Rather, it should be conceptualized in terms of exaggerated psychological stress that can lead to breakdown or seriously handicapped functioning. In the initial phases of the operation, confronted with so much violence, starvation, and death, a few workers had breakdowns requiring hospitalization in Bangkok or being sent home. Volag representatives, who were unprepared for such contingencies, were distracted from the urgent tasks at hand. When working hours were "round the clock," the brief sleep available was the only escape for many, but they, too, were not spared nightmares and stomach cramps. Some workers seemed prepared to ignore their own stress ("They didn't have time") as they worked feverishly, sometimes mobilized by guilt feelings from within or induced by co-workers. Some came to believe that their work had greater meaning if they themselves suffered a bit, just like the refugees they had come to serve.

Mental stress was usually signaled by strong emotional reactions, complex interpersonal behavior, and psychosomatic concerns. Gastrointestinal, respiratory, and dermatological symptoms were common, as well as disturbed sleeping and eating patterns. A fair percentage of those who were phobic about infections were given to antibiotic pill popping and health personnel tended to abuse drugs and alcohol. Staff members were noted to have fits of irritability, withdrawal, and moodiness. Suicidal thoughts, temper tantrums, and feelings of "just wanting to run away" were common. Since identification with the aggressor is common among persons working with violent individuals and their victims, it was not unusual for relief workers to vent their anger even on the refugees. There were AWOLs (workers absent without official leave) and blatantly inappropriate liaisons with fellow co-workers and even refugees. Minor irritations would be built up, and paranoid reactions easily evoked. Deep emotions were aroused over such matters as renewal of contracts, unanticipated crises at home, and delays in the mail.

Culture shock revolved around ·real and imaginary fears: fears of being robbed or victimized or of getting lost were the most common. Devoid of their accustomed support networks, relief workers would become oversensitive and suspicious or feel hated and out of place. This sense of isolation caused many to identify closely with the plight of the refugees and therefore to feel displaced themselves. The refugees, too, felt displaced. Communication with the refugees in the camp and with the indigenous Thais after hours was difficult for some. Unfamiliar greeting gestures were confusing, and since nonverbal behavior is a major part of Asian interaction, faulty interpretations often led to akwardness. A faux pas or an error in etiquette—to which sensitivity is always heightened in stressful situations—often led to some clumsy and distancing responses. Some relief workers were known to have behaved like "ugly foreigners" outside the camp.

There was a strong tendency to blame others when things went wrong. This could be seen very regularly in the form of disputes between the agencies. Such dissonance has its roots in tension. People of diverse backgrounds working together in a tense atmosphere, as in the border zone between Thailand and Cambodia, are bound to get in each other's hair. When nerves are raw, minor differences assume huge proportions. Dissatisfaction with the way things were being done would become huge issues. There were major confrontations over such matters as a particular surgical technique, treatment, or immunization procedure; bottle- versus breast-feeding; teaching English as a second language versus revival of indigenous art or music; screening of refugees by immigration officials to prevent the emigration of refugees with excludable diseases versus resettlement regardless of past illness or "previous attacks of insanity"; religious activities (proselytizing versus building a temple); patient care (allowing exhausted patients to sleep versus waking them up in mid-afternoon so that medical students and their professors could conduct "ward rounds"); and the management of unaccompanied minors and rape victims (a Western social-work approach versus something culturally appropriate).

Interviews with relief workers who had completed an overseas assignment revealed that nearly 70 percent experienced much anguish when about to leave the camp and also considerable re-entry stress and reverse culture shock. Several weeks prior to departing from the camps, relief workers tended to withdraw or find distraction in planning side trips to other countries en route to their home destination. Relationships with colleagues and attachments to refugees became strained. For some, there was a strong need mentally to review their entire relief-work experience. On returning home, many felt a compulsion to talk about their experience but felt puzzled when people at home were not as interested as they had hoped. This led some to ponder over the real value of their service and to wonder if their compassion was genuine. Besides much soul-searching and preoccupation over the meaning of life, disturbed sleep and eating patterns were noted, as were depression, anxiety with flashbacks, and many other physical symptoms

Clearly relief work is hazardous as well as rewarding. There is no way to measure the enormous amount of human effort expended in behalf of the Cambodian refugees, but certainly the rewards outweighed the strains. The following sentiments were echoed in every setting that I visited: "These people contributed much more to my life than I did to theirs"; "I felt more freedom than I had in my own country, a function of being in a culture but not of it, and free of cultural restraints"; "Here I am someone."

Unprotected persons require much more than food, medicines, and shelter. I appeal for the introduction of mental-health services as critical and essential programs for refugees and relief workers in the confined camp settings where they reside. There is a role for a "mental-health sanitarian" or a mental-health engineer sensitive to psychological issues for both refugees and relief workers, and to psychosocial factors pathogenic to the camp community. A team of such individuals, working in collaboration with traditional public-health workers and key refugee leaders, could develop preventive approaches, mechanisms for defusing stress, and coordinate appropriate mental-health programs.

HOLISTIC HEALTH CARE

Virginia Veach

Refugee camps by their very nature are comprised of people who have suffered not only physical hardships, but also mental, emotional, and spiritual ones. Therefore, our first team was interdisciplinary: a doctor, five nurses, a priest, three psychologists (who also had degrees as physical and acupunctural therapists), an educator, two paramedics, and a laboratory and x-ray technician.

When we arrived in Khao I Dang in early December 1979, about two weeks after the center opened, we were first taken to see our future ward. Upon entering the bamboo shelter, we found a small group of dancers teaching children classical Cambodian ballet. They were somewhat dismayed to see us and expected to be told to leave. Instead, I told them that I was pleased that they were both strong enough to dance and still wanted to dance; I also told them that they were welcome to stay and use the building as long as it was under construction and we were not using it as a hospital unit. When the building was completed and it opened as a ward, we promised to ensure that they would have a place to continue their dancing school.

Virginia Veach was Coordinator and Director of the Family Practice Ward at Khao I Dang, while working with the International Catholic Migration Commission from December 1979 to September 1980. She is now a psychologist, physical therapist, and minister at the Ting-sha Institute, Pt. Reyes Station, California.

The head teacher, Mrs. Mom Kamel, responded with pleasure and gratitude. She explained that they had been moved from one building to the next ever since the camp opened, and that they feared that the school would have to stop without someone to help them to continue. She told me, "We cannot survive unless we remember where we have come from—unless we have an identity and a sense of dignity." She added, "Many people from all over the world have come to help us with medicines and food, for which we are so grateful that our hearts can never express it; but you are the first people who have come who care how we are as human beings."

There was a great concern among the volunteers that there was no adequate outreach program. There was no way to get to the sick people of the camp unless they came to the hospital, and often they were brought in when it was almost too late. The Cambodian people were fearful of Westerners and of Western medicine, so it was quite a problem. Nevertheless, early on, the only outpatient department was swamped with patients—often a thousand people in a single day. Because people too sick to stand were waiting for hours in the hot sun only to be turned away at the end of the day and told to return the next morning, we decided to start an auxiliary outpatient department in our as-yet-to-be-completed ward. Some of our team members offered to help in the existing outpatient department; others stayed in our newly formed auxiliary outpatient department. We had the dancers at one end of the ward and the outpatient department at the other. Mrs. Kamel came to me the next day with great concern. "Sick people need quiet," she said. "Perhaps we should stop our dancing." "That's true," I replied, "and sick people also need joy." She smiled.

The Khmer people began to trust us, and gradually began coming in to ask for medicine for a relative too sick to visit the outpatient department. We told them that we could not give them the medicine until we had seen the patient, but that we would be willing to go to the relative's home. Then the negotiating began, "Please don't take him to the hospital." We assured each one that we would do what we could to treat the patient at home, but if he was too sick to do so, we would have to bring him to the hospital. We were always able to reach an agreement. We were very pleased to be able to go to their homes and treat those who had been too afraid to come to the hospital, or too sick to stand in the long OPD lines. This kind of outreach took a lot of work and much time, but was very rewarding in the increased care and trust that began to develop.

We discovered that many of the Western teams were supplying baby bottles to undernourished or dehydrated mothers who were unable to breast-feed, due to their own lack of an adequate diet. Feeding a baby by bottle in a refugee camp is tantamount to signing a death certificate for the child. The water is contaminated, the bottles difficult to boil. On our ward, baby bottles were outlawed. We hydrated the mothers and fed the babies by dripping milk onto the mother's breast. The baby would nurse as though the milk was coming from the nipple, thereby stimulating lactation. These mothers needed not only nourishment but support and encouragement, for they were naturally quite frightened that their babies were not getting enough to eat. Our approach to caring for the dehydrated mothers and infants was well rewarded when the infant mortality rate markedly dropped.

We had patients with diseases ranging from cerebral malaria, tuberculosis, pneumonia, terminal cancer, polio, leprosy, and measles to beriberi and parasitic worms. We had patients recovering from shrapnel and bullet wounds, and amputees who were victims of land-mine explosions. We had patients suffering from anxiety reactions, and women who, having been victims of rape on the border, would wake up at night hysterical and hyperventilating. We were sent patients who were not responding to medication in other wards, or patients who were too difficult for other wards to handle. We were sent the terminally ill and the mentally ill. It was impossible to separate the physical ills from the emotional, mental, and spiritual suffering. Among our patients, there were those who, because of the extreme shortage of food, had been forced to make the unbearable decision of whether to give too little food to several children and possibly lose them all, or to give all the food to one child in the hope that at least one would survive. Sometimes, when families had made the agonizing decision to sacrifice all but one child, one of the starving children managed to live long enough to be brought to the refugee camp. When the family was given food in the hospital ward, it would often be the healthy well-fed child who would be given the food, not the starving one. The doctors and nurses in the other wards could often not understand this behavior, and became frustrated and angry with the parents. In our ward, we would simply sit with the family and talk, or play with the well child, encouraging the feeding of the starving one in a supportive way, understanding that the family members already grieved for the starving child, and found it too difficult to hope for his or her survival when there was still such a strong possibility that he or she would die, and they would have to go through the grieving a second time; also that it was too painful to face the guilt of what they had had to do. Gradually, once the child grew stronger, the family could then again begin to incorporate him or her into the family structure.

We also cared for women who had given birth in the hospital after suffering the loss of their other children. These mothers were often too emotionally depleted to make a connection and care for the new baby. They would tell the doctors or nurses that they did not want the newborn and ask that the baby be taken away. In such cases, instead of taking the newborn baby to the unaccompanied children's center, we took care of both the mother and the baby next to one another. After four or five days of care and support, when the mother felt stronger and somewhat nourished, she would then become interested in her new baby, and the bonding would occur, thus avoiding our having another unaccompanied child or infant death.

The day after our ward opened, we bought a Spirit House to be placed outside. In Thailand and Cambodia, each home and each place of business has a Spirit House, a tiny replica of a temple, set on a pedestal. Inside each Spirit House is a small statue of Buddha; outside are placed flowers, incense, and an offering of rice or some other food. Each time anyone passes a Spirit House, either entering or leaving a home or place of business, he or she bows and says a prayer or gives thanks.

When we brought the Spirit House to the ward, the Cambodians were speechless with amazement. Hundreds of people watched in silence as our guards and interpreters placed it in its proper relationship to the sun and to the entrance to the ward. Finally, they began to murmur quietly, and I asked my interpreter, Chao, what they were saying. Chao told me that they were amazed that anyone outside of Cambodia or Thailand would have heard about Buddhism, and that Westerners would value and honor their traditions and beliefs. Whenever a patient wanted to burn incense and say prayers for a relative or friend, he or she was encouraged to do so.

We were fortunate enough to locate a few Cambodian monks. When there was a death in the ward, we would ask a monk to come in and perform a service, both before the death and after. We were the first people in the camp to make the death and burial process a personal one. This was of great moment not only to the immediate family but also to the entire ward. The general mood and feeling in the ward was raised, uplifted, as each one in his or her way participated in a religious service for the first time in five years. It was apparent that in our ward we really cared how each person was, not only physically but emotionally and spiritually.

We encouraged all the members of a family to care for the patient whenever possible. Patients got better much faster when what was left of the family could be kept together. There was always a great deal of anxiety about the well-being of the absent members when visitors were restricted. So we had many children in the ward, well ones as well as sick. We began a children's program at one end of the ward where the children could color, paint, model in clay, and look at books. Many of these children had never seen books or crayons before, as all schooling had been stopped for the past five years under the Pol Pot regime. They did not know what to do with the crayons and paper until we showed them that marks could be made on a page.

The children were eager to learn and to communicate. They wanted to let us know what they had experienced. At first, the pictures they drew were all of fighting—blood, guns, helicopters, tanks, fire, death. But after only a few weeks, they began drawing the sun, flowers, trees, houses, fish, birds and people. The healing took place remarkably quickly once they were given the opportunity to express themselves. As the children improved, so did the entire ward. The adults became interested in painting, sewing, basket making, embroidery. We bought them materials in the nearby town, gathered leftover bamboo fronds from the thatched roofs, and dug up clay from the ground around the ward for modeling. The Khmer began to realize that their talents were appreciated and valued by us.

Now, in addition to their traditional dances, the Khmer refugees had other things to share and to give. In order not to rob one another of dignity and a sense of self-worth, it was essential for the recipients of our giving to be able to give to us as well. If we did not encourage this, our help would become demeaning and ultimately be resented.

At Christmastime, the dancers prepared a performance of classical Cambodian ballet, and invited all "the foreigners" to attend as their gift to us. Many of the Western volunteers did not understand the value of accepting the invitation—it was the only gift the Cambodians had to give, and it was important to them that we be willing to receive it. When so many refugees were in need of treatment and care, it seemed frivolous and wrong to be going off to a dance performance. The importance of the event, however, gradually began to come through, and by Christmas, many volunteers as well as Cambodians enjoyed a magnificient dance celebration.

After the opening of our ward, we began and supported the cultural program, the children's activities, the sewing center and an English and educational program, designed not only for the people in our ward but also for those in the other wards as well. We started a medical program to teach emergency care and paramedical and first-aid training to eighty Khmer students; we participated in and supported a new physical rehabilitation center.

We placed a particular emphasis on working with Khmer doctors and shamen for the treatment of many ills for which Western medicine alone had no solution. It is important for the patient to believe in or to feel trust in the treatment prescribed. Our doctors worked closely with the Khmer doctors and shamen to develop a course of action that would best benefit the patient.

We found the Khmer to be a very bright people, full of warmth, courage, love, integrity, and with an amazing capacity for life. We felt privileged to be able to meet and know these people who will remain an inspiration to us all, reminding us of what the human spirit is capable.

Medicine alone is not enough for the survival of refugees. For them to be able to survive the continued effects of hardships and disease they must be able to maintain a sense of their own identity, their culture, and their worth as human beings.

TRADITIONAL MEDICINE

J. P. Hiegel

Traditional medicine centers (TMCs) in refugee camps, functioning both independently and in cooperation with OPDs and hospital wards providing modern medical care can provide invaluable services. On behalf of the ICRC, I promoted cooperation with traditional healers who were refugees themselves and created a TMC in each Khmer holding camp in Thailand. This program started in January 1980. It was supported by the ICRC through July 1981, then by the French relief body of the Order of Malta, which took over the project until the end of 1981. Later some voluntary agencies convinced of the usefulness of such centers opened them in a number of other camps.

Widespread cooperation between modern medical teams and traditional healers, whenever these are present in the camps, can significantly reduce the need for chemical drugs without reducing the quality or efficiency of care.

Refugees are dependent upon humanitarian organizations for their survival. This situation is humiliating. Supporting the activity of their traditional healers contributes to their dignity.

Dr. Hiegel, a French psychiatrist, went to Thailand with the International Committee of the Red Cross to coordinate the traditional medicine centers in the Cambodian refugee camps in January 1980.

The herbs that the Kru* mix to prepare various concoctions (by boiling to extract essences), powders, pills or ointments undoubtedly have healing properties. I shall not discuss this further here, although these preparations can occasionally cure physical illnesses resistant to modern medical treatments. I emphasize the role of the Kru in providing adequate answers to the psychological needs of refugees. These needs are often neglected, and even when there is an awareness of the refugees' psychological suffering, the relief workers can easily feel helpless. In some cases, they are helpless because their own psychological needs are not fulfilled. Sooner or later many refugees complain of somatizations; that is, they actually suffer in some part of their bodies although they are not physically ill. Their pain has a psychological origin; the suffering has been diverted to the physical body. Sometimes misunderstandings, misinterpretations due to a cultural gap and Western frames of reference, may lead to inappproriate solutions for particular problems. The Kru possess natural psychotherapeutic abilities. They have the same cultural identity as other Khmers, and they are usually much respected. They are wise, and they are in a position to cope with almost every particular psychological stress provided that their own psychological needs are also met.

The Khmer often discussed the hardships they had endured. Some victims had also to face their own guilt because their survival had required compromises that in hindsight were hardly acceptable. This might occur anywhere from several months to several years later, and the relief workers provided an important psychological support by listening and showing esteem, interest, and sympathy.

---

*Kru is a phonetic adaptation in Khmer of the Sanskrit word *guru*. It is a general designation for any person who is endowed with a specific form of knowledge. Thus the Khmer traditional healers are called Kru. The term does not imply that they have healing capacities, but shows that the persons thus referred to possess some form of knowledge. A second noun can be added to the original term Kru, further qualifying the particular kind of knowledge. The Kru Thnam, for example, treats his patients using medications prepared by mixing in various proportions the bark, root, fruit, and leaves of medicinal trees. The Kru Thmop is expert in magical therapy.

Sooner or later, however, the ego mechanism of defense operates increasingly in the relief workers who, being closely involved in the refugees' care, cannot get enough personal benefit from their work. Some may feel sad, useless, more or less disappointed, or unmotivated. Unconscious aggression and rejecting attitudes toward patients may occasionally occur, especially when the complaints manifest themselves as somatizations.

At a time when health and nutritional conditions had much improved in the camps, we were able to make an instructive observation. One modern doctor had obviously unconsciously organized her consultations in such a way as to protect her own ego. She sat at a table, the patient stood behind her. The interpreter translated questions in a quite mechanical way without regard for the patient's real understanding. Then the doctor said, "They come, but they are not sick. They are happy if they can get an injection." Being a placebo distributor is not satisfying to the doctor who knows that this is not in fact the proper answer to the patient's needs. Refusing such a position is also unsatisfying to the doctor who has the illusion that he or she would make the patient happy by giving a drug, seen as a gift.

During the emergency phase, medical people are obviously saving lives. This situation provides much gratification to doctors and nurses, but their narcissism may easily be wounded when they have only routine work to do. As a consequence, unconscious aggression may come to pervade the doctor-patient relationship. In this context, the physician refusing to give "a drug gift" cannot know if his or her decision is based upon a wise medical attitude or if it is the consequence of unconscious aggression toward the patient. In consequence, both the patient and the doctor are dissatisfied with the consultation.

The kind of doctor-patient relationship described above is of course, an exception among physicians participating in relief activities. But many modern practitioners have difficulty in dealing with patients with psychosomatic complaints. They feel more frustrated in a refugee situation than in their homeland because linguistic and cultural barriers may prevent them from providing their patients with adequate psychological aid. It is not satisfying to give an inactive substance to a patient and make him or her think that it is an active one, because this, in fact, is just fooling the patient. Fooling the patient with a placebo may be the physician's answer to his or her own personal feeling of having first been "fooled" by the patient. It is, furthermore, unwise to try to solve a psychological problem with a placebo, especially in caring for people from a Third World nation. Encouraging patients to regard modern drugs as panaceas for all suffering is inappropriate.

The longer the refugees remained in the camp, the more somatizations occurred. This was a real concern to the medical teams. Many patients came to the OPD saying that they suffered. When asked, "Where?" they responded by saying, "I don't know" or by indicating almost any part of their body: one day the head, the next, the chest. The fact was that they did suffer, even if there was no clinical evidence of any organic disease. The traditional healers' approach to their patients and traditional remedies is a valuable resource for such patients.

Symptoms are, of course, the expression of a somatic or psychological pain, but to a certain extent, they are also influenced by social codes. They are part of the relationship between the person and the group to which he or she belongs, being a means of communication with that group. That is why, mainly in the psychological field, a wrong diagnosis could easily be made by practitioners referring to Western psychiatric nosology.

On various occasions, Khmers were referred to the TMC with the diagnosis of acute or chronic schizophrenia. In many cases the Kru were categorical that such patients were not chkuot (mad), but possessed; and, in fact, the patients immediately recovered once a magical ritual was performed. Western medical people are usually not familiar with the role and importance of magic in many societies. The belief in a supernatural world populated with various spirits, which are not hostile but, if offended, potentially revengeful, is deeply rooted in the Khmer culture. When a Khmer, like many people belonging to other ethnic groups, thinks that he or she is being punished by an offended spirit or that a spirit has been driven into his body through witchcraft, he or she unconsciously adopts a certain kind of behavior as a consequence and proof of possession. Western people behaving in the same way would probably be severely mentally ill. The Khmers are highly sensitive to the meaning of this sort of special behavior. They are often afraid to approach a possessed person, fearing that the spirit will possess them as well. A reinforcing situation is created because the patient's feeling is confirmed by the group's attitude which reflects the image of being possessed.

According to traditional Khmer belief, a spirit is tenacious and only a Kru Thmop (a healer having special magic powers) has the ability to deal with such cases. Western people often think that beliefs in a supernatural world populated with spirits, which can interfere with humans' existence, are nonsense or that these beliefs are actually detrimental to the people. In fact, if we admit that such spirits do not exist, we must regard them as projections of the unconscious. Such beliefs help to express and resolve psychological conflicts. We, therefore, should respect these beliefs and allow people to find appropriate help from their own traditional healers. Moreover, we show our esteem for people by showing respect for their traditions and culture. Disregarding someone's cultural identity is not only offensive, it may also cause a psychological trauma, especially in the case of a refugee.

Some popular beliefs may be at the origin of misunderstandings and therefore have consequences for patients. For example, many Khmer mothers, during menstruation, will not approach their child if he or she is suffering from measles. According to popular belief, if the mother did so, the disease would become worse. This explains why some mothers refuse to stay with their hospitalized children and assist in their care. Traditional healers are in a good position to teach us about all beliefs and interdictions which have to be observed during specific events. This knowledge prevents us from offending or frightening patients who have different medical concepts. Modern medical treatment is more easily accepted when patients feel that their own beliefs have been taken into consideration.

Among relief workers, those who have only an ethnocentric approach to problems have difficulty under certain circumstances in providing refugees with adequate psychological support. The Khmer medics and social workers who had been trained by foreigners were in a better position to furnish this psychological support, because of the common culture. We must, however, be aware of the fact that we offer them a Western model of identification in which they may become imprisoned. There is always some danger in unconsciously or implicitly urging people to separate themselves from their own culture and submit to our values in order to please us.

A Kru Thmop has magical power and knowledge of formulas and mantras. He will train and teach only those known for their good morality. The student has to pay respect to his Thmop and promise that he will lead a correct and honest life, using his skill to do only good.

Traditional healers are respected by the Khmers. They receive the respect traditionally given to anyone having knowledge, and are also revered because they usually keep to ethical rules in their own private lives and in their public calling. They themselves respect the Kru who taught them. They believe that his spirit keeps an eye upon them and that they will lose their power if they do not keep the promise made to him. The respect and trust given to the Kru enable them to play a truly psychotherapeutic role. They can be quite directive in their interventions, as in the case of a suicide attempt.

After a suicide attempt in the camp, people are taken to the admissions (emergency) ward and are then usually referred to the TMC. The Kru listens and talks to them, and gives them showers with lustral water in order to clear their minds. Patients are required by the Kru to promise them not to try again to take their own lives. The healers are convinced that the strength of this promise is sufficient protection from another attempt. This promise made by the patient to the Kru represents a link with a respected, revered person. It has actually proved more effective in preventing further attempts than any other method available to us. The TMC staff usually accompany the Kru to the patient's house for home visits during the days that follow.

On various occasions, Khmer refugees were brought to the
TMC or the Kru were called to the hospital for conditions diagnosed as hysterical. In many cases, most of the symptoms of
what we would term conversion hysteria were present. The
Khmer people usually believe that such a person is possessed
by a spirit. The healing process consists first of urging the
spirit to speak through the patient's mouth. In this way, his
internal conflict can be publicly aired, whereas according to
Khmer social rules, one can hardly ever discuss directly one's
personal feelings and internal conflicts. The belief in possession includes the idea that not the person but the spirit itself
is speaking. In this way the patient is, in fact, socially allowed to
speak about personal matters while avoiding "losing face."
The spirit, moreover, is considered responsible for feelings, such
as love or hate, that the patient does not accept as his or her
own. This opinion, of course, helps to reduce any feelings of
guilt, provided that the possession is recognized and thus certi-
fied by a Kru Thmop. Then this spirit is driven out of the
person's body through either a simple ritual using lustral water
or a more complicated one in severe cases. It was plain that the
Khmer belief in a supernatural world populated with spirits
helped to express and solve psychological conflicts in a socially
acceptable way.

The acute psychiatric cases with which the Kru dealt were
the most spectacular, but they represented a small percentage of the average of a thousand patients a day who came to
each TMC in the main camps to receive daily treatments. Many
had somatic diseases, but a great number suffered from somatizations. The Khmer staff in each center numbered about 50,
including helpers and healers; therefore, the Kru themselves
had time to listen to the patients and to care for them. Both
patients and healers spoke the same language. This meant that
they not only spoke Khmer but also that their concepts about
illnesses, their origins, and the ways for recovery were rooted
in the same cultural background.

Some traditional and popular concepts about illnesses have
no direct equivalent in modern medical ways of thinking, but
they are meaningful both to patients and to traditional healers.

That was why a discussion with a Kru was really significant and reassuring for the patient who felt that he was understood and understandable that consequently the treatment prescribed was appropriate to his case. A Khmer who complained of being "hot inside" usually had no fever. The feeling could only be understood through its pathophysiology. One of the elements of living creatures—the wind—does not circulate in the body. The traditional treatment of the patient's condition was to rub the edge of a coin, previously soaked in paraffin oil, on the thorax of the patient or to pinch the skin repeatedly in various places. In each instance, superficial cutaneous hematomas were produced.

We have emphasized the traditional healer's role in the psychological and psychosomatic field because this approach to these problems is more adapted than the one we ourselves offer to these patients. This does not mean that the role of the Kru is to be restricted to this field. In the treatment, for example, of skin diseases, cutaneous infections, and conjunctivitis, the various preparations that the Kru use have proven efficacy. A wise and expert practitioner should not disregard traditional remedies unless he or she has good reason to do so. The Kru prepare herbal mixtures with great care, and we have never been aware of any ill effects or intoxication.

Westerners sometimes find it difficult to accept one particular traditional treatment, namely the burns that are quite common practice in Khmer traditional medicine. These burns are only superficial, and the Kru do not apply septic elements to them. No tetanus cases following this treatment have ever been reported among Khmer refugees. The only complication occasionally noted is local infection, but with no real danger to the patient. Westerners may feel that this treatment is aggressive, but the Khmers do not. It would be unwise for foreign workers to exhibit a hostile attitude to this practice, as this might only serve to induce fear of disapproval; therefore, if a patient actually needed modern medical treatment, but had previously had traditional burn therapy, he or she might not come to the Western medical services because of fear of disapproval.

Traditional and modern medicine are complementary. It would be meaningless to try to prove the superiority of one over the other. The experienced Kru are well aware that modern medicine may cure cases that are beyond the reach of traditional remedies.

A patient coming to a TMC instead of going to a modern OPD clearly indicates his or her choice. He or she expects to see a traditional healer. We must respect the patient's choice. We do not have the right to subject him or her to examination by a modern doctor first. The Kru ask our advice when they think that the disease may require modern care. They agree that it is unwise to take risks and that we should avoid competition of any kind between the two ways of healing. The Kru are not reluctant to refer patients to the hospital. They resist only when newly arrived nurses, not yet familiar with their healing capacities, want to refer patients whom the Kru know they can cure. In such a situation, they try to persuade the nurse in charge of their ability to manage the case, and they indicate how long the cure will take. Nurses are very impressed when they see that the Kru are right.

Modern practitioners who fear that the Kru are overpossessive and unaware of their limitations are precisely those who would not refer a case to traditional healers. We, on the other hand, cannot expect the Kru to be willing to cooperate with modern doctors if the latter scorn their practices and reject them as ignorant. Genuine cooperation can be obtained only if we establish a relationship based upon mutual respect, esteem, confidence, and understanding. Modern doctors and nurses feel allowed to make mistakes, like any other human being. Traditional healers should also be allowed the same latitude. In the TMC, the well-trained and the more experienced supervise the practice of the younger.

Many Khmer mothers whose children are hospitalized are afraid of modern technology. Sometimes they wonder if by taking their child to the hospital, they have made the right choice. There have been cases where mothers have run away with their severely ill children because they felt that a Kru in the TMC or in the camp would provide better therapy.

At the request of the medical staff of a pediatric ward, traditional healers from the TMC have been visiting this ward daily. They may be able to provide traditional remedies in addition to the modern therapies being used. In this way, the mothers feel that nothing is being neglected in their children's behalf. In the case of a child's dying, this open-minded attitude helps to prevent the mother from having regrets and feelings of guilt which might arise if only modern methods had been used. In every ward, patients should be permitted to receive additional help from traditional healers whenever they want. Doctors reluctant to admit the physical benefit of traditional medicine should at least acknowledge the psychological support that it gives to enable the patient to recover.

The way that the Kru handle babies and young children is particularly delightful to watch, and the children are rarely frightened of them. The healer sometimes utters some magic word and blows on the child. Mothers feel more secure because the spirits will be disposed to help the child recover.

Another example of the benefits of involving the Kru in modern health services comes from a maternal and child health center. The health workers in this center used to spend much time and effort trying to convince some of the mothers to continue breast-feeding, instead of bottle-feeding, their babies. Sometimes the women did not have enough milk because they did not take enough fluid, but they could not be persuaded to drink more water. In other cases, they felt that their milk was of poor quality and that artificial milk would be better. Traditionally, Khmer mothers drink three or four liters a day of a special concoction which is said to increase the quantity and the quality of their milk. This concoction is prepared every day in the TMC and distributed to the mothers in the maternal and child health center, in the pediatric ward, and in the TMC. In this way, they agree more easily to take enough fluid and breast-feed their babies.

The Kru occasionally have also to cooperate with surgical teams; they do not practice surgery themselves. When a patient arrives at a TMC with an abscess, the healers cover it with a special ointment, and when the pus has collected, they refer the patient to the hospital where it is drained. Occasionally they have been asked to convince patients opposed to surgery to accept it. The Kru, sometimes after long discussions, persuade them that there is no alternative for saving the patient's life. After land-mine injuries, most people, especially the young, cannot accept to have a limb amputated, and they are very depressed. The Kru, on request, visit them. They provide psychological support to the patients, which enables them to undergo the operation in a better psychological condition. This preoperative support along with postoperative support prevents reactional depressions from occurring.

Traditional healers can give valuable support to patients with incurable conditions—for example, there was a woman who could not be operated on for a large tumor of the parotid. She could not open her mouth; she was unable to speak or eat. Moreover, she was planning to commit suicide because she could no longer endure the severe shooting pains. The Kru treated her with their remedies for more than three months. Her general condition improved, and she seldom suffered.

In conclusion, cooperation with a group of traditional healers in some Khmer refugee camps has proved to be workable and useful for both patients and relief workers. The realization that traditional and modern medicine are complementary and the creation of traditional medicine centers in refugee camps gives patients a better chance to find the appropriate solution to their suffering.

Scene of mass murder, torture, and rape by Khmer Rouge during Pol Pot regime.
(Drawing by Bun Heang Ung.)

Scene in Khmer Rouge hospital, depicting forced labor, broadcast propaganda, dispensing of "medications" by untrained personnel, and injections of non-sterile fluid kept in soda bottles. *(Drawing by Bun Heang Ung.)*

Cambodian refugees crossing Thai-Cambodian border in 1979. *(Photograph by Tadao Mitome.)*

Western relief worker rushing moribund child for emergency medical assistance at Thai-Cambodian border in September 1979. *(Photograph by Tadao Mitome.)*

Severely ill and malnourished patients resting and receiving treatment on ground at makeshift hospital at Sa Kaeo camp in October 1979. *(Photograph by Tadao Mitome.)*

Top: Cambodian men constructing addition to obstetrics ward in field hospital at Khao I Dang in early 1980.
Bottom: Typical ward with approximately 100 cots, gravel floor, and sheet plastic roof at Khao I Dang in early 1980. *(Photographs by Barry Levy.)*

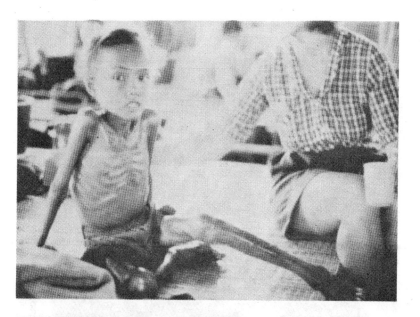

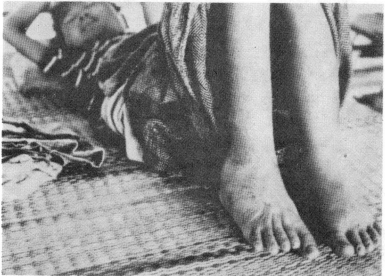

Khao I Dang intensive feeding ward in November 1979.
Top: Relief worker putting oil on dry skin of child with severe wasting typical of
marasmus (protein-calorie malnutrition).
Bottom: Child with swollen feet, puffy face, wasted arms, and skin changes typical
of kwashiorkor (severe protein malnutrition). *(Photographs by Daniel Susott.)*

"Landbridge" in Nong Chan camp on Thai-Cambodian border, where people received international donations of rice in 1979 and 1980 to carry home by oxcart home to northwestern Cambodia, in order to prevent further starvation. *(Photograph by Tadao Mitome.)*

Refugee camp on Thai-Cambodian border in 1979, whose appearance was similar to that at Khao I Dang shortly after its opening, before its trees were cut for firewood. *(Photograph by Tadao Mitome.)*

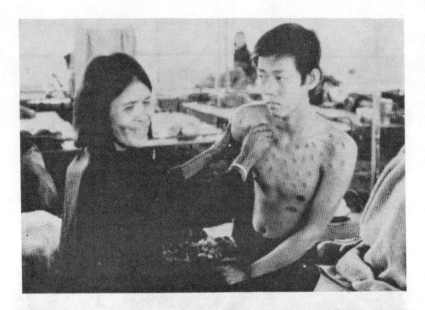

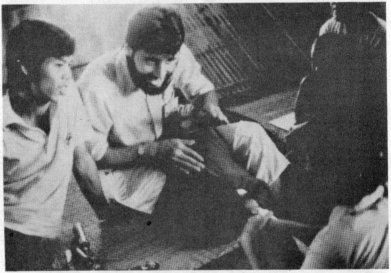

Top: Cambodian woman pinching skin of patient with gastrointestinal problem in traditional Cambodian medicine practice.
Bottom: American medical student clapping ("cupping") chest of child with pneumonia in Western medicine practice. *(Photographs by Daniel Susott.)*

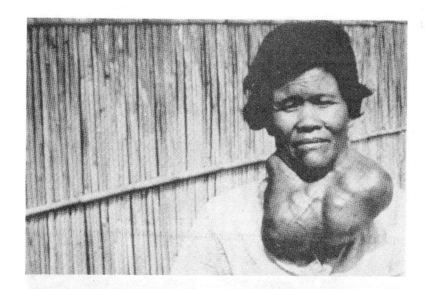

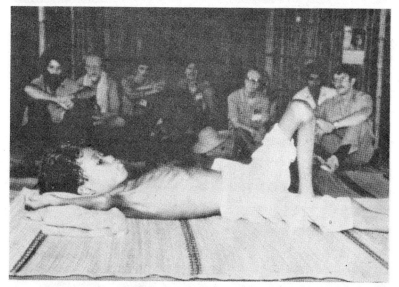

Top: Cambodian woman with severe goiter due to iodine deficiency and lack of medical care. *(Photograph by Daniel Susott.)*

Bottom: Cambodian child with apparent mental retardation, diarrhea, and skin changes, suggestive of pellagra (niacin deficiency), being presented at weekly medical grand rounds for Western relief workers at Khao I Dang in early 1980. *(Photograph by Barry Levy.)*

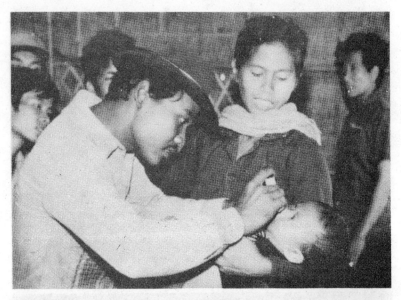

Khao I Dang in early 1980.
Top: Cambodian public health worker administering oral polio vaccine to child.
Bottom: Thai public health worker administering contraceptive injection to Cambodian woman. *(Photographs by Barry Levy.)*

Khao I Dang in early 1980.
Top: Cambodian classical ballet troupe members performing at Buddhist temple.
Bottom: Cambodian orphans making clay statues of Buddha at handicraft center.
(Photographs by Daniel Susott.)

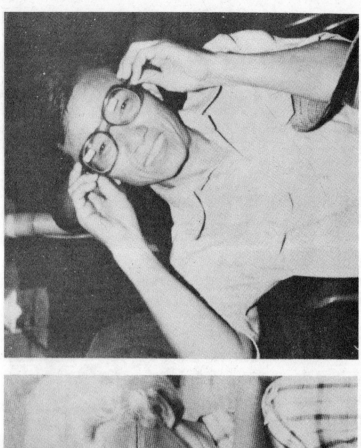

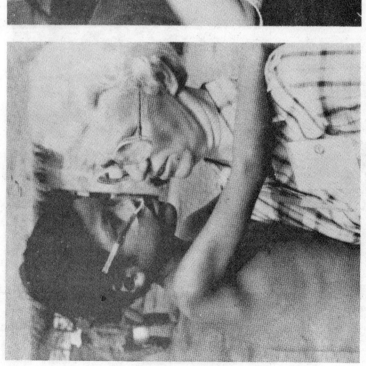

Left: Western relief worker with emotionally disturbed Cambodian orphan, unable to see since witnessing the murder of his parents during the Pol Pot regime.

Right: Cambodian man elated at receiving new pair of glasses at eye clinic at Khao I Dang in early 1980; during Pol Pot regime, wearing glasses symbolized education and often marked one for death. *(Photographs by Barry Levy.)*

Cambodian public health workers attending course on communicable disease control at Khao I Dang in early 1980. *(Photograph by Barry Levy.)*

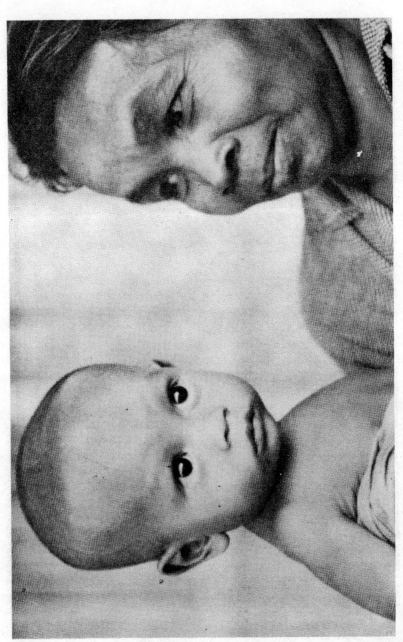

Faces of Cambodian mother and child reflect pride, dignity, and hope for a brighter future. (*Photograph by Barry Levy.*)

PART 3

PUBLIC HEALTH, NUTRITION, AND EDUCATION

THE PERSPECTIVE OF
AN AMERICAN PUBLIC-HEALTH NURSE

Charlotte J. Knaub

Public-health conditions in any of the refugee camps in Thailand can only be described as depressing. During my 13-month tour of duty in Thailand, I visited 12 of the Cambodian and Laotian camps, spent from days to months in each, and surveyed the general health status of the refugees in relationship to environmental conditions, availability of food, and quality of health-care services. Regardless of the age, the size of the population, or the location of the camp, the common denominator was the inadequacy of preventive health programs.

The health services in the older established camps were centered entirely on treatment. The medical staffs, supplied by a variety of international agencies, had neither the background nor the interest to initiate health-promotion activities outside their own particular clinical areas. The hospital wards and outpatient clinics claimed virtually all the staff's time, and few attempts were made to teach patients how to avoid the recurrence of the common, prevalent conditions that accounted for most hospital admissions.

Charlotte J. Knaub served as a Public-Health Nurse and Epidemiologist in the Cambodian relief operation from November 1979 to December 1981 with the International Rescue Committee, UNHCR, the International Committee of the Red Cross, and World Concern. She is now Team Leader, Primary Health Care Project, assigned to the National Headquarters of Health, with the World Health Organization, Western Pacific Region, Port Moresby, Papua New Guinea.

As I visited and worked in the various camps, I inwardly writhed at the environmental hazards I encountered. I could only make recommendations to the authorities to improve the cramped huts, drain stagnant pools, spray the hordes of flies, and increase the water supply. Few seemed to care that these conditions contributed to the general ill health of the refugees.

Every experienced "gum-shoe" public-health worker knows the formula to approach health problems: Assess, Analyze, Organize, Evaluate. Public health in refugee camps follows the same format, as I had to keep reminding myself, passing through military checkpoints to reach the maze of bamboo-scrabble huts, long thatched wards, and black-market stalls that were the basic design for most refugee camps in Thailand. Objectively *Assess* the pungent smells of excrement, sweat, illness; assess the stillness and silence of lethargic children. *Analyze* the decision to contain thousands of the starving and dispossessed sick while denying them the basic right to enough clean water to sustain life. *Organize* pitifully inadequate resources in an attempt to prevent further catastrophes. *Evaluate* —later, when my senses were anesthetized and I could function with professional detachment.

I began work àt Khao I Dang in early 1980. As its population increased, so did the public-health problems. In response, the volags collaborated with each other, with the United Nations, and with the refugee doctors to organize a public-health department. Several of the Cambodian doctors had been public-health officers in Phnom Penh, and after much encouragement, they assumed leadership responsibilities for public-health activities in the camp. Divisions for nutrition, sanitation, water, mosquito spraying, safety, health education, immunizations, and statistics were formed. Refugees were put in charge of the various departments with relief workers acting as advisers. Weekly meetings were held, and the public-health department quickly became the place for providing information on immunization programs, family-planning clinics, and spraying schedules. Section leaders could bring their concerns and problems to the department about shortages of water and food rations or about the need for an outpatient clinic.

I was working closely with Dr. Donald Allegra [see the chapter "The Role of Epidemiology in Disease Prevention" by Donald T. Allegra and Phillip Nieburg] in ICRC's epidemiology unit. Although a reporting system for disease surveillance, deaths, and births was organized in the hospitals and outpatient clinics, it seemed an impossible task to devise a system to collect statistics from outside the clinical area. Refugee aides with an interest in statistics were identified and trained to use simple reporting forms for a census of births and deaths. Six aides were responsible for teaching each of 20 section leaders to collect the required information weekly. These data, which were reviewed, tabulated, and recorded in a central registry, were available to all agencies and became invaluable in planning, performing surveys, and operating special clinics. Sometimes information about the purpose for which the data would be used would induce a section leader to inflate his census count, usually in the hope of receiving more food rations. An instant recount would be requested, but the figures might still be considered inaccurate.

IRC was the first volag to recognize the urgent need for a public-health team in the camp, and after the withdrawal of the ICRC-supported epidemiologists, I assumed the full responsibility for surveillance. But as in almost every bureaucratic system, IRC moved slowly in supplying their public-health team, so I was a one-member team for several months. Meanwhile, more refugees were being trained to perform essential tasks.

Children were the focus of our attention. Children under five years of age constituted over 20 percent of the population of Khao I Dang. Assessing their health status and their nutritional and immunological needs, I was often overwhelmed by their sheer numbers. I admired their tremendous tenacity to cling to life, persisting in surviving with all the odds against them. They needed all the assistance we could offer in their struggle to survive; vaccinating as many as possible against preventable diseases became our major goal. There had apparently been no immunological vaccines in Kampuchea for five years. We considered children under the age of six at highest risk and vaccinated them first.

"Jet guns," designed to use multiple-dose vials, can administer vaccine rapidly to thousands of children. Two teams of 25 refugee volunteers each, few of whom had any medical training, were trained to use the guns supplied by the CDC. The mass clinics were held at the established feeding centers and operated by different volags. Refugee aides were assigned other tasks, such as registering children, making out health cards, swabbing arms, and maintaining order.

Sustaining the "cold chain" essential to assure potency of the live-virus vaccines was a daily challenge. Packed in dry ice and transported from Bangkok, the vaccines were stored in the ICRC pharmacy refrigerators. Due to frequent power failures, the pharmacy had its own emergency generators, but there was still a constant risk to the tens of thousands of stored doses. The camp, 30 kilometers away, did not have storage facilities, so the vaccine was carried in ice-packed coolers, and extra ice was brought to maintain the cold throughout the day. Once clinics were scheduled, they continued for 21 days without interruption. This required a person to organize daily the collection of vaccine, guns, ice, coolers, and supplies at the pharmacy; obtain transport; and arrive at the camp early enough to organize the immunization teams. As anticipated, the obstacles that could arise were numerous. Although my agency—IRC—had assumed overall responsibility for public-health activities, I was expected to organize my own support system, including transportation, to carry them out. Many a time I was left standing by the side of the road with six coolers, six cartons, and 23 jet guns—with no transport. Several times I thumbed a ride on a volag bus. When IRC finally placed the other members of the long-promised, long-awaited public-health team in Khao I Dang, we were assigned our own van shared by all six members.

Perhaps because of the many obstacles, conducting the clinics became a personal challenge to me. Although thousands of children were vaccinated, it seemed as if we would never get ahead of the epidemics. The initial epidemic was measles, and a special ward of 200 beds was opened for those cases with complications. The mortality rate remained high, and it took over six weeks of administering vaccine before it declined.

DPT (diphtheria-pertussis-tetanus) immunization clinics were scheduled next; but polio cases were being reported from the border camps, so polio vaccine was given, after which the DPT clinics started. We hoped to complete the required doses, but with the vast numbers and constant mobility of people within the camp, record keeping was unreliable. Both typhoid and cholera epidemics threatened, and in between, there was an increasing number of reported cases and deaths due to meningococcal disease. Meningococcal vaccine was then made available by the United States and 20,000 young adults were immunized.

It took months, but as the general health status of the children improved—bolstered by the efforts of the immunization teams—a first week, then a second, and a third passed without reports of new outbreaks of preventable diseases. The need for mass clinics—the urgency, the headaches dealing with obstacles and breakdowns, the early awakenings and long days, the worries about the continual quality and quantity of vaccines—were over, as were the unnecessary deaths.

An important component of our epidemiologic surveillance was the collecting and recording of information on all the refugees who died, either in the hospital or out in the camp. With the departure of the CDC epidemiologists, I assumed this responsiblity.

This duty was not among my favorite tasks, and although I continued to train refugee aides, more expertise was required to obtain the required information for mortality investigations. Sometimes the causes of death were clear-cut, but often many different disabilities had afflicted a patient, and it was difficult to determine which was the major cause of death. Deaths due to trauma were common. On the border, the fighting continued, and patients severely wounded by shrapnel or gunshot were brought into Khao I Dang. Within the camp, there were stabbings and physical assault and occasionally a gunshot wound; information about these victims was almost impossible to obtain. And always there were more deaths of women in childbirth, adding yet another orphan to the already overcrowded children's centers. (Because there were few people beyond the age of 45, no one was ever reported to have died of "old age.")

All too often my investigative work was made more difficult by the lack of transport. The camp covered a wide area, and a foray into the inner sections became a major trek. With the aid of a translator, I would spend many hours tracking down and interviewing a dead person's relatives; but all too often, as in the case of a trauma death, the fearful refugees preferred not to admit any relationship with or knowledge of the deceased.

Cremation would have been the preferred method of final interment by the majority of the refugees, who were chiefly Buddhist. Permission to construct a crematorium had been denied by the camp authorities, however, and the designated area for burial was in shallow ground. Due to the shortage of wood, coffins were also unavailable, so the dead were simply placed in superficial depressions in rocky soil. Unfortunately, when the monsoon rains raised the water level, the bodies were also raised, creating yet another environmental hazard.

* * * * *

I often wanted to reach out and talk to the refugees, about the terrible feeling of not belonging—of having nowhere to go, of the impermanency of their lives—and yet it seemed so futile for me to experience such intimate contact with them, sharing these desperate times in their lives, when I would never see them again. They themselves did not share this hesitancy. With few options open to them, they talked with compulsive urgency about the horrors they had witnessed, experienced, and survived. Without passing judgment, many wonderingly questioned why it took so long for the outside world to react to the disaster that was wracking their country. They were unable to comprehend that the outside world was not aware of their misery— or was it that originally no one had really cared?

I had no explanations; I could only offer encouragement that when their dying cries were at last heard, we had come to do what we could to relieve their plight.

THE ROLE OF EPIDEMIOLOGY
IN DISEASE PREVENTION

Donald T. Allegra and Phillip Nieburg

Most refugee operations are characterized by an acute shortage of money and manpower. The limited objectives pursued are often based more on the "perceived" needs of the refugees or on projects with a great deal of emotional appeal, such as feeding undernourished children, than on the "actual" needs of refugees based on objective data. It is difficult not to accomplish some good in a situation where the needs are great; but the real challenge is to accomplish the most good with the limited resources available.

The massive influx of Khmer refugees into Thailand in 1979 and 1980 presented a unique opportunity to approach refugee health assistance in an organized way. The plight of the Khmers caused an enormous outpouring of financial assistance and health personnel from a concerned international community,

Donald T. Allegra and Phillip Nieburg are physicians who, in 1979 and 1980, were medical epidemiologists in the Bureau of Epidemiology, Centers for Disease Control, United States Public Health Service. They served in the Cambodian relief operation on loan from the Centers for Disease Control to the International Committee of the Red Cross. Dr. Allegra served from November 1979 to February 1980, and Dr. Nieburg served from November 1979 to March 1980 and made a subsequent trip to Thailand in January and February 1983. Dr. Allegra is now in private medical practice, specializing in infectious diseases, in San Antonio, Texas. Dr. Nieburg is a medical epidemiologist with the Division of Nutrition, Center for Health Promotion and Education, Centers for Disease Control, Atlanta, Georgia.

and the hospitality of Thailand enabled the assistance operation to pursue goals rarely achievable in most operations. We and other epidemiologists worked under the auspices of the ICRC.

We were among the first epidemiologists who arrived in Thailand early in the relief operation. We worked for the United States Centers for Disease Control (CDC), but each of us had had differing prior experiences in epidemiology. Some of us had worked primarily as epidemiologists assigned to state health departments; others at the CDC headquarters in Atlanta. Each of us was assigned a refugee camp, and one of us was appointed overall coordinator. We had no predetermined guidelines as to our roles. We were instructred to do what epidemiologists usually do—that is, to collect, analyze, disseminate, and use information in decision making and rational planning to solve public-health problems. We had been working as epidemiologists in already-functioning systems, such as systems of surveillance and information dissemination, in which our specific roles were fairly well defined. Our roles in the relief operation were less defined and often involved creating new approaches to problems.

How do a few epidemiologists have any impact at all in a crisis situation where no surveillance system is in place and where many of the "tools of their trade," such as serologic tests [to measure blood antibody levels for diagnostic purposes] are unavailable? Since we had no specific guidelines from previous refugee experience—either our own nor anything that had been published—we set out initially to establish a crude surveillance system, and then to expand the system gradually and to apply other simple tools of epidemiology to the prevalent health problems. We encountered six types of problems almost immediately:

Acceptance. While other health workers were working very diligently performing "hands on" tasks, we were initially viewed as bureaucrats creating needless paperwork. We were called "statisticians," and most health workers thought it was a tremendous waste of time for physicians to be simply statisticians keeping track of such things as the number of refugees and the number and causes of deaths. It was nearly impossible to get other health workers to assist us for any extended period of time. They might assist for a few days, but as soon as they could relocate with a ward or clinic participating in active curative patient care, they would leave. It was only gradually that other health workers realized our role and utility, and accepted us as an integral part of the health system.

Cooperation. As expected, most health workers were anxious to discard record-keeping functions, often seen as a burdensome part of their jobs in industrialized countries. In an emergency situation, however, the ability to make decisions based on objective data, rather than on hearsay or anecdotes, is essential, but it was only after showing the utility of our data that we were able to encourage cooperation with simple record-keeping. Getting accurate information daily on such parameters as hospital census and numbers of deaths and births was often a difficult task. To encourage record-keeping, we often bought rulers and notebooks for hospital staff, and even labeled the pages of the notebooks, to try to get someone to fill in the appropriate information. Although none of us spoke the Khmer language, we did speak a little French—the second language of the Khmer —which was sometimes helpful in soliciting aid from refugee helpers.

Shortage of resource materials and expert advice. Although we were all well-trained physician epidemiologists, we certainly did not consider ourselves experts in all aspects of nutrition, sanitation, and tropical medicine. We also did not have immediate access to a medical library or to a cadre of public-health and academic professionals. We did consult with university physicians in Bangkok when possible and intermittently made calls to the United States. But basically we drew on our own experiences and those of our fellow workers and tried to use a heavy dose of common sense in dealing with the myriad of health problems that presented themselves each week.

Lack of adequate laboratory resources. Epidemiologists often rely heavily on laboratory analysis, such as serologic testing and stool cultures, to help their investigations. Although a field laboratory was available, it performed only simple tests, such as hematocrits and blood smears for malaria, it was unequipped to perform bacterial cultures or any sophisticated tests. Furthermore, the lab from the beginning was overwhelmed with work and could not be expected to participate in large-scale epidemiologic surveys. Confirmation of outbreaks of polio or cholera, for example, was therefore difficult, since specimens had to be hand-carried for several hours to Bangkok and arrangements to perform special tests had to be made. Transport media, freezers, and other supplies and equipment are not routinely available to be used in transporting specimens to referral laboratories.

Language barriers. One of the major epidemiologic tools is the survey questionnaire. Extensive questionnaires, however, could not be used because of the shortage of personnel to administer them, time constraints, and most importantly, the problem of communicating with the refugees. Although there were some English interpreters in the camps, they were in short supply and could not all be justifiably appropriated for use by the epidemiologists. Questionnaires had to be kept simple. Although the official language in the camp was English, many health workers from Europe and Asia spoke and wrote English only as a second or third language. Therefore in soliciting their help for surveys or in disseminating the results of epidemiologic surveillance, the wording had to be kept straightforward and in very simple English.

Logistics problems. Once all these problems had been taken into account and a plan formulated, the next step obviously was to implement the plan. Logistical problems then became the next barriers to overcome. For example, once it was recognized that measles was occurring in one of the camps and that a mass-vaccination program was needed, the vaccine had to be shipped from Europe and transported to the camp, vaccine jet guns had to be borrowed, refugee workers had to be recruited, an advertising campaign had to be launched to encourage compliance, and finally an adequate "cold chain" had to be established to maintain vaccine efficacy in an area where refrigeration was not routinely available.

* * * * * * * * *

Establishing the surveillance system. We began by setting up a simple surveillance system and then gradually expanded our role to include simple surveys, rapid initial health screening, investigation of disease outbreaks, health program planning, consultations on infectious diseases, and other more complex activities.

The initial surveillance system consisted of simply counting the numbers of deaths occurring in the hospital. When these numbers were matched with the total burial data collected by Thai health authorities, it quickly became apparent that more than half of the refugee deaths were occurring outside the hospital. Expansion of the case-finding program to seek out sick refugees in their tents and bring them to the hospital resulted in many more referrals and an associated rapid decrease in out-of-hospital and total deaths.

The epidemiologists who arrived at Sa Kaeo set as their first priority a register of hospital deaths by age, sex, and diagnosis, so that accurate information on these factors could be available daily. Each day an epidemiologist or public-health nurse collected information from the ward clerks on the patients who had died in each hospital ward. After a few days, the system was expanded to include the total number of and reasons for hospital admissions. Still later, other facilities in the camps, such as OPDs and supplementary-feeding centers, were used to collect further information, such as nutritional surveillance data, to evaluate the effectiveness of these programs.

Similar surveillance systems were set up in each of the other Khmer camps in Thailand as they opened. The data collected in the surveillance systems allowed relief coordinators to demonstrate to themselves and to others the effectiveness of the assistance effort in decreasing illness and death rates among the refugees.

Age, sex, and diagnostic data allowed resources to be focused on specific problem areas. For example, hospital admission data at Sa Kaeo indicated that, by late 1979, malaria remained the major reason for hospital admission. Resources were accordingly shifted to various programs for reducing the prevalence of malaria in the camp with subsequent success.

Epidemiologic surveys were an important part of our work. For example, once the surveillance system was set up at Sa Kaeo, a community survey was undertaken in order to identify other current problems. A small team of health workers and interpreters used a map to randomly select several sites in the camp and examined those refugees in tents immediately adjacent to these sites. Information collected on each person examined included age and sex (for camp census data), height and weight of young children (to determine rates of malnutrition), and blood smears for malaria. The very small proportion of young children (only 9 percent were under five years of age compared to the expected 15 to 20 percent) and older adults (only 7 percent were more than 45) suggested that the death rates in these age groups had been very high in the recent past. The 16 percent malnutrition rate found in the survey was only the tip of the iceberg. Hundreds of severely undernourished children had already been hospitalized in the camp's pediatrics and intensive-feeding wards, and this survey actually represented the proportion of undernourished children among those who were not sick enough to require hospitalization. Finally, about 40 percent of those on whom we performed blood smears had evidence of current *P. falciparum* malaria infection. Thus, a "quick-and-dirty" survey using few resources provided important information on (1) the composition of the populations, suggesting that, for example, the relatively small number of children meant that fewer resources than anticipated would be needed for mass-immunization campaigns; (2) nutritional status, indicating a great need for supplementary-feeding programs; and (3) malaria prevalence, providing a partial explanation of the large numbers of malaria-related hospital admissions and deaths.

Health screening of new arrivals. Rapid health screening was also an important part of our work. For example, at Khao I Dang, where relief workers had the benefit of having had both several weeks of prior experience at Sa Kaeo and several days of planning time before the refugees arrived, a system was devised to assess rapidly the health status of all arriving refugees. The purpose of this health-screening process was (1) to identify, by history and brief examination, those refugees in need of hospitalization or other immediate care; (2) to identify other specific but less urgent health needs, such as undernutrition; (3) to determine the extent of possible long-term health needs, such as the number of children eventually needing immunization and of pregnant women eventually requiring obstetric services; and (4) to distribute systematically some simple health services, such as by referrals to prenatal clinics or to measles immunization programs. This screening system, staffed by health workers from various voluntary agencies and Red Cross teams, collected the same type of information that had been collected by surveys at Sa Kaeo and other camps, but it did so more efficiently and completely. Immediate hospital referral of ill refugees may have been partly responsible for the lower death rate at Khao I Dang, as compared to other camps.

In addition, the people being screened were surveyed for measurements of immediate interest. For example, because of the seriousness of the malaria problem among refugees at Sa Kaeo, a problem of similar magnitude was anticipated among those entering the newer camp at Khao I Dang. Initially each arriving refugee was given a dose of an antimalarial drug. In addition, 200 refugees arriving in the first two days had blood smears taken for malaria testing. Within a few days, the blood smear results were available and indicated a surprisingly low prevalence of *P. falciparum* infection. The program of malaria drug distribution—costly in terms of money and staff—was therefore discontinued, and resources were diverted to more important needs.

The screening system was staffed by teams of nurses and interpreters. Some teams included a physician. Depending on the number of refugees arriving on a particular day, between two to eight teams would be screening refugees simultaneously. This screening system processed 120,000 refugees who entered Khao I Dang. Daily arrivals ranged from less than 100 to 7,700; they averaged 2,000 to 4,000 per day during the first few weeks of the camp. The system provided much information that was essential for rational planning of camp health activities.

Outbreak investigations. Investigation of disease outbreaks is one of the traditional roles of epidemiologists in industrialized countries. Refugee camp environments are ideal for the spread of disease for many reasons. Refugees are generally undernourished, lack knowledge about sanitary practices, and often have not had prior access to preventive care such as immunizations. The camps themselves are crowded and have poor sanitation facilities.

Rumored and actual disease outbreaks investigated by epidemiologists in the first few months of the Khmer assistance effort included measles, polio, bloody diarrhea, suspected beriberi, cholera, vomiting due to water contamination, and meningococcal disease. The following is a description of an outbreak of gastroenteritis which was investigated using simple tools of epidemiology.

More than 60 people came one night to the admissions ward with severe nausea, vomiting, dizziness, and lethargy. With these symptoms occurring less than 30 minutes after drinking water, chemical intoxication was suspected. Leftover water from patients' homes was analyzed with a crude swimming-pool chlorine counter. Chlorine levels were found to be more than five times the acceptable level for drinking water. Water truck deliveries and chlorination schedules were reviewed, and it was discovered that some trucks were being chlorinated at the water source two hours away from the camp and again on their entry to the camp. All the cases had occurred in sections of the camp supplied by water trucks which had been chlorinated twice. When the second chlorination at the camp entrance was stopped, the outbreak came to an abrupt halt. Some cases, however, were apparently not associated with water consumption, and several cases of nausea and vomiting continued to occur each day. Further investigation revealed that all these individuals had eaten a small palm plant that some of the Khmers had gathered from a nearby mountainside to supplement the meager vegetable rations. Once this plant had been implicated, loudspeaker trucks went through the camp warning the refugees about the danger. Only one additional case occurred after these warnings. A botanist later confirmed that the plant was poisonous.

The information leading to the resolution of both these outbreaks was obtained through simple questionnaires, interviews with sick patients, and crude laboratory tests, involving such tools as swimming-pool chlorine chambers.

Preventive medicine programs. Epidemiologists were involved in all stages of preventive-medicine programs in the camps—planning, implementation, and evaluation. In some cases this occurred because one or more of us had some knowledge of the disease in question. In other cases, our involvement was for planning of the ongoing data collection and evaluation of programs. These programs included nutritional supplementation, tuberculosis control, childhood immunizations, malaria control, and sanitation.

Infectious disease and public health consultation. The epidemiologist's role often included consultations requested by other health workers. Some of these consultations were related to infectious-disease problems of individual patients. In these cases, our contribution was knowledge of the diseases endemic to the area or endemic to the Khmer population, and knowledge of what diseases were being found in other camps or in other wards or clinics in the same camp. In other situations, we were able to offer advice on survey planning, such as to the staff of the supplementary-feeding center who were planning a nutritional survey. Our consultation role was encouraged formally by our participation in committees and attendance at regular camp meetings and informally by our making ourselves as available and accessible as possible.

Dissemination of epidemiologic information. Especially in situations of limited resources, the collection and analysis of health data only make sense if the information is given as soon as possible to those who "need to know." Returning home to analyze the data and write an erudite paper based on it would defeat the whole purpose of having epidemiologists on the scene early in refugee-crisis situations. Rapid surveillance, analysis, and dissemination of results, even if preliminary, are essential. We did our best to disseminate information as quickly and as widely as possible. We gave weekly briefings at meetings of health workers and published a biweekly epidemiology newsletter. Surveillance and screening data were displayed on blackboards and updated daily.

Monitoring the health workers. Many health workers who participated in the relief operation had had little prior experience in developing countries, and in some cases, had had inappropriate personal-health preparation for this assignment. Some, for example, had been vaccinated against smallpox—a nonexistent disease by this time—but were unprotected against polio, a common problem in Southeast Asia. When a polio outbreak occurred among the refugees in Khao I Dang, much time and effort were expended in identifying and providing unimmunized health workers with polio vaccine. Others had taken cholera vaccine, which was of limited potential benefit, and erroneously believed that malaria prophylaxis was unnecessary in the dry season. Still others were uncertain about how "careful" to be about food and water. Most workers took appropriate measures to protect their own health once they were supplied with accurate information.

The epidemiologists participated in organizing the dissemination of accurate information and helped to arrange treatment for those health workers who became ill. In addition, a rudimentary surveillance system was set up to detect unusual kinds or incidences of illness among health workers. This surveillance system also proved to be useful as a biologic monitoring system. For example, data about malaria risk during the dry season was conflicting. Some people used this as an argument against taking malaria chemoprophylaxis. The finding of a few health workers who had become infected with malaria clarified this issue quite clearly and reinforced the importance of continuous chemoprophylaxis.

Setting health priorities and evaluating the relief operation. In refugee operations, it is extremely important to set priorities and to evaluate ongoing health programs continually so that available health resources are used in the most efficient way possible. Although we did not do an entire program evaluation in Thailand, we did attempt to analyze disease trends, to make long-term recommendations, and to evaluate a few specific health programs. At Sa Kaeo, for example, information from the surveillance system indicated continuing high numbers of outpatient visits, hospital admissions, and deaths due to malaria, and this helped convince the camp health authorities that mass antimalarial treatment was needed to reduce illness and death. Similarly, information from camp surveys was combined to indicate that very high proportions of young children and of lactating women were receiving supplementary feeding but that the coverage among pregnant women was much lower. These types of information were of immediate use to the camp health administrators. In addition, we also evaluated the utilization of lab services, the appropriateness of various food donations, the use of drugs, and other parameters of care. We gave to camp administrators and relief-organization staff members the results of these surveys and our recommendations based on these results in an attempt to improve the efficiency of the ongoing relief effort and potentially to influence planning for future activities.

An ongoing need for health-data collection and analysis will exist as long as the refugee population exists. Only a limited training of Khmer health workers was possible during the first few months—the "emergency phase" of the operation. Supporting the autonomy of the refugees was, however, a major goal of the assistance operation and efforts to integrate them into epidemiology—and all other areas of public health—began in earnest as soon as the emergency phase of the operation was completed.

FOOD AND NUTRITION PROGRAMS

Elisabeth Eie

As nutrition coordinator at Khao I Dang, I supervised all the activities and personnel involved in food and nutrition; planned and taught in nutrition and primary health-education programs for Khmer staff and mothers; visited feeding centers, hospital kitchens, and warehouses; consulted and advised on dry-ration composition, foodstuff availability, and the use and nutritional values of these products; planned and supervised necessary nutrition surveys; developed a policy for vitamin and iron distribution; and kept up with developments in Bangkok and on the border.

We faced two overall problems in our work. First, the general view—even among medical personnel—is that illness is cured by medical treatment, even when patients are suffering from malnutrition. In the Khmer refugee camps, malnourished children died despite medical treatment from what under other circumstances would not have been a fatal disease: measles, pneumonia, diarrhea. Second, most medical personnel lack a basic knowledge of nutrition, yet they often become responsible for the hospital feeding and even other feeding programs. They

Elisabeth Eie, a Norwegian nutritionist, was Nutrition Coordinator of Khao I Dang for the International Committee of the Red Cross from January to April 1980. She is currently Senior Officer, Norwegian Ministry of Development Cooperation, Oslo, Norway.

do not know the human body's physical need for nutritients, nor the nutritional composition of most foodstuffs, and they have little idea of how to prepare the food to keep its nutritional value.

Most camp residents existed on the dry ration, which, if received in full quantity, provided sufficient protein and energy. The original daily per capita dry-food ration at Khao I Dang was 500 gm rice, 30 gm cooking oil, 50 gm mung beans, 5 gm fish sauce, 15 gm fresh frozen meat, and 70 gm vegetables. Although even this amount of ration did not meet the daily requirements of energy and nutrients, both the rice and the oil rations were reduced for no apparent reason.

Food was available from UNICEF/WFP (the dry ration), the voluntary agencies, and at the supplemental-feeding centers (primarily for malnourished children and pregnant and lactating women). In addition, there were markets in Khao I Dang and some of the other camps; but these usually closed after short periods, and even when they were open, few refugees could afford to buy food at their inflated prices.

Several suggestions to improve the composition of the dry ration were made. The energy content could easily have been improved by increasing the oil ration—thus preventing valuable protein from being wasted on energy, by purchasing whole rice at the village level, and by increasing the bean ration to meet the daily requirement of vitamins B_1 and C. Unfortunately none of these suggestions was acted upon. The quality of the vegetables varied greatly and was often bad. The supplies also arrived very irregularly, complicating distribution. In March 1980, the amount of food received in each section varied between 60 and 90 percent of their allotment. Receipt of food at the family level also varied greatly. Distribution of dark-green leafy vegetables, which were locally available and part of the traditional Thai or Khmer diet, was recommended to compensate for the uneven nature of the other vegetables.

Donated foods, shipped in by voluntary agencies, supplemented the dry-food ration. Up until early February 1980, these foods consisted of—controversial—milk products, cereal products, and canned baby foods. There was much complexity in some of the donated food items. For example, nearly a dozen varieties of dried-milk products were available. Packages varied from bags of 25 kilograms to half-kilogram cans; quantities varied from half a ton to 70 tons. There were also three types of canned liquid-milk products. The huge variety of products created logistical and usage problems. For example, usage and turnover of powdered milk was very low, partially due to a decision not to distribute it in bulk through the general food-distribution program.

The only milk product familiar to the Khmers was sweetened and condensed milk (SCM). Formerly available also in the local markets, it was mainly used as a sweetening agent—it contains 46 percent sugar. The practice that already existed among the women of giving infants diluted SCM was strongly discouraged. In our program, the only relevant use of SCM was as a sweetening agent in certain dishes served in the hospitals and feeding centers.

Other forms of milk were of little use. Evaporated milk was disliked by the Khmers, unless sugar was added. Although it is of limited use in feeding operations, the stocks available were vast. "Ready-to-drink" milk in small cans was an example of how water is transported in an expensive package, making the cost per nutritient extremely high. Infant formulas were required only for those—rare—orphans or infants whose mothers could not breast-feed them. A restrictive policy on their use was enforced in order not to discourage breast-feeding or create a later dependence on this kind of product.

The huge donations of Western-type baby food packed in glass jars or bottles caused a number of problems. The various fruits and vegetables contained basically only carbohydrates, having lost most of the original vitamins during processing. The taste of the fruit was artificial in comparison with that of available fresh fruit. The logic of sending from Europe at great expense mashed banana packed in glass jars to a banana-producing country is difficult to understand! The baby food itself was made according with Western habits and tastes, and did not fit into the customary Khmer diet. The only possible use for some of it was to mix it into the salty soup served at the feeding centers. The small jars were also very impractical. Mass distribution of such products to a refugee population is not advisable because the cost of transporting and storing food of so little utility cannot be justified.

Although the warehouses were filled with many kinds of donated food, a need for certain foodstuffs that would be adequate to this operation was recognized. A list of suitable and desirable food was prepared so that the donors were advised to donate food acceptable and familiar to the residents, nutritionally valuable and hygienically safe, and unlikely to cause logistical problems.

Supplementary foods were provided as an extra ration to those who were malnourished or particularly vulnerable to malnutrition: children under the age of five, pregnant and lactating women, the elderly, the socially disadvantaged (such as unaccompanied children), and people with TB, severe anemia, and certain other illnesses. Initially, the pattern for supplementary feeding varied greatly in method and effectiveness among the holding centers and the border camps.

At Khao I Dang, the voluntary agencies were assigned responsibility for running one or more supplemental-feeding centers, serving highly nutritious meals—usually a rice-based porridge or thick soup—twice a day. Khmer workers organized the centers under the supervision of voluntary-agency personnel. A home-visiting program sought out any registered beneficiaries who failed to attend for two consecutive days. By February 1980, Khao I Dang with 130,000 refugees had nine supplementary-feeding centers. They were attended by 85 percent of the children under five and lactating mothers, and by 55 percent of the pregnant women.

Early surveys gave us useful information about the numbers of potential beneficiaries for supplementary feeding and greatly facilitated program planning. Nutrition surveys were conducted from November 1979 to May 1980 in Sa Kaeo, Khao I Dang, and the border camps. At Sa Kaeo, 10 to 18 percent of the children were "wasted" (that is, below 80 percent of the standard weight for their height) and some 2 percent were "seriously malnourished" (below 70 percent of the standard weight for their height) and in need of intensive feeding. The majority of those in need found their way to the hospital, although others had to be tracked down in the camp. Surveys taken two months later indicated improvements in nutritional status, but unexpectedly, there were no substantial improvements after that time. At Khao I Dang, in March 1980, 6 percent of the children under five were found to be "wasted," and 41 percent were "stunted" (less than 90 percent of the height-for-age standard, which indicates adaptation to a low intake of nutrients over a long period). This indicated that the success of the feeding programs was relative. Only 1 percent of the schoolchildren, aged six to 12, were "wasted," and 72 percent of them were equal to or above 90 percent of the weight-for-height standard; however, 19 percent were anemic (hematocrit, or blood count, less than 30) and alarmingly 39 percent showed some signs of vitamin-A deficiency. In the border camps of Mak Mun and Nong Samet in early 1980, 9 percent of the children under five were found to be "wasted," and, a cause of much concern, about two-thirds of them did not attend any supplementary-feeding centers.

The nutritional survey of the schoolchildren in Khao I Dang verified a growing suspicion that they were being neglected, that they only rarely attended any supplementary-feeding program. A school feeding program was therefore organized, consisting of a daily nutritious meal.

In order to avoid overdosage and wastage, detailed guidelines were developed so that the distribution of supplementary iron and vitamins would only take place in the feeding centers, maternal and child health clinics, hospital wards, and in the OPDs only when the need was increased by the presence of certain specific diseases or the use of certain medicines. The therapeutic use of vitamins or iron only took place in the hospitals. We met, however, with many problems in our efforts to develop a safe, preventive distribution program of iron and vitamins for those outside existing feeding programs, some of whom were at high risk of developing vitamin-A deficiency. An accidental intake of a double preventive dose of 200,000 IU of vitamin A can be toxic. Besides, we were unable to obtain adequate amounts of the right vitamin-A preparation and were thus unable to carry out, for example, a safe, preventive vitamin-A distribution program on the border. Meanwhile, multivitamins, which were included in the dry ration, continued to be distributed in a basically uncontrolled way in the border camps. The only function of this hazardous distribution policy was the emptying of the overfilled warehouses of 40 metric tons of donated expired multivitamins.

In mid-1980 at Khao I Dang, a general educational program of basic nutrition and feeding, health, and sanitation was developed for Khmer residents working in the camp kitchens and feeding centers to provide them with information about the planning of feeding programs (recipes, cooking methods, and nutritional needs). Its goal was to minimize the refugees' dependency on foreign assistance.

Medical personnel in relief actions very often become responsible for food distribution and feeding programs without being appropriately prepared. This problem can be minimized by providing medical personnel with education in food and nutrition and by providing sufficient professional nutrition and dietary assistance. The international relief organizations should arrange briefing programs and develop and distribute educational materials, including a detailed handbook on food and nutrition operations.

I also suggest that international relief organizations develop and disseminate guidelines on necessary foodstuffs, the handling of milk products, bottle feeding, commercial breast-milk substitutes, the minimal educational level required to occupy various staff positions, and the mass distribution of medicines, multivitamins, iron preparations, and deworming cures.

Unquestionably, the distribution of emergency food is a humanitarian action. Nevertheless, controversy often occurs regarding the choices and appropriate uses of foods, in part because there sometimes is competition between using such food to improve the nutritional status of the recipients and using it to meet the interests of the donor societies. Food-aid programs should also be based not on the availability of surplus foods but on the particular needs of the recipients, on demand and not supply. Food-aid planning should be regarded as important as medical care. This is especially true in emergency situations, where uncomplicated and well-known basic foods and feeding services must rapidly become available. Food aid in emergencies should conform to the following principles: The number of food products, of varieties and packages, should be kept small to minimize logistical problems. Foods of a low nutritional value, such as those containing high proportions of water or carbohydrates, should not be used. Foods that may be used or handled inappropriately, thus causing harmful effects, should be avoided—this applies especially to those products that require dilution with water, which may be contaminated. Instructions on food packages should be in appropriate languages. Food packages should be able to withstand transportation and storage. Food products whose safe consumption dates have passed should not be used. Familiar foods are preferable to foreign ones. Also, dependency on imported food which may become available after the relief effort has ended (sometimes at very high prices) should not be created. Commercial food industries should not be permitted to use the relief situation as an opportunity to create a new market.

SUPPLEMENTARY FEEDING:
A REFUGEE'S PERSPECTIVE

Sichantha Neou ("Kassie")

CARE's supplementary feeding program at Khao I Dang was a remarkable success because of the compatible combination of CARE and the voluntary Khmer staff. Much of its success was due to the "50-50" management policy in which CARE allowed the Khmer staff to have half of the management responsibility.

It was a blessing that we shared a common purpose: devoting our time to serve our people. We recruited workers for required positions from center supervisors to kitchen staff. We had frequent meetings to convince the staff to share our beliefs and purposes. We believed we were not working *for* CARE but *with* them. Most staff members participated in making our rules and regulations. To maintain the quality of our work, discipline in behavior, working manner, and interpersonal contact applied to everyone. The words *honesty* and *honor* were frequently mentioned. When problems arose among staff members, the nondependables got corrected, and the uncorrectables got fired in a most peaceful way.

Although recipients of the supplementary feeding program were refugees in vulnerable groups, some of the international relief workers, misunderstanding the program or allowing their

---

Sichantha Neou ("Kassie"), a Cambodian, was overall supervisor of the eight CARE supplementary feeding centers at Khao I Dang from December 1979 to July 1980. He is now self-employed in the service station business in Washington, D.C.

compassion for the refugees to hold sway, gave permission for others to get food in this program. This caused many problems.

Food was prepared by the Cambodian cooks we selected. As Cambodians ourselves, we knew what could be accepted or rejected by our own people. The food had to contain a specific amount of nutrients recommended by CARE and UNHCR nutritionists, and it had to be prepared in Cambodian style, so it would be completely consumed.

When operating this program, we received both help and hindrance. Problems arose one after another. Some Western relief workers, including voluntary staff of CARE, turned out to be a hindrance because of their misunderstanding and inadequate knowledge of Khmer customs. The problem of the water supply was also a hindrance. Flies from the neighborhood and latrines severely disturbed our approaching the goal. The UNHCR had spent some money for spreading water on roads to prevent blowing of dust. I felt they should have that money to build better latrines instead; to the Cambodians, dust is not as bad as flies from the latrines. The drainage system also seemed to be a problem for the feeding centers, but compared to what we had during the previous four years and compared to where we had come from, UNHCR had done great things for us.

A common problem in society, even in a Communist country, is stealing possessions, money, or food when one is indefinitely or desperately needy. So security must be among the first things considered. Of course, Cambodians do not like to steal. But how could I assure myself that the food warehouse would remain constantly safe, when it was in the midst of crowds of people who had been hungry and needy for four years and were then with an insufficient supply of dry rations?

INTENSIVE FEEDING

S. N. Chaudhuri

In the early days of Sa Kaeo, many children, especially "unaccompanied minors," suffered from the effects of chronic food deprivation and disease. They had muscle wasting, thin limbs, and dull sad looks on their faces. Skin infections, chronic limb ulcers, chronic diarrhea, and respiratory-tract infections were some of their specific health problems.

A special hospital tent was filled with severely malnourished children who were being intensively fed. Some food items used were milk products, fish and fish derivatives, cereal-milk-based porridges, and biscuits, which were purchased from Bangkok by the international agencies or brought in by individual donors or volunteers. At first, the malnourished children said they disliked milk products, and wheat-based products like biscuits and porridge. They liked rice, fish, meat, fresh fruits such as bananas and watermelons, and leafy green vegetables, and were fond of a porridge made of rice, fish shreds, and leafy vegetables. Most children who came into the ward with wasting, but without severe malnutrition, recovered rapidly on this diet.

Severe malnutrition was often complicated by diarrhea, dehydration, malaria, acute respiratory infection, tuberculosis, worm infestations, and/or anemia. Mortality was very high:

S. N. Chaudhuri, a physician, worked from October 1979 to February 1980 as Nutrition Coordinator at Khao I Dang for Catholic Relief Services. He is Director of the Child In Need Institute in West Bengal, India, a nutrition and health care program for 150,000 people.

in each of the first three weeks at Sa Kaeo, there were about five deaths among the approximately five hundred unaccompanied minors.

In the initial stages, groups of Thai and foreign volunteers from church-based organizations and the diplomatic community came to Sa Kaeo to supplement the efforts of other volunteers from the international agencies. They brought milk formulas, biscuits, clothes, and toys for the children. Entry to the camp was unrestricted, and the sad plight of the refugees, in general, and the unaccompanied children, in particular, received wide publicity in the Bangkok media.

The possibility of repatriating the unaccompanied minors to third countries for adoption was being discussed in the foreign and Thai media as early as November 1979. This attracted many expatriate individuals who were living in Bangkok and representing families or organizations in Europe and the Americas to visit these children and explore possibilities of resettling them. While medical personnel were treating and attending to these unaccompanied minors in the hospital tent, those interested in adoption were screening and selecting the children!

Meanwhile, at Khao I Dang, the severely malnourished children and adults, after initial screening, were referred to our intensive-feeding ward. It had a capacity of 120 patients, was approximately 40-by-80 feet in size, and was built of polythene sheets and bamboo. Folding plywood cots, placed in rows, rested on the gravel floor. Each ward had a toilet area at the back with dugout latrines. Water was stored in tanks outside the ward, being replenished regularly by tankers. Electricity became available within a few weeks, but only for lighting. Standard hospital meals twice a day were provided from the central kitchen, managed by CRS.

Mothers with their malnourished children were made welcome and provided with a bed. A history was taken, regarding the causes of the malnutrition. Occasionally another relative was allowed to stay in the ward with the child if the mother was burdened with the care of other children. Members of the family visited the sick child often during the day, especially during mealtimes. The average duration of stay of the malnourished mothers with their children was about three to four weeks.

The children were nutritionally rehabilitated in Khao I Dang as they were in Sa Kaeo. To ensure an optimum intake of calories and other nutrients vital for quick recovery, we studied Cambodian food habits in depth.

Severely malnourished children under three years of age posed special problems in nutrition rehabilitation. Intravenous feeding through scalp veins as well as through intragastric tubes had continuously to be closely monitored. Mothers cooperated very well when the temporary nature of this intervention was explained to them, and they were persuaded to feed the baby mother's milk to ensure rapid recovery. Family members, with free access to the ward, often took turns nursing the child. Sometimes mothers put their children in hammocks of black material they strung up in the ward. The personnel requirements to run such a ward would obviously be high, even though much nursing care was done by the mothers themselves.

FAMILY PLANNING:
THE PERSPECTIVE OF
A THAI PUBLIC-HEALTH WORKER

Surangkana Pitaksuntipan ("Oy")

In 1979, I was doing field work for my master of public health degree at the University of Hawaii. I was working in Chiang Rai province of Thailand with Khun Meechai Viravaidya, focusing on his specialty of family planning integrated with community development. He is widely recognized and respected in Thailand and throughout the world for his innovative and successful approach to family planning.

At this time, the sudden influx of Khmer refugees into Thailand occurred and redirected our efforts to the Thai-Khmer border and led to the birth of a Thai refugee-relief organization. Khun Meechai, working closely with the Thai Ministry of Public Health, established the Community Based Emergency Relief Service (CBERS) to work in parallel with his successful Community Based Family Planning Services (CBFPS), already present in a third of Thai villages.

Initially we set up our office at Khao I Dang, close to the Thai military and the UNHCR, and acted as liaison between the foreign relief workers and the Thai authorities. CBERS

Surangkana Pitaksuntipan ("Oy") was from November 1979 to August 1982 Health Coordinator for the Community Based Emergency Relief Services (CBERS) and then Nutrition Field Assistant with the World Food Program as part of the United Nations Border Relief Operation. She is now Primary Health Care Project Officer for UNICEF in Accra, Ghana.

was responsible for a wide variety of activities which would improve and maintain the well-being of the Khmer "illegal aliens" while they were guests of the Thai government. Besides family planning, CBERS was responsible for sanitation, parasite control, and skills development (in handicrafts and agriculture).

The most significant opposition from the expatriates came in response to the family-planning programs. We felt that, although the Khmer had lost many children during the difficult years behind them, the time was still not right for them to reproduce: many were still quite ill and malnourished, and attention needed to be given to the children they already had, and to build up the people so that when they returned to Kampuchea they would be strong and healthy. It had been rumored that the Thai government was responsible for a house-to-house campaign in Mai Rut and Kamput holding centers, injecting every three months all the women and girls with DepoProvera, a contraceptive hormone used widely and with good effect in Thailand. Efforts to start a program of family planning at Khao I Dang using DepoProvera injections as the mainstay met with severe opposition and outright sabotage in a few instances. The foreigners said that the drug was banned in their home countries because it might cause cancer in high doses in beagle dogs, not recognizing that *any* form of contraception is preferable to having a baby in a refugee camp with an uncertain future ahead. Eventually, most people and agencies came to agree with Thai policy on this matter.

In my opinion, the problem with the family-planning program was the timing: it was introduced too soon, and the cry of "Genocide!" showed that the foreigners really did not understand it at all. It is true that we should have given more education to the Khmer people—and to the expatriate relief workers. We were careful to offer alternatives to the "shot": the "pill," IUDs, or condoms, if requested. Sterilization and vasectomy were encouraged but never forced on people.

FAMILY PLANNING:
THE PERSPECTIVE OF A
CAMBODIAN PUBLIC-HEALTH NURSE

Pheng Eng By

Any women who wanted to have an injection for preventing pregnancy for three months would receive a chicken. But problems arose within families: husbands did not want their wives to have the injections because they thought that Thai people would not have sympathy toward Khmer people; it was feared that they may have wanted to destroy our race, which was already partly massacred. A lot of criticism was directed at CBERS' contraceptive methods because most of the women did not understand much about what was happening and there was not enough education for that; but CBERS still continued the program.

CBERS was successful because a lot of women in the camp came to have injections, even me. Rumors spread over the camp that a woman had died of a hemorrhage due to the injection. [To our knowledge, such a death was never confirmed—Editors]. Three months later, I decided not to have the second injection because I had a lot of irregular bleeding during the first three months, and my mother was afraid that I might get cancer if I continued to have the injections.

One time, CBERS brought in many condoms. They blew them up and threw them out over the crowded people, especially the children. The people did not know they were

Pheng Eng By is a Cambodian public health nurse and a survivor of the 1979 forced repatriation at Preah Vihear. She escaped to Thailand a second time, after her second daughter was born, and worked in public health at Khao I Dang.

condoms; they thought that they were balloons. They ran under each other, laughing but also crying because they got hurt by trying to catch the balloons. The CBERS staff laughed as they threw more blown-up condoms to them. For the children, it seemed like money from heaven, but I felt angry and sorry because I could not stop the crowd; I could not help the children who cried, who got hurt; and in our culture it is not fair, it is shameful to use such things for a game.

UNACCOMPANIED MINORS:
A UNHCR VIEW

Martin Barber

When the Kampucheans entered the holding centers, about three thousand "unaccompanied minors"—those under the age of 18 who had been separated from their families—were identified. Between the years 1975 and 1979, the Khmer Rouge had taken children as young as nine or ten, from their parents and put them in special youth brigades. When the Khmer Rouge retreated, they took the members of these youth groups with them, some even into Thailand. Other children had watched their parents being taken away, and a few had actually seen their parents die or be killed. Even in these cases, the children might eventually be reunited with other adult relatives. Others had been separated from their parents or relatives in the confusion just before crossing the border into Thailand. Finally there were those families who having seen that special facilities had been established for unaccompanied children in the holding centers, and either fearing that they themselves would be unable to look after their children, or else hoping that being parentless, the children would receive preferential treatment, had asked neighbors to take the children to the children's center as though they had no family. Children in all these categories, especially the younger ones, when asked what had happened to their parents, would often say that they were dead, since this was the easiest explanation of their parents' absence for the children in their own minds to accept.

As soon as the dimensions of the problem became apparent, we were besieged by people wanting to *do* something. An important minority of these people set out to do all they could to remove as many of the younger children as possible for adoption in Western countries. In the initial chaos that surrounded the sudden opening of the holding centers, they were sometimes successful.

From the start, my colleagues and I were implacably opposed to this trade. The argument put forward by the adoption lobby was essentially very simple: these poor children had suffered appallingly during the Khmer Rouge regime; how much better off they would be in nice homes in Europe or America where they would be loved and cared for by enthusiastic foster parents. When this argument failed to sway, these people would then point to the conditions in the holding centers and the fear that the children might have to return to Kampuchea to face more hardship. The point that was never addressed was that very few of the children could be proved to be orphans, and that almost all of them had a reasonable chance of locating some adult relative. In order to look after these children, UNHCR invited a number of voluntary agencies to establish special centers.

As time went on, pressure built up to allow many of the youngest children to be adopted in Western countries. Sixty-two children left Sa Kaeo for France "in time for Christmas" in 1979. This was a major blow and aroused sufficient opposition among the voluntary-agency staffs working in the camps to encourage us to resist other applications for some months to come. As we learned more about the children and as the number of cases where relatives were found began to increase, so our resistance to the idea of resettlement gathered force.

One of the great successes of the whole relief operation was the tracing operation. Put together by the ICRC, Redd Barna (Norwegian Save the Children) and IRC, this used a variety of exciting techniques to help the 3,000 unaccompanied minors locate their relatives. In 18 months, in about two thousand cases, we met with success. Had it been possible to extend the program to the interior of Kampuchea, I am convinced that almost all would have found a relative. I hope that agencies working with those children who have come out of Thailand to new lives in the West will vigorously pursue efforts to locate the parents or relatives.

As time went by, the debate intensified. The future of children in different age groups was analyzed and discussed, the chances of family reunion were endlessly debated, and gradually more young Kampucheans were removed to uncertain futures in the United States or other Western countries. Many of them will do well and be happy. I sincerely hope that all of them will in the end feel pleased with the decision taken on their behalf, but I have seen enough of the psychological consequences for young people of separation from their families to know that the first priority must always be to promote family reunion. The immediate aftermath of an emergency is not the best time in which to make irrevocable decisions regarding the long-term futures of the youngest victims.

UNACCOMPANIED MINORS AT KHAO I DANG

S. N. Chaudhuri

There were many unaccompanied minors at Khao I Dang. The healthy ones went to a central area next to the hospital zone where a few tents had been put up, and when their numbers exceeded 500, Catholic Relief Services (CRS) and the United States Catholic Conference were entrusted by UNHCR with equipping, provisioning, and administering special children's centers. These children's centers were built in each section to enable the children to live with their own people and to have a chance of being recognized by relatives.

The children in the centers were cared for by housemothers chosen from the young widows among the newly arrived refugees. Later, housefathers were also chosen. The population of each center was usually limited to 100 children and ten houseparents. Each center had three or four dormitory-type houses in which boys and girls lived separately.

On arrival at the centers, the children were given thorough medical examinations and referred to clinics as necessary. A work schedule for each center was prepared. For younger children, cultural activities such as music and dance were emphasized; older children were taught sewing, tailoring, basketmaking, and preparation of nutritious foods. In one center, elderly people started to visit the children and teach them skills such as basket weaving and fan making. Very soon, the unaccompanied minors attended schools that were established in the camp. Other children in the camp mingled freely with the unaccompanied minors during play and vocational training.

Orphan children throughout the world and from time imme-
morial have struck tender chords of human sympathy and affection in well-wishers. Cambodian children are among the most
beautiful gifts of God on this earth. When they smile and play in
the arms of a woman of either European or American origin who
wants children but is not able to bear her own and is thus desperate to adopt one, the sequence of events is not difficult to imagine. Intense emotional ties were generated when there was free
access to the camps initially, and many such women offered to
take care of these beautiful children; these offers were accepted
with gratitude by the authorities.

Individuals or groups made unsuccessful attempts to take these
children out of the camps, some arriving with gifts to entice or
influence the children to accompany them. The houseparents
took adequate precautions, especially with the smaller children,
to prevent such occurrences. At a meeting of the houseparents,
it was even decided that they themselves would adopt the children under their care, as many of them were childless widows.
ICRC and UNHCR continued their tracing while the controversy
raged about allowing the unaccompanied minors to be adopted,
and more children were reunited with their parents.

Children and houseparents were frightened of the Thai soldiers who were the custodians in the camp. The Thai soldiers
carrying their weapons reminded them of the oppression and
terror let loose by Pol Pot's forces earlier in their own country.
Stray incidents of Thai soldiers abusing teenage Cambodian
girls reinforced their fear. Usually prompt action against the cul-
prits by UNHCR and the Thai military reduced tension and fear.

In part, due to concerns voiced by volunteers and agencies,
ICRC and UNHCR intensified tracing and developed a detailed
coding, information storage, and retrieval system. This led to a
decrease in the number of unaccompanied minors.

Whenever and wherever famine occurs and is reported by a
well-developed international-news network, many individuals and
international-aid agencies respond in a natural humane manner
by rushing in resources and skills or by mobilizing support
through fund raising. Yet it is humiliating and sad to think that
famine still stalks the face of this earth when so many resources
are scandalously wasted on a meaningless arms race by both the
rich and the poor nations.

SANITATION

Richard Swenson and Terrance Rahe

When we arrived at Sa Kaeo in December 1979, we were greeted by a hospital nurse: "Boy, I'm glad you're here! We've been waiting for you to solve all the sanitation problems." We were dumbfounded as we thought we had come to support others in addressing these problems—not to be the principal problem-solvers ourselves.

The camp reeked of feces, both in the hospital and in the general "housing" areas. Flies were just getting their life cycles tuned to maximum reproduction. Waste and litter were scattered everywhere. Refugees were lined up at the water taps, waiting for water. Since the camp was located on an old rice paddy, which was bound to be underwater during the rainy season, there was no practical way the camp could be prevented from being inundated when the rains came. Our first thought was that the camp must be moved.

Few visitors went where we did. The latrines, at the back of the camp, were hurriedly constructed and a disgrace to humanity—no privacy, nonfunctional except for fly breeding. Hospital personnel had their own pour-flush latrines, kept under

Richard Swenson and Terrance Rahe worked in the Cambodian relief operation as Public Health Sanitarians with the International Rescue Committee. Mr. Swenson participated from December 1979 to September 1980, and Mr. Rahe from January to March 1979. Mr. Swenson is now Director of Environmental Health at the Benton County Health Department in Corvallis, Oregon. Mr. Rahe is Environmental Health Consultant with Cascade Earth Sciences, Ltd., in Albany, Oregon.

lock and key, with individual compartments. Supplementary water was trucked in and obviously contaminated as it was dipped out of the water bins with dirty buckets.

The hospital wards we visited were crowded but orderly. Adjacent to the ten hospital wards was a 20-foot space surrounded by a four-foot-high wall. We looked over it and saw mounds of feces and flies.

The environmental conditions in the camp were so poor that continuing reinfection and rapid spread of disease were imminent—if not already occurring. A program had to be initiated to protect the health of the 30,000 refugees, several hundred hospital workers, and surrounding Thai population.

The Thai public health authorities had been charged with the responsibility of protecting health in Thailand, including the health of the refugees. Of course, the already overworked Thai public health officials had their own normal duties to perform—let alone to take on with no added resources additional responsibility for many thousands of refugees. The Thai sanitarian for the area, including Sa Kaeo, realized that the present conditions in the camp could easily spread disease to the Thai community via flies, waste water (draining into the surrounding rice paddies), and mosquitoes. He spent much time at the camp. Refugee and Thai work crews were assigned to him to work in camp sanitation and vector control. He was helpful in interpreting as well as in identifying what local materials were available for building latrines, improving drainage, making inexpensive tools, and performing other necessary tasks.

It was the responsibility of the UNHCR field officer to provide protection to the refugees. We viewed protection to include not only protection from physical violence and harm but also protection from disease and pestilence. The UNHCR had a difficult role in administration of camp activities as there were many organizations and agencies involved, all of which were present by grace of the Thai government. UNHCR had the responsibility but lacked complete authority for the coordination of resources. At one point, when the number of hospitalized patients became very low, new medical teams arrived and actually took patients from other wards in order to have something to do. At the same time, thousands of refugees had no decent, safe place to defecate. Unfortunately, few voluntary agencies were concerned with disease prevention; curative medicine in the hospital wards was given highest priority.

The medical coordinator attempted to integrate camp medical activities. There were more than 20 volags in Sa Kaeo, and most were involved in curative medicine. The medical coordinator was, by virtue of position, a leading influence in the camp. Such public-health activities as immunizations and camp sanitation were largely affected by the interest and cooperation of the medical coordinator.

Environmental health programs were fragmented in the camp. At times, purported solutions created more problems. The water supply was under the control of an engineer. Combination concrete bathing and water-storage platforms had been built. Apparently, however, no one was responsible for the drainage from the bathing areas. The engineer indicated that the disposal of the waste water was not his responsibility. Soon pools of stagnant waste water formed in the housing areas causing a serious problem. The architect in charge of the hospital-area building program installed sinks without regard to waste-water disposal. As a result, the hospital area became full of stagnant waste water. Latrines that required pumping were located where it was impossible to reach them with the pumper truck. No one wanted to deal with the latrine problem. At one point, there were 5,000 refugees and no usable latrines. Food for the hospital kitchen was infested with rats; amazing to us, this did not seem to concern anyone else, even though simple measures could have been instituted to "rodent-proof" the structure.

Because these and other environmental health problems were not dealt with by anyone, there were often critical gaps that exposed the population to health hazards. The fragmentation of work among various agencies contributed to no group's accepting responsibility for maintaining a healthy camp environment.

Nothing can be more important to the success of environmental health programs in a refugee camp than knowledge of cultural habits and practices. In the Cambodian culture the women, both young and old, are responsible for obtaining clean water for family use; they also do the cooking and disposing of wastes. We therefore encouraged as much female participation as possible. We gave classroom education to 30 refugee workers —mostly women—on the life cycle of the fly, germ theory, and common diseases.

An interesting discovery about the preferences of refugees provided a vital clue to the motivation of refugees in the battle against the fly. The farm-oriented population was not accustomed to the abundance of flies in the camp. We were able to improve waste management more easily when we explained that the changes would help reduce the fly population.

The camp wells could not produce enough water to meet the demand, so the supply was augmented by trucking in water. The trucked-in water was distributed, through plastic hoses, into 1,000-liter metal storage bins. The personnel were not trained in how to protect the drinking water from contamination. Once as we rounded a corner, a worker had just picked up the end of a hose from a ditch full of sewage and was about to put it into the drinking-water storage tank of a hospital ward.

It was also not uncommon to encounter a driver filling his water truck from a "local watering hole" rather than from the approved safe source. Many thought that the water from the trucks was quite safe, but the quality depended on a long chain of factors, often broken at some point. The trucked-in water was supposed to be chlorinated, but this was rarely done. We did not have the facilities to test the water for microbial contamination and to determine if it had been properly chlorinated.

Once water pipes were laid, expectations rose that there would finally be a steady supply of safe water. This never occurred: the three camp wells could not produce the needed quantity. Parts of the distribution system were turned off on a rotating basis in order to keep at least some pressure in the pipes. Not surprisingly, this caused problems. Refugees would dismantle the pipes when there was no water. Then when

the water was turned back on, it would run out of the dis-
connected pipes. Maintaining an adequate uncontaminated
water supply was a constant battle.

In the beginning, the camp latrines consisted of slit trenches
two feet wide, four feet deep, and several hundred feet long.
The latrine floor was made of boards. A rickety four-foot-
high, bamboo-screen wall was constructed along the trench,
but once inside the latrine, there was no privacy. Many refugees
waited until dark to defecate; but there was no light in the
latrines, and they were afraid of entering lest they fall in. Consequently, feces were deposited outside the latrine areas.

Any type of excreta-disposal system would have required
some capital. Usually latrines are inexpensive, but when one
needs to construct 4,000 of them, expenses can become great.
Refugees working at low wages helped to lower construction
costs. They also helped to sensitize other refugees to using the
latrines. Nevertheless, many refugees at Sa Kaeo were poor
farmers who had never before used a latrine; they preferred to
defecate in the open field, away from the smell of the latrines.
The bamboo screens used for the latrine walls soon disinte-
grated. Small pieces of bamboo were broken off because there
was no toilet paper available. Finally, latrines with individual
compartments were constructed. These provided the necessary
privacy. Work crews were organized for cleaning and maintenance. A grass-woven mat was used as a door. At night, children would remove the strings that were used to weave the grass
together. The next windy day, kites would be at the end of the
strings.

Excreta disposal, although necessary, is not a glamorous
subject. Volags have a much easier time raising funds by
showing a child being saved by medical treatment than by showing a sanitary latrine. Funds to provide adequate latrines and a
supportive educational program were hard to find. No one
wanted to take on this important responsibility. Latrine technology needed to be improved. And an intensive effort was
needed to bring about a change in refugee behavior to use and
maintain the new latrines.

With so many facilities, so many refugees, and so few Thai

and volag workers, the tasks often seemed overwhelming. There were 25 workers for latrine construction and maintenance, drinking water, solid-waste management, drainage maintenance, and all the other needed environmental-health services for 30,000 people. Only we two volag sanitarians and five Thai public-health workers had any experience in public health.

Refugee camps come with a chain of command. The structure is useful in keeping track of the population, food distribution, medical services, and other information. This chain of command proves very important in achieving public-health goals. The structure develops leaders who can be relied upon to help organize activities within a particular group. In our case, these leaders provided public-health representatives from their sectors. Collectively assembled, we formed a public-health council. After we had selected a chairman, we got the council to determine what should be done to improve conditions. First, they wanted a building for public-health meetings—not a poor start, for it gave them status and position. The building was a symbol of public health. Their next task was to train volunteer workers to build their own privies. Existing refugee workers from the Thai health team became the training staff. Sector by sector, the privies were built. This time they were built by the people who used them and who eventually became responsible for their care. This sense of personal control and accomplishment spread into the other areas of public health, such as solid waste and drainage.

Control of solid waste was a particular problem. Simply adding rice water, which is a cooking waste, to dry dust and otherwise inert thatch residue creates ideal fly-breeding conditions in a hot humid climate. Daily removal of this material appeared essential to fly control. Initially, woven baskets, each of which contained half a cubic meter of waste, were scattered throughout the camp. Each day a contract garbage hauler would come in and empty the baskets into an open truck and haul the waste to a burn site outside the camp.

The woven baskets were soon worn out, and replacement became necessary. The logical solution seemed to be used oil drums; they were made of metal and should last a long time. After spending two weeks finding funds for their purchase, we finally distributed 200 oil drums with the tops cut out. When we distributed them, we emptied the worn-out garbage baskets into the oil drums to demonstrate their function. The following morning, when we returned to the camp, not a single drum was in sight. All the garbage was there, right where the cans had been, but no oil drums. It did not take long for us to discover the error of our ways. The drums had been traded to the neighboring civilian population for fresh fruit and vegetables. The drums were highly prized for water storage and were simply too valuable to remain in service.

Two weeks later, 200 drums were again distributed, each drum having been perforated numerous times to render it useless for water storage. All went well as long as the drums were not full; it required at least four strong Thai workers to lift one full drum into the truck. Because of this, we decided to redistribute woven baskets. They were light, could be handled by one person, and were worth so little that they could not be traded.

Clearly not every problem has a practical solution. Problems and their solutions must simply be evaluated in the context of the situation. In retrospect, this whole episode seems illogical; but when you are facing problems in six major environmental health areas at once, it is easy to find yourself "doing something even if it is wrong." Not only is this approach wasteful of both energy and financial resources, but also it raises questions about the entire program.

This sort of problem can often be avoided by consulting closely with the refugee and host-country health workers, letting them make a critical review of the proposed program. Once input is obtained from all sources, one can proceed with enthusiasm and common sense. In this way, much support is obtained from co-workers and one is seldom caught completely off base. If wrong decisions are made, at least everyone can laugh at themselves together.

There are many other issues, such as garbage disposal, vector control, fire safety, hospital hazardous wastes, food protection, housing, waste-water disposal, and health education, that are important aspects of a good environmental health program in a refugee camp. The variety of the problems and the opportunity to help people at a tragic time in their lives made this work very meaningful.

* * * * *

A refugee asked a fellow volunteer after seeing him work in the camps for several weeks what nationality he was. He said, "I'm from the United States." The refugee did not think this was possible. "You can't be," he said, "the United States bombed our rice paddies." The two men then became friends.

FORTY-EIGHT HOURS AT
MAI RUT

David I. Cooper, Jr.

Five hundred yards to the east, the gray-green tropical forest climbs in lush density to the top of the low ridge, whose serpentine spine forms Thailand's southeastern border with Kampuchea. Five hundred yards to the west, the Gulf of Thailand stretches away from calendar-photo beaches to island-dotted horizons. In between, along some three kilometers of a sandy sliver of Thai territory, was the Mai Rut Holding Center for Kampucheans, where, during 1980, some 14,000 refugees, 40 Thai, many United Nations and foreign voluntary-agency relief workers, and 30 Thai military personnel struggled to create a refuge, a community, and hope.

Thursday

My wristwatch alarm sounds at 5:55, announcing a third blue-gray dawn of drumming rain. I cannot imagine six more months and more than 200 inches of rain falling before the monsoon will end. As I shave, the Voice of America (VOA) news announces that the Thai government and the UNHCR are evaluating a "voluntary" repatriation program for Cambodians.

David I. Cooper, Jr., is a Senior Health Policy Analyst in the Office of the Secretary, United States Department of Health and Human Services, Washington, D.C. On leave from that position, he served in Thailand from January to December 1980 with the International Rescue Committee and UNHCR.

Since the refugees never miss VOA news, I expect to find the camp in a state of shock.

Tea and toast in the restaurant next door with my co-worker, sanitarian Dennis Kalson; Stephen LaHusen, our young German UNHCR field officer; and Rolfe Schumacher, the camp's German dentist. By 7:30, the garage boys have jacked up our pickup and snaked it clear of the parking morass, and we are making our customary round of errands—we buy six more squat plates and cement for toilet repair, pick up our resoldered backpack sprayers, and stop at the Trat hospital lab to get results on our weekly water-sample analyses. (A significant coliform-bacteria count confirms our concern about the camp's hospital kitchen well.)

By 8:15, the rain has stopped, and we head east on the superb Klong Yai highway, past pale-green rice seedbeds, mist-shrouded mountains, the mysterious "Queen's Camp" for Khmer children (no foreigners allowed), and a new Japanese dam site. The 62 kilometers pass quickly as Dennis and I weigh the day's plans. The rains have made the camp's half-kilometer-long entry road a bog. A bamboo-laden truck, sunk to its axles in mud, convinces us to take the longer cross-country approach, an unmarked track we have dubbed the "safari route," across the sand and through the scrub bush. We enter the "old camp" (1975) from the south, past the token barbed wire, the thatched longhouses, the sprawling MSF hospital, and the wooden Thai Ministry of Interior office. We pull up at the small bamboo building we share with the UNHCR and dash in through the downpour; the sound of the radio link with Bangkok is already crackling like a comforting hearth fire. Before I can get my poncho off, our Khmer insecticide-spray team takes my keys and sets about siphoning gas from the truck for the motorized backpack sprayer and unloading the manual backpack sprayers we use for spraying chlorine solution in the toilet houses. I can see the United Nations field officer in hushed and earnest conversation with the senior refugee leaders, trying to calm anxieties related to the VOA report.

Our Khmer sanitation chiefs, Chhin Thun and Dy Rann, are

waiting. We blow the bamboo dust—from boring insects—off the papers and tables, and set out tasks for the day. Garbage pickup is always first priority, but the camp's main road is impassable, and we have been unable to pick up the garbage at Bamboo Camp or New Camp for two days. The military have not yet given us permission to break down a portion of the embankments lining the now-submerged road so that the tractor can cross. I put it on my list of items to take up with Major Norachai. Dy Rann reports his crew will work on the 14 squat plates that were broken when the farmers in the Old Camp dipped out raw sewage to fertilize their gardens. Chhin and Dennis will work in the New Camp rebuilding the recently installed asbestos sewage drain pipes that have been crushed by construction contractors building the New Camp, cracked by shifting sand, or plugged or misaligned during installation. Bruce Cobb of the Thailand Baptist Mission (TBM) and Cara Kelleher of Concern arrive, and we work out today's schedule for the tractor and trailer: hauling garbage away for us, refugee food rations down to the New Camp for distribution by TBM, and bamboo for Concern's new supplementary-feeding center.

UNHCR and some voluntary-agency personnel arrive crammed into the Land Rover. Dennis and I consult with a Thai UNHCR social worker, than draft a radio message to UNHCR Procurement in Bangkok asking for a third time that they cancel the toilet-pump truck contract: the contractor has driven over and broken toilet-holding tank covers, his hose is too short to reach an entire section, we often have had to buy gas for the military trucks to pull him out when he becomes stuck, and now that the monsoon has inundated the holding tanks, he is mainly pumping water. Part of the control problem is that UNHCR/Bangkok wrote the contract with a Thai middleman in Bangkok who, having no pump truck himself, spot-hired the present trucker. We have frequently asked Bangkok for permission to do our own sewage and water-truck contracts and to buy bamboo and food locally, but their rules do not seem to have enough flexibility to permit it. A second message goes to ICM for 800 doses of measles vaccine and a replacement for our clogged Ped-O-Jet vaccination gun.

I slog down to the hospital to show Dr. Vincent David, the MSF camp medical coordinator, a draft design for the new isolation-room addition. On my way, I can see the Khmers wading in water above their knees out behind the toilet houses and picking what they call *pak*, a green leafy stalk eaten as a vegetable. This same water has inundated the toilet holding tanks, and the effluent is floating all over the place.

At the hospital, I find that Dr. David is away. Dr. Bouhier gives me a note scrawled on the flap of a pharmaceutical carton with the name, age, and house number of a man who died of tuberculosis. (I make a mental note for the fourth or fifth time to design and reproduce a standard death report form.) The man's body has been moved into one corner of the ward where the members of his family, who have surrounded the corpse with food and candles, are now mourning. I promise to arrange with the military to remove the body. Guillaum asks if our tinsmith can repair a gutter that is leaking into the TB section and confirms that the campaign to stop patients throwing garbage out the windows is reducing the fly population. I tell an MSF Nurse that we will move a water tank under one of the gutters so that we can close the contaminated well. I check the OPD records and am surprised that they do not show a rise in gastrointestinal illness—perhaps the Khmer outreach workers are not finding the cases that must be occurring. I will check what the Concern nurses are seeing in the supplementary-feeding centers. I wait out the remainder of a slashing rain squall by watching three small children splashing joyously, naked, under a downspout.

Dy Rann catches me outside, shows me the toilet repairs, and in our usual Khmer-Thai pantomime, lets me know that the military bulldozer did not cover the garbage at the dump. They are three days late, and we will soon have another heavy fly-breeding cycle and another visit from irate, neighboring Thai farmers.

As I stop by the office to pick up my poncho, I find three Khmer boys proudly displaying their plastic bag full of rats' tails, eager for Dennis's bounty for one baht per tail. With help, I explain that redemption of the rats' tails takes place on

Friday afternoons. This rat-catching incentive plus Dennis's attention to potential harborage sites has significantly reduced rat sighting, except at the hospital where they race about above the bamboo-mat dropped ceiling, occasionally tumbling into patients' water buckets. As I leave for the new camp, the Thai social worker is immersed, as usual, in an intense discussion with a family of five—family reunification, marital discord, plans to emigrate, I cannot tell.

The Thai guards do not bother me today about not wearing my pass and wave me on past the hubbub around the New Camp gate. By avoiding the road and cutting across the sand, I soon reach the New Camp outpatient clinic a quarter of a mile away. A Thai Catholic nun and an American nurse promptly corral me and ask why I have not found them a new clinic site; the military has rented space ten feet from the clinic door to Thai meat and vegetable vendors, and the smell, noise, and flies are placing added burdens on an already hectic clinic practice. I move the problem up on my list of priorities and walk down to look at one of the newly constructed refugee barracks as a possible site. The barracks are about 25-by-80 feet in size, and open along the front; they have plywood floors, cement-panel walls, corrugated tin roofs, and cement piers on which they stand. Arranged in four-building quadrangles, with two wells in the middle and fiberglass Aqua Privy toilets at two corners (at $900 a piece!), each building is to hold eight families. I select a building along the road between Bamboo and New camps—accessible to the residents of both—and track down the two Khmer area leaders. I explain that we need the building for a clinic and ask them to have the few people in it moved to another building by next Wednesday.

I walk through the New Camp to find Dennis and Chhin for lunch. Each day I am amazed anew that in the short weeks since they arrived, the ethnic Chinese Khmer from Khao I Dang have created such a thriving market economy: stalls between the "quads" sell stamps and aerograms, thread and fabrics, cigarettes, soft drinks, and sweets. There are barbers and even a watch repairman. Since the Thai contractors hired refugees as construction laborers paying twice what I could pay, there has been some money in the camp. There is also a considerable bustle and flow of goods, and it is clear that their reputation as merchants has not been exaggerated. I find Dennis's crew trying a new method of shoring up the fragile asbestos pipe with a bamboo framework where the pipes lie on the surface of the ground. They are putting wet cement patches over the small cracks. Over lunch, we exchange doubts as to whether the repairs will work.

At 1:00, I meet my class of English teachers at the Bamboo Camp school for a twice-weekly, two-hour class. The energy devoted to language classes by the refugees is very impressive. Even though prohibited by the Thai authorities, English is taught every day in dozens of small clandestine classes, hidden away in the houses. But the teaching of teachers is apparently within policy and we laugh and act our way through one of the series texts. There is such a demand for these books that the school-supplies shop in Trat cannot keep them in stock. One of my favorite students is a middle-aged woman with no front upper teeth for whom "th" is impossible, but her determination and great good humor carry us all along with her. At times, the rain drums so heavily on that thatched classroom roof that we cannot hear even the boldest student. I have great enthusiasm for this teaching, and the two hours pass with much laughter and several sharp questions which keep me on my toes.

On my way back to the office, I muster my energies and stop at military headquarters to see Major Norachai. He is dour, a bit imperious, and sometimes hot-tempered, and I have found that patience, a sympathetic "we're-all-in-this-together" attitude, and a ready pocketful of quid pro quos are the best approach to him. I take note of his complaints about volag personnel driving too fast in camp and not stopping for the flag-raising ceremonies. I raise the need to breach the entry road embankments, so that the garbage tractor can pass, and renew my request that the bulldozer cover the dump before the villagers come to him to complain. The major promises to raise these problems with the camp commander, and laments the command's lack of fuel for the bulldozer. I parry with a promise that we will pump out the officers' quarters toilets tomorrow (and hope that UNHCR has not recalled the pump truck yet). I also remind him of a visit next week from someone from the Bangkok office of IRC—my agency.

With military-volag relations at a cyclical low point, the military have taken (capriciously in my view) to denying entry to visitors even though they have passes from the Supreme Command in Bangkok. We did not have this problem when Colonel Kosol was in command, but he was ambushed and killed just outside the camp, and the new commander is being more hard-nosed just to remind us who are the hosts and who the guests. I find I must actively monitor myself to avoid slipping into a we/they view of the military. It can happen gradually and subliminally, and usually leads to bitterness and reduced effectiveness. However petty and grating the security and administration at Mai Rut, we have only to reflect on our colleagues' tales of the military's fearsome security behavior up around Khao I Dang.

When I reach the office, I am met by Dr. David. A baby has been born with exposed intestines (omphalocele) for which he needs specialized help at once. I radio to the UNHCR medical adviser in Bangkok, but he is up-country at one of the Lao camps. I try Dr. Daniel Susott at the medical coordinating committee, but there is no answer. Finally we reach Dr.Philippe Laurent at MSF headquarters, and ask him if he can make arrangements for Bangkok General Hospital to receive the baby if we put him on tonight's UNHCR courier car. He reminds us that it is late on a holiday afternoon in Bangkok (groan!), but while pessimistic, he is willing to try. The deadline for reaching the courier car before it leaves Trat is already very close. Laurent calls back to say he has reached the director of Bangkok General who has agreed to receive the child. Military-command permission is readily given, and I pick the baby up at the hospital. An MSF nurse carries the baby on her lap with a saline bottle rigged to keep the abdominal dressings moist.

While my best combination of care and speed, we bounce out across the "safari route" praying that we will not get stuck. As we reach the highway, my heart sinks as I see that when my workers siphoned the tank for the sprayer that morning, they left me insufficient gas to reach Trat. I know that the courier rarely waits, no matter what, but I have no choice and turn south toward a gas station 15 kilometers away. Pushing the truck up to 150 kilometers an hour, we reach the station on fumes, fill the tank, and rocket back north toward Trat. Gathering storm clouds and failing light cut our speed to 100, then 80, as black-clad rice-field workers, bound for home on foot or unlit bicycles, share the shoulder and edge of the highway with lumbering two-ton water buffaloes. I hunch forward over the wheel, scanning for a telltale flutter of cloth or the glint of an eye, willing the rain to hold off.

We are nearly an hour late for the courier when we finally swing into the Trat Hotel and—the courier has waited. We meet his anger with relief and profuse expressions of appreciation, but he is impatient to be off for Bangkok, 400 kilometers away and hurries us along. He tells us curtly that the area around Bangkok General is flooded and he will not be able to get close, but off they go. (I learn later that, arriving in Bangkok at 11:00, he patiently drove roundabout routes and backtracked until he was able to deliver nurse and baby to the hospital door. It was typical of a generosity we were to experience often at his hands.)

Dennis and some Thai school teachers are going to a Chinese movie and invite me, but I am too tired and decline. After a *moo pat hom yai* [spicy fried pork and big onions] from a marketplace restaurant cart, I go up to bed with two letters from home and some prayers of thanks for the day.

Friday

A blistering-hot crystal-clear morning. At breakfast, I meet an MSF doctor on his way to the Vietnamese boat people's camp about a hundred kilometers up the coast to investigate an epidemic of conjunctivitis. I send a note with him to the Thai part-time UNHCR field officer saying that Dennis and I will come on Tuesday with the Swedish well-drilling team to look for a well site and to evaluate alternatives to the camp's current toilets—stalls on wooden piers over the cove where refugees bathe and fish.

When the UNHCR driver does not show up, Dennis drives their Land Rover to the camp while I wait for the bank to open so I can draw the weekly payroll for the sanitation workers ($.50 per day). I spend the spare hour laboring crossly over my IRC and UNHCR accounts and picking up plywood and screws, so that our production crew can make a couple of reusable coffins. I arrive at the camp about 10:00, past groups of boys sidearm skimming rubber flip-flops at a target ball—their usual chorus of "OK, bye-bye" trails in my wake.

I am just in time for the weekly program coordinators' staff meeting. Squeezed with a dozen other people into Stephen's ten-foot-square office, we jockey for places next to the best bilinguists while Dennis washes the mud off his feet outside the door. Brown faces peek in the windows, and the dull thud of artillery in the next valley intrudes, incongruously mixed with the sounds of children's chanted recitations at the school across the way. (How different from the Washington staff meetings to which I am accustomed.) Stephen runs the agenda: we expect a movement of 8,000 refugees to come from Khao I Dang in ten days—the third schedule we have heard. The Thai military has decided to allow refugees to go to the beach for two hours on Sunday (previously, only the unaccompanied minors have been allowed to go once a week). The camp commander has asked for participation in a market committee to monitor prices and goods, but it looks like a political mine field and no volag volunteers. Two TBM workers give a report on the tenor of re-fugee-military relationships, and state that since the American Embassy abruptly canceled the only movement ever scheduled for Old Camp refugees, wife beating, drinking, prostitution, fighting, and theft are on the rise. The meeting closes with announcement of a name-the-pig contest for the orphan center's four new piglets. After the meeting, Dr. David and I agree on a final design for the hospital isolation room addition and nego-tiate a cost-sharing arrangement: I will pay for materials, and he will pay for the labor. I talk with two Thais who run an orphan center about their immunization schedule.

Major Norachai interrupts by walkie-talkie to ask me to come to see him right away. He immediately launches into a tirade about not working together. Although his English is excellent, it takes me a minute to realize that he is complaining about my instruction yesterday to New Camp leaders that a building should be vacated for use as a clinic. I kick myself for forgetting to touch base with the military since I know how seriously they take their refugee control responsibilities, and I apologize. I review at some length the advantages of that particular building and conclude by pointing out that as soon as the shift takes place, the military can rent the present clinic space to more Thai merchants (without mentioning the financial advantages that will probably accrue). I mentally resign myself to an endless process of memos and meetings and negotiations, but surprisingly Major Norachai agrees to the change and says he will fix it with the base commander.

I walk to the Concern supplementary-feeding center in the Old Camp for another in the series of seemingly interminable meetings intended to work out an agreement between Concern and MSF over who will be responsible for the "under-5" clinic— MSF nurses in the OPD or Concern nurses at the feeding center. Concern is stubborn (this is a countrywide issue that its director is constantly raising in Bangkok); so is MSF. A trial plan emerges which is grudgingly and skeptically agreed to by both sides.

Dy Rann intercepts me outside to show me the toilet repairs and ask again if we can fix the lights in the toilets (women are frightened). I point out maggot-ridden fish heads in a pile near the well. Situation normal. I give him the payroll for his workers.

The sun is glaring off the white sand, and without our usual onshore breeze, smoke from the refugees' charcoal ovens just hangs in the shimmering heat waves. Sweat-soaked, I take a quick Coke at TBM and then head back to touch base at the office. I send a message to my IRC co-worker at the Kamput camp (150 kilometers north) saying that I will come up tomorrow to review the contractors' percolation tests. (The soil "percs" inadequately; the contractors refuse to make changes, and the system later fails, just as predicted.) I plan to stay for a Sunday meeting regarding a proposal for Kamput's New Camp pipeline.

Chhin says that there is great discontent among many Khmers in the New Camp because the ethnic Chinese among them have been elected and appointed to the leadership positions, loudspeaker announcements and music are often in Chinese, and even the Khmer dental assistant, who is an ethnic Chinese, gives them priority. This has been coming on for some time—the ethnic Chinese have taken to referring to themselves as Chinese and to the others as Khmers. Also, a relief group from Taiwan has set up a "Chinese Quad" with classical Chinese opera performances, foreign Chinese-language newspapers, language classes, and special help in locating Chinese relatives abroad with whom reunification would provide emigration priority. All refugees are welcome, of course. . . . I suspect that the roots of these quarrels run deep and doubt that I can do much, but promise to take it up with the field officer. I pay Chhin the payroll for his crew, while Dennis redeems 86 rats' tails.

The towering cumulus clouds that have been prowling off shore all day provide a stunning sunset as the truck fills up with soldiers and volag staff going into Trat. Unlike last night, I intend that before last light we will be off on what everyone agrees is a very dangerous highway. But as I near Trat, it is very nearly dark, and the carbide lamps of the frog hunters are already bobbing through the marshy roadside ditches.

I pick up a *Bangkok Post* and relax over an orange drink. The Thai social worker comes in with Dennis. She tells me that she has heard that about 50 Vietnamese boat people are at Ao Cao, ten kilometers to the south, and will I take her down to see how they are. It is raining hard again, and it takes us nearly an hour to find the right place. By flashlight, we sort through the 63 men, women, and older children huddled among the wooden piers under the police station. The police commander tells us they have been there for three days. He buys them food prepared by local residents for which the Ministry of Interior will reimburse him. The local wat [temple] has contributed some mosquito netting and a few blankets, but the mosquitoes are the most voracious I have ever seen. Two Vietnamese regale us with tales of their voyage and being set upon by "corsairs," but other than an infected hand (caught in the boat motor), they seem to be in an adequate though somewhat emaciated condition. A slit-trench toilet out against the hedgerow is shallow among the roots, and there is little privacy. We decide that before I go to Kamput tomorrow, Dennis will bring down two squat plates (though high ground water makes disposal problematic) and some plastic sheeting. We will also try to scrounge some mosquito netting from TBM. Within 15 days or so, the ministry will move all these people to another camp.

Finally we drive back to Trat. A quick bowl of noodles, a cold shower, a letter to my family, and an early lights-out, with the "tock-tock" of the village watchman's patrol signal echoing through the now silent market.

MEDICAL TRAINING PROGRAMS
FOR REFUGEES

Barbara Bayers

I had several goals in mind when in February 1980 I met with nine Khmer physicians who were "illegal immigrants" at Khao I Dang. The meeting was prompted by a nurse who was about to leave and who had proposed structured classes for those refugees who were hospital workers. The classes would provide a basis for medical self-help among the refugees, encouraging their withdrawal from a dependency upon the whims of Western-oriented relief. We tried to convince the Khmer doctors that (1) it was possible to form such a school; (2) they were still doctors even though they had worked as farmers for the previous four years; (3) their ability to speak Khmer was a distinct advantage that far outweighed their lack of recent medical experience; (4) we would provide them with more French medical books and eyeglasses so that they could read the books; (5) we would find a building for the school; and (6) it was *their* responsibility, and we would be there to assist.

Barbara Bayers was for most of the period from January 1980 to April 1983 Coordinator for Medical Education for Khmer Refugees, International Catholic Migration Commission of Geneva, performing work that was supported by a grant from Caritas Denmark. From June 1982 to January 1983, she worked as Assistant Medical Coordinator for the United Nations Border Relief Operation at Aranyaprathet, Thailand. She is presently working as a charge nurse at a private hospital in California and as Executive Director for a non-profit teaching corporation, Self Education Programs International (S.E.P.I.), Inc., Mill Walley, California.

During the previous four years, these nine physicians had survived by hiding their professional identity. Eyeglasses, medical books, and precious certificates had been thrown away and replaced by the dress and veneer of a peasant. The survival habits of the past years were hard to change as they were reluctantly drawn into the hospital wards to function as doctors. Although their theoretical knowledge was sound, their clinical skills were rusty. Resuming their old work threatened and embarrassed them. They fumbled with stethoscopes and other equipment that they had not seen in years. "We're only refugees," they often said. "We can't be doctors or teachers."

Each little hurdle had to be overcome. The books they had could not be read without eyeglasses. That was clear after we received several hesitant requests for glasses and our noting one physician squinting at a text, his nose inches from the page. Coincidentally, shortly after the February meeting an optometrist from Minnesota arrived in the camp with boxes of glasses discarded by his previous patients. We immediately went to see him, and all the Khmer were soon supplied with the glasses they needed. The fact that several doctors were now wearing the eyeglass frames of Miami Beach matrons stirred something inside me as did their joy in being able to read again. Their dignity went far deeper than external wrappings. They could read again. *Yes,* they agreed to teach.

Notices were casually placed in a few spots about the proposed course. We expected enough applicants for a class of from 20 to 30 students. Instead over 400 applied! With no building, only a few books, no desks, no curriculum, and no money, we were completely unprepared for the response.

I located an empty bamboo hospital ward. Fifty refugee carpenters, using a pile of scarce bamboo that had somehow been dumped next to the building, set to work and in three days produced desks, benches, a lecture podium, and bookcases for the library. The poor acoustical qualities of bamboo and the fact that the hospital generator was located next to the ward sent me off on a mission to Bangkok to ask a milk company to donate a microphone, an amplifier, and a speaker. Using a blackboard made of wood and green paint, whatever books we could beg, borrow, or steal, and a curriculum written by French-educated, theoretically based physicians who had farmed for the past four years, the Khao I Dang School of Nursing, with an enrollment of 80 students, began its first day of a three-month course on March 1, 1980, exactly three weeks after our first meeting.

I had three objectives when we started: (1) to train hospital workers, (2) to enable the Khmer medical doctors a graceful reentry into their profession, and (3) to prepare replacements for the eventual departure of the international volunteers.

No one really knew how long the international agencies would be allowed to stay. By late January and mid-February, the Vietnamese army was only five kilometers from the border, 11 kilometers from our "safe haven." The proximity of 50,000 Vietnamese soldiers posed the constant threat of imminent evacuation. Without knowing whether the three-month course could or would be completed, we proceeded one day at a time.

Since all the students accepted for the first class spoke French, the second language of Kampuchea, I asked nurses from the French medical team to conduct the lectures during the first few weeks. I had concluded that the students had already had to adapt to enough without adding courses in another language —English—and another approach to medicine than that of the French. God bless the French nurses! They were wonderful. They may have thought, as many did in the beginning, that such a program was impossible under the circumstances of a refugee camp. Just two months earlier, people had been dying of starvation and disease. When asked, the French nurses neither argued, nor refused. They taught as if it was a responsibility they felt was natural. Without books, without a well-defined curriculum, day by day, a school began to take shape. These were nurses teaching, from memory alone, students who were 95 percent male, coming from four years of terror, and with prior educational experience in such fields as chemistry, pharmacy, law, education, the military, engineering, and religion. It was a remarkable process to watch.

Despite the reluctance of the Khmer physicians to say it

was *their* school, I kept insisting that it was and that I was there only to assist them. It meant letting go of a lot of my own ideas and accepting a curriculum which I considered overly esoteric.

They appointed a director, a librarian, and a secretary for the school. The library was still quite bare, for the books that the French team had also promised to help me get had yet to arrive. While waiting quite impatiently for the books, we used the few volumes in English which were already there, and I again borrowed a book by David Werner entitled *Where There Is No Doctor.* Since there were several workers in one ward who had learned English quickly, I asked them to translate portions of the book into Khmer for handouts to the students. The Khmer physicians, however, coming from their French base of education, thought the book much too simple and would not participate in its translation.

On the other hand, the Thai authorities, seeing the value in preparing these displaced people to meet their own needs, were encouraging from the beginning. Dr. Tom D'Agnes, an American working for the CBERS branch of the Thai Public Health (Service), offered to assist me in duplicating the original translations. Because of his encouragement and his trust, I was allowed to run up a bill of 33,000 Baht (more than $1,500)— a bit risky I thought, since I was making $100 a month—and most of that went for notebooks, pens, chalk, wire, and green paint.

By April, 14 Khmer ward workers had translated 80 percent of Werner's book. I was by this time long overdue to return to California and my then 12-year-old daughter. (I had originally only planned to be in Thailand for six weeks.)

The first three-month class was half finished, and the director, Dr. Lim, and I decided that before I left, we had better arrange for clinical practice for the students. The camp had 18 hospital wards, staffed by volunteer agencies from all over the world. We wanted the students to have practical experience working in medicine, surgery, pediatrics, and possibly obstetrics. Because of the large number of students, unless every ward agreed to help us, clinical rotations would not be possible.

Dr. Lim and I made a list of the wards and divided the students into rotations. Each ward had to take the maximum number, some as many as seven at one time. Dr. Lim and I visited each ward. Already working as hard as they could, we asked their staffs to devote yet more time to teaching the students, mostly without any medical background, to work in a hospital ward. Miraculously, not one of the head doctors or nurses refused. The positive reaction of each meant, in my opinion, that they had by now accepted the school as theirs and not mine. It was a Khmer school, representing the displaced, the homeless, the survivors pulling together to try and help themselves, by sharing their knowledge and courage.

We had German surgeons teaching French-speaking Khmers, and Japanese nurses showing refugees how to take care of patients. Irish, Swiss, English, Thai, and American volunteers found the time and the patience to bridge huge language and cultural barriers to share their knowledge and leave behind some of their skills. That motive was very important. To leave behind something of yourself when you are no longer there makes leaving a little easier. To simply come and administer to the sick may be satisfying to you at the time and helpful to them at the time, but what about the gap of time after you go? Who will fill that gap? We were beginning to see.

The goals were starting to be met. The students were learning how to work in hospital wards. The doctors were again beginning to think of themselves as physicians. When I returned to California in mid-April and left the school to run on its own for two and a half weeks, I worried like an anxious mother. But when I returned, there on the wall of the school hung a beautiful sign, which looked very professional:

School of Nursing
Director: Dr. Hean Meng Lim
Secretary: Mr. Man Kiri (Sophin)
Librarian: Mr. Bun Yan
Administrator: Ms. Barbara Bayers

I felt a tremendous amount of pride. The director, the secretary, and the librarian took their positions very seriously. They trained their own assistants and selected guards for the library. The books had arrived from Paris just before I left. Ours was the only building from which there was no stealing. Bun Yan was a very strict librarian and would not even allow the doctors to check books out of the building. It was *their* school. They designed a school crest which was a combination of the United Nations seal, the Red Cross badge, and a depiction of Angkor Wat. Diplomas were designed and issued to those who passed very strict final examinations conducted by the physicians.

With the end of the first three-month class, the committee of physicians called a meeting with the director and myself. They openly criticized several aspects of the first course, demanding that we delay the opening of the second class and offer instead a refresher course for the 72 Khmer nurses in the camp. There was no longer any doubt about who was in charge. Although we argued with them through interpreters, what a joy it was to see them standing firm; the refresher course began two days later. After 64 hours of lectures, the more confident nurses returned to the hospital wards. With the end of the refresher course, another nursing class began, this time following a more practical curriculum based upon the book *Where There Is No Doctor*. Now we stressed more clinical skills than theoretical knowledge, an attempt on my part to begin withdrawal from the French system.

This was our beginning. Other medical programs followed. The Irish nurses did a fantastic job of teaching midwives. I attempted a pilot study to train paramedics along the border, but was blocked by doctors in the camp who could not tolerate my designing a program without consulting them. Though by this time I had the dubious title of medical-training coordinator, I dropped the study, letting them restructure the program I had written and teach it in their own way. Looking back, I realize that it did not meet Khmer needs but the need of the foreign volunteer for control and authority.

By now I was a volunteer agency of one, supported by a private grant from Caritas Denmark. Being small has definite advantages. You can move quickly and create. When I returned to Khao I Dang in 1982, the programs which had been started that first spring were still running, teaching more students to replace those who had gone to other camps, third countries, or back to Kampuchea.

In mid-June 1980, I was surprised to receive my first letter from the Oxfam consortium working in Phnom Penh [see the chapter "Voluntary Aid Inside Kampuchea" by Joel R. Charny and Joseph Short], inquiring about the status of the translation of the book. The letter was delivered to me in a holding center, all the way from Phnom Penh, a place in my mind as inaccessible as Atlantis. The minister of health in Kampuchea wanted the book for "the interior."

What excitement! It renewed my interest in translating, checking, correcting, and revising. The Khmer physicians who had originally refused to participate in the translation of the book because they felt it too simple now formed a medical translation team. They were very aware that there were few doctors left in Kampuchea. Whenever a minor roadblock left them discouraged, such as someone reclaiming the typewriter we had borrowed or the translation team being split up, I would push them on, reminding them of the people left behind where there were almost no doctors. The translation-team office was set up in the empty pediatric ward. Dead rats and litter were thrown out, wiring and extra lighting installed, and I bought tables and chairs. The translators were paid in extra food. It was difficult work. One by one, they were called away for re-settlement, and it seemed as if we would never finish.

Being medical-training coordinator at Khao I Dang and initiating a book translation was not the only area in which my one-woman volunteer agency was involved. By August 1980, I was also finally on the border. My first target area was a camp called Nong Samet, six kilometers from Khao I Dang, which needed a teaching program. Due to the instability of the military situation, medical teams were allowed there only from 9 A.M. to 4 P.M. During periods of fighting and shelling, there were times when no medical teams were allowed on the border for several days. Those refugees who had come to the Thai border for rice or to attempt to enter Thailand were virtually trapped among the Thai army and an antitank trench on the west, a Vietnamese army to the east, and Khmer political factions fighting each other in between. The border had been treacherously mined by several military strategists, either to keep the refugees inside Kampuchea or outside Thailand, or to prevent rapid movement anywhere. Too often these land mines were stepped on by the innocent, the elderly, the young, by women and children. All too often there was no medical personnel to tend these wounds, which, if not fatal, would be so badly infected by the time they did reach medical care that amputation became an all too common necessity. The rehabilitation wards of the holding centers grew, and the need for providing prostheses became another problem.

Because of the instability of the border war zone, I had designed a program that would allow for interruption. The four-module, eight-week program could be taught simultaneously in several border areas, allowing for frequent movement along the border caused by the military action. The program was tight, condensed, and only available to English-speaking Khmers with hospital experience, who did not want to go to a third country and were willing to become teachers. Subject matter was divided into four categories: (1) theoretical, including anatomy, physiology, nutrition, sanitation, and hygiene; (2) medicine, mainly acute infectious disease; (3) surgical, including trauma care and first aid; and (4) pediatrics and obstetrics. The program allowed for only three or four students at a time in a two-week module.

After trying to gain access to the border area, which was controlled by the ICRC, I was finally offered a pass by a German team (Soforthilfe) which had an OPD there and had been allowed to stay on the border only because they had preceded the ICRC to the area.

Although attempts to establish a workable teaching program with the German team failed, it did awaken interest in the proposal, and the ICRC agreed to help to implement the program. This program was designed to train English-speaking

Khmers how to become trainers of non-English-speaking Khmers, using as a base the now nearly completed translation of *Where There Is No Doctor.* The program's purpose and structure were carefully explained to the Khmer administration who not only approved but took an active part in student selection. The Khmers taught each other, covered wards for each other, and began to assume responsibility for their future health care. People who had worked in surgery helped teach those whose experience was in pediatrics. Students who were midwives taught those whose experience was in acute medical care. Since most refugee hospital workers had become "specialists" by staying in one area, we needed to complete their knowledge, so we selected one student from each area for each module, and they formed a study team, responsible for each other.

Each module was composed of a surgeon, a midwife, an instructor, and specialists in medicine and pediatrics. Those with expertise taught those without. There was a lot of crossover, with the instructor serving primarily as a guide and as someone who could provide techniques of teaching. With a somewhat shaky foundation, we carefully selected students, and in consultation with the Khmer administration of the camp, began the first eight-week modular training program. The most difficult thing was trying to get the teachers to accept this approach to teaching. Too often they would slip back into the position of lecturer and use complicated medical terminology. Keeping things simple is often very difficult.

The students were allowed to progress to the next module after successfully completing the first. Once the course was completed, most students not only had the skills for clinical practice but roughly half of them had also acquired or demonstrated an ability to teach those skills to others. I was allowed to recruit teachers for which another volunteer agency would pay. With a $750 cash donation, I was able to reimburse the airfare of one teacher and pay for the initial costs of setting up the experimental program. Finally, people were teaching. Even surgeons on relief-agency teams gave classes. What a sight it was to see a surgeon teaching microscopy on the top of a bunker where the light was best and there was the least chance of being run over by an ambulance. There they were huddled around the microscope: "Can you see the malaria parasites on this slide? What type are they?"

By the time we were in the third module of the program, I willingly turned the project over to the ICRC and the ARC so that I could oversee the final phase of the translation of *Where There Is No Doctor*. It was October 1980, and half the translation team had been called to the processing center at Chonburi, leaving behind in Khao I Dang one physician, two typists, and an artist. What could I do? The UNHCR had already sent their Khmer language expert to the holding center for three weeks to help in the grammar check of the book. Still, there were many changes to be made and so little time. I was getting exhausted from traveling back and forth between Khao I Dang and Chonburi in my pickup truck. One night, in Aranyaprathet, I asked the man in charge of UNHCR in Bangkok if we could transfer three people to Chonburi so that the translation work could be completed. He agreed. I drove the three kilometers to Chonburi the next day after overcoming several last-minute obstacles that at the time seemed insurmountable.

For the next month in Chonburi, we raced the clock. Each chapter received a final check for medical accuracy, grammar, consistent phraseology, phonetics, and typographical errors. All the illustrations were redone. Pages were renumbered and interfaced for photo offset, and I then began feeding them to the Ministry of Health in Phnom Penh for final approval. Through frequent correspondence with the ministry—with the help of Dr. Hennie Brown of Oxfam, we made the changes, additions, and deletions they required for acceptance by their government and hopefully ultimate distribution to the people. The book had been carefully translated to ensure that it remained politically neutral. We worked tirelessly.

Finally, the book was finished. On January 30, 1981, I left Bangkok for San Francisco with the completed manuscript, after sending one complete duplicate copy to Phnom Penh and leaving one locked in an office of the United States Embassy. Safeguarding the fruits of their labor had become routine by now, and each draft was duplicated and stored in Bangkok, just in case something happened in camp.

Shortly after returning to the United States, I went to Washington, D.C., to copyright the manuscript of the Khmer translation. The translators and all the other Khmer people responsible for producing the work had chosen to remain anonymous. The book was to be a gift to the Khmer people, without acknowledgments. Many people, however, now recognized the value of this labor of love, and although their perception was accurate—albeit rather delayed—their attempts to climb on the bandwagon were somewhat clumsy at so late a date. Offers to pay for the printing and to help arrange for shipping came from everywhere, all with the hope of registering credit for someone or some group. I am very pleased that 10,000 copies of the book are now in Phnom Penh and that 8,000 copies have been distributed along the Thai-Kampuchean border.

LESSONS LEARNED IN THAILAND

When a crisis occurs and people are in need of immediate assistance to remain alive, the media alert international communities and their agencies. "MASH"-type medical units are indeed needed, but their response to human needs should immediately signal the beginning of the second phase of relief—teaching, which should begin as soon as the mortality rates begin to drop. Before beginning any teaching, I suggest the following:

1. *Orient yourself:* Understand in depth the political, cultural, and traditional belief patterns of the people involved and those of the host country. Do not discredit any traditional beliefs of a culture.
2. *Find the cause of the crisis.* Look beyond the rumors. Has the cause been eliminated? Do not be too judgmental.
3. *Learn the religious beliefs of the people:* Do not interfere with their right to practice the religion of their choice. Support their right to practice their own religion.
4. *Learn the sort of medical problems and care that were available before the crisis and what will be available afterward:*

Try and find out what the approach to medical problems was, including the role of traditional medicine. Traditional medicine should not be discredited or underestimated in its effectiveness, value, or position it holds in the culture. Try to introduce a standard of medical care which the people will be able to maintain after you leave.

5. *Be neutral:* Be both politically neutral and religiously unobtrusive. Health care is a human right, not a political or religious privilege.

6. *Know the work of other agencies:* The goals and objectives of international relief agencies are not always the same. This demands compromise if you are to avoid not only conflict or competition but also duplication of services.

7. *Know the coordinating bodies:* International agencies have years of experience. Respect their advice, and educate yourself to their goals and perspectives. Work with them, not against them. Keep them informed.

8. *Break the habit of dependency:* Instead of saying, "Here, take this," say, "Here, do this for yourself and tell me what you need."

ASSESSMENT AND PLANNING

Assessment is necessary to prioritize needs and to determine what resources are immediately available and what will subsequently be. As soon as possible begin a realistic plan for training the people involved to meet their immediate needs and allow for your gradual withdrawal. Keep these teaching programs simple, aimed at educating all the people and not creating an elite group of trained refugees. The programs should be designed to "fill the gap" which will occur when you leave. People from within the population should be involved in the design of the program, student selection, and actual training using the native language. Great caution should be taken not to conflict with or discredit traditions.

Keep the classes small. Act as an adviser. Adapt and adjust your programs to meet changing needs. Always remain flexible

—bend like the bamboo reed in the wind. Do not make yourself indispensable. Keep a low profile. Examine your motives.

I have learned from the past two years' experience that nothing is impossible if you care enough to share. The kindest, most humane aid you can offer to displaced people is not necessarily money or equipment, but your self and the methods and the directions which may make it possible for them to help themselves using the resources available. Programs of *self*-help in medicine, food production, and housing, which are simple and clear and presented in the people's own language, following their cultural and traditional patterns are the most useful. Working your way out of a job means freedom from dependency. As soon as possible, give them the strength to stand alone, and if at all possible, do it as quietly and gently as possible. You can return for reassurance and "postevaluation" if necessary. Do not remind them of all you have done by placing stamps and signs on everything. This you really only need to protect yourself from other "relief agencies."

Be able to accept confusion and contradiction along the way. Know your own limits, discover theirs, and strive to reach appropriate goals.

TAKING ADVANTAGE OF THE SITUATION

A displaced person should not be considered a liability, for not all displaced persons are resettled and many, when possible, are repatriated. While they are displaced, there is a unique opportunity to prepare them for this repatriation, by teaching them practical skills for maintaining life, through self-education programs in health care, self-support in food production, low-cost energy sources, and housing. Do not waste your precious time and theirs teaching them technology which will most likely not be available to them after they return to their own land. When they return, life will be determined by food, shelter, clean water supplies, and the *basics* of health care. Keep in mind the resources with which they will have to work.

Improving the quality of their lives will depend on their

ability to be self-sufficient in the basic requirements of survival. What we can do is to try and "fill the gap" with clear, simple self-education programs whose sole purpose is to maintain life after the "emergency buttons" have been turned off, and the attention of the international community has gone elsewhere, along with its financial support.

CONCLUSION

Displaced persons are often in a particularly receptive state for learning. Because they are off-balance and they have no government of their own, there is also no infrastructure to prohibit teaching them. This can apply to small-scale agricultural programs, basic health programs, appropriate technology, or almost anything else. The vehicle of modular teaching, adapted to the geography, culture, tradition, and language of the persons involved, is the most efficient and most practical method of educating the most people in the least amount of time, and requires on their part the least amount of preparation. The host country will welcome this approach since it will decrease the dependency of the displaced, which is viewed as a political liability.

Generally, those persons who survive to become refugees are often the most resourceful and most flexible. Regardless of the land that they temporarily inhabit as displaced persons, refugees—or "illegal immigrants"—are responsive and receptive to almost anything you wish to teach. The opportunity to use this time to the best of their advantage must not be overlooked, for in many cases, neither you nor they may ever have a second chance.

PART 4

AID BEYOND THE HOLDING CENTERS IN THAILAND

VOLUNTARY AID INSIDE KAMPUCHEA

Joel R. Charny and Joseph Short

"Unless we act now we will see the possible extinction of Kampuchea before Christmas." It was with this urgent message for the Western press and international relief organizations that Jim Howard, the British Oxfam's disasters specialist, returned after a visit to Kampuchea in August 1979. Kampuchea's economy and communications infrastructure were in shambles, and the country's rice lands were largely unplanted for the fall harvest on which the people's food supply always so critically depended.

Over the next two years, the world mounted an extraordinary relief effort to save the Kampuchean people. By early 1981, there was undeniable evidence that the nation would survive and perhaps be firmly on the road to recovery by the end of the year. The fall rice crop of 1980 had been more than twice the size of the crop of the disastrous previous year and more than half of a normal year's yield.

What have we learned from the experience of helping the Kampucheans to survive and to rise above their cumulative

---

Joel R. Charny was an administrative officer with the Oxfam Consortium Team in Phnom Penh from July 1980 to February 1981, and continued to perform some work on Cambodian relief after that period. He is now Southeast Asia Projects Officer with Oxfam America in Boston. Joseph Short was Executive Director of Oxfam America from October 1979 to September 1984. He is now International Consultant with the American Council for Voluntary International Action, New York and Washington, D.C.

tragedies, and particularly from the experience of those voluntary aid organizations that operated *inside* Kampuchea? Our tentative answers are from the perspective of Oxfam America, which mounted a major media and fund-raising campaign in the United States for Kampuchea and was an active member of the Oxfam/NGO (nongovernmental organization) Consortium, which included 27 voluntary agencies and provided about $42 million in assistance by air and sea through Kompong Som and Phnom Penh between October 1979 and December 1980.

In Western countries, particularly in the United States, the crisis for the Kampucheans was initially portrayed by the press as mainly a crisis for the "refugees" in Thailand or along the Thai-Kampuchean border. Much public attention was fixed on aid to these displaced people, and this obscured the fact that most of the Kampucheans in need still remained within the borders of their native land and that-it was there that perhaps 60 percent of the millions of dollars in Western aid for Kampuchea would ultimately be distributed.

The immense challenge to whatever humanitarian relief agencies chose to work within the borders of Kampuchea was to ensure that the aid reached some five million people in a territory with ·a shattered transportation and communications infrastructure, an inexperienced and wary government installed by a Vietnamese force of occupation, and a population just emerging from one of the greatest traumas ever inflicted upon an entire nation.

The Joint Mission, composed of UNICEF and the ICRC, was entrusted with the difficult task of coordinating the entire relief effort. It is estimated that the Joint Mission, including affiliated United Nations agencies (WFP and FAO), spent more than $600 million on Kampuchean relief, of which approximately $320 million was spent inside Kampuchea. The major inputs of the Joint Mission program included 250,000 metric tons (MT) of food aid (mostly rice), 26,000 MT of rice seed for the 1980 rainy-season crop, 1,600 trucks, thousands of notebooks and other school supplies, and tons of medicines and hospital equipment. ICRC supplied medical teams for the hospitals in five cities and towns. UNICEF contributed port engineers, dock workers, and mechanics to service the huge fleet of vehicles that it provided.

International voluntary agencies responded with programs of significant but smaller magnitude. Consortia of small agencies were formed to increase coordination and impact; other agencies preferred to mount independent programs. Total non-governmental organization (NGO) expenditures amounted to almost $100 million; the Oxfam/NGO program alone spent $42 million.

While emergency food aid was the initial focus of the agencies working through Phnom Penh, most programs quickly evolved into support for the massive reconstruction efforts required in Kampuchea. Voluntary aid involved supplementing Joint Mission inputs in certain sectors, especially agriculture, and providing key and timely equipment and supplies that the Joint Mission was unable to provide. The voluntary agencies actually contributed as much rice seed and a greater amount of fertilizer, irrigation pumps, insecticide sprayers, hoe heads, and plow tips as FAO. Aid to industry, an irrigation rehabilitation program, and the refurbishing of a pediatric hospital in Phnom Penh are but a few examples of the unique contributions of the voluntary agencies.

Some of the items that the Oxfam/NGO Consortium shipped to Kampuchea were nearly 2,000 irrigation pumps, 13,500 MT of rice seed, 6,950 sprayers, 216,000 hoe heads, two garbage trucks, 200 wheelbarrows, 550 MT of aluminum sulfate fertilizer, 209 trucks, three ferries, 500 Khmer script typewriters, 150 sewing machines, and spare parts to rehabilitate textile, plastics, and fishnet factories.

No part of Kampuchean society was left untouched by the relief effort. International food aid provided rice rations for both government officials and peasants throughout 1980. In the countryside the average peasant family planted an international rice variety, fertilized it with imported fertilizer, and lessened insect damage with imported insecticide. Men and women gave up the black apparel of the Khmer Rouge for colorful *kromas* (scarves) and sarongs made from cloth manufactured with the aid of Western spare parts. Small diesel-powered irrigation pumps helped to irrigate additional hectares of rice in the dry season. When not helping their families with food production, one million Kampuchean children returned to schools equipped by UNICEF and the voluntary agencies. These inputs reached the provinces in trucks supplied by the international aid agencies. With the beginning of the harvest in December 1980, it was clear that the people of Kampuchea would survive.

Humanitarian aid in disaster situations often has political implications; this seems especially so in the case of Kampuchea where the struggle for governmental control of that country continues, where the near demise of an entire nation derived from political and diplomatic failures, and where even today the ultimate security of the people cries out for political and negotiated settlements.

With considerable justification, it has been argued that food to aid the Kampucheans in Thailand was diverted to bolster the resurgence of the Pol Pot forces—and that humanitarian aid inside Kampuchea indirectly fortified the present Vietnamese occupation. Because humanitarian aid may affect the balance of political forces within and among countries, diplomats of any nationality are tempted to block humanitarian aid to those people in "enemy" areas; but as the case of Kampuchea also demonstrates, they may temper their political cynicism with human kindness, or at least a more "flexible pragmatism." Asked if the government of Heng Samrin would object to assistance to the Kampucheans in Thailand, one minister replied: "We cannot deny help to our people in the refugee camps, although we do object to aid *over the border* which helps our enemy, Pol Pot." At the same time that an American diplomat was telling his colleagues, "We must bleed the Vietnamese so they will come to the bargaining table," the United States government was overcoming its initial reluctance to see any humanitarian aid routed through Phnom Pehn—which might help the Vietnamese—and was agreeing to provide food and financial assistance to intergovernmental agencies working inside the country.

What might the humanitarian-aid agencies have further done

to overcome or sidestep the political obstacles to meeting the life-or-death needs of literally hundreds of thousands of people in Thailand and Kampuchea? Humanitarian-aid agencies operating in disaster situations must hone in on the survival and emergency needs of people without primary reference to ultimate political goals and consequences. This response is more than rhetoric and easier said than done; it is an approach that will not please and may even antagonize the proponents of "playing hardball with the enemy." The corollary is that in an area of military conflict humanitarian-aid organizations have a moral and practical obligation to assure that the aid goes effectively and efficiently only to noncombatants. If humanitarian-aid organizations either deliberately or unwittingly use their resources to advance particular political or military objectives, they can readily forfeit their moral and practical standing that enables them to play a useful role.

One of the most practical lessons of the Kampuchea experience is that humanitarian-aid organizations should coordinate their efforts, so that acting together they can straddle political divisions and reach the maximum number of persons possible wherever they may be. It was very difficult for a single aid organization to operate in both Thailand and Kampuchea. Some like UNICEF finally did, but it was also advantageous that other organizations chose to accept the constraints of the political situation in order to operate more effectively in either one land or the other. The Oxfam/NGO Consortium, for example, consciously chose to work only inside Kampuchea, in the knowledge that many other Western aid organizations were moving rapidly to assist the Kampuchean refugees in Thailand. For this reason, in October 1979, Brian Walker, the director general of British Oxfam, was able to achieve the first formal aid agreement with the government of Kampuchea, providing a detailed framework for potentially massive aid from a Western source—perhaps as much as $50 million in assistance. Walker agreed that the Oxfam/NGO Consortium, contemplated by the agreement, would provide aid exclusively for humanitarian purposes and strictly avoid interference in the internal political affairs of Kampuchea. In particular, it was agreed that the consortium as such would not provide relief aid to the Pol Pot forces along the Thai border: it could, however, provide aid through Bangkok for Kampuchean refugees settled well within Thai borders. Privately Walker understood this as meaning that the consortium should accept the constraint of not providing any aid beyond the Thai border, because the Kampuchean government held that any cross-border aid was aid to Pol Pot. Again, Walker acted in the knowledge that other aid organizations were rushing to assist refugees in and through Thailand and with the conviction that practical constraints would need to be accepted to open desperately needed aid channels through Phnom Pehn.

The Oxfam agreement with the Kampuchean government also provided that consortium aid would be exclusively distributed by government ministries to Kampuchean noncombatants in cooperation with a Phnom-Penh-based team of seven consortium representatives. These representatives would be given full facilities to monitor the use of resources through on-site visits and regular government reports.

Thus, in zones of political and military conflict, voluntary relief agencies, especially those with little or no government funding, may have a special opportunity to be of service. If they abide by their professed standards of meeting emergency human needs, by whatever principled and practical means possible, they are able and willing to take risks to reach people who would otherwise be defined as beyond the pale of governments vying mainly for political advantage. British Oxfam took such a risk in initiating the consortium that worked through Phnom Penh.

Helping the majority of Kampucheans who remained within the country and averting the further migration of refugees became guiding principles for the Oxfam/NGO Consortium, and for other voluntary agencies. In retrospect, that approach seems all the more sensible and rational, but it can easily be forgotten how difficult and risky it was for voluntary agencies to establish operations within Kampuchea. Political and logistical obstacles might well have deterred any Western involvement there, as they actually did through months of inconclusive negotiation in the spring and summer of 1979. Later, the Oxfam/NGO Consortium had to weather unjustifiable charges that it was—by providing aid inside Kampuchea—acting as either a witting or unwitting tool of Vietnamese expansionism.

Another lesson is that wholly private voluntary agencies can often be of service in politically conflicted disaster situations which require rapid humanitarian action that governments, government-funded voluntary agencies, and intergovernmental agencies are unwilling to take. Oxfam America, for example, became the only United States voluntary agency to have a major funding and policy role in the predominantly European Oxfam/NGO Consortium, and this placed it among the few domestic organizations that could directly channel aid into Kampuchea, and with a steady flow of information from that country, interpret events and needs there to the American public. This probably would not have been possible if Oxfam America had been wholly or even partly dependent upon the United States government for its funding.

In just about every major disaster situation in modern history, voluntary-aid agencies have been faulted, however justifiably, for not concerting and coordinating their efforts to give assistance. The Kampuchea experience, by contrast, may have yielded more examples of successful interorganizational collaboration than any other comparable situation in memory, with the notable exception of the European Marshall Plan. Perhaps the main reasons for this cooperation were circumstantial: the monumental needs of Kampuchea dwarfed the means of any one organization and morally and practically demanded cooperation among aid givers. Within Kampuchea the expectations of the government, and minimal accommodation and transportation for resident aid teams virtually *required* cooperation. But even if necessity was the mother of invention, the lessons of successful cooperation may serve again in the future.

For this reason, the Oxfam/NGO Consortium may be an exemplary model for future consideration. The joint fund raising, decision making, and field administrative performance of the Consortium surpassed even the highest expectations of Oxfam and its other 26 fellow members. Although the Oxfam agreement originally provided a framework for aid in the general magnitude of $50 million, the members actually surprised even themselves by raising $42 million for the effort. None of the members was very experienced in interorganization decision making, and certainly none fully anticipated what voracious information-sharing needs would have to be met for effective policy making, administration, and attention from the press. Nevertheless, to provide joint policy direction for operations, an effective council of members was established, which met periodically in various Western European capitals. A management committee of several members, chaired by Oxfam, gave sustained leadership to the council. From its headquarters in Oxford, England, Oxfam managed a dramatically successful information clearinghouse. A complex supply-acquisition and shipping operation was established in Singapore.

By agreement with the Kampuchean government, the consortium fielded for 15 months a team of seven representatives based in Phnom Penh. Oxfam regularly provided the team leader and two other personnel, and the other members posted specialists in agriculture, engineering, medicine, and nutrition. The consortium also deployed several staff members to Phnom Penh for special purposes, such as water purification, vehicle maintenance, and general administration. Some of the many lessons from this collaborative experience deserve particular mention.

First, collaboration within the consortium and among other aid groups obviated the excessive foreign penetration so often associated with laissez-faire and organizationally chaotic foreign-aid programs, such as afflicted Bangladesh in the early 1970s. This was the effect, if not the intention, of Kampuchean government policies which restricted and closely regulated the terms of foreign agency operations inside Kampuchea.

Second, a consortium of aid givers can potentially create synergistic effects in field administration, fund raising, host government relationships, and the media that are more than the sum of the contributions that individual members might otherwise have contributed by themselves. Economies of scale and of division of labor were achieved in field administration and in delivering resources. Twenty-seven different members could leverage more donations in their respective countries by justifiably promoting the program of the entire consortium and by extolling the merits of collaborative action. The strength of numbers and the national diversity in the consortium added to the credibility and influence of the whole enterprise in the eyes of the Kampuchean government. The heterogeneous nature and effectiveness of the consortium gave it, in turn, a relatively high standing with the world press.

Third, it is probably imperative that one or a few members of any large and complex consortium have preeminence in policy direction and administration. British Oxfam was the senior partner of this consortium in initiating, directing, and administering the entire operation. It made the largest organizational and financial investment in the common enterprise, and incurred more risks and responsibilities. It also gained corresponding organizational credit and accomplished a far greater total impact.

The other members, at the same time, had to give up a measure of organizational identity and defer to Oxfam leadership for the common good, even when their sense of priorities was different from that of their senior partner. For leaders and followers alike, there were both benefits and costs; but the common purpose was indisputably well served. This, in the end, was due to the skill and commitment of individual leaders to making the consortium work and to creating a flexible framework of cooperation that utilized rather than obliterated the individual members' interests and outlooks.

Fourth, the field staffs of all the agencies involved were generally able to overcome the normal conflicts, jealousies, and insistence on individual organizational priorities, partly due to reasons unique to the Kampuchean context. The intense isolation of Phnom Penh helped to create a spirit of "We're all in this together." This isolation included the lack of Telex communication, the unreliable cable service, and the dependence on chartered flights which could be canceled at the whim of the Kampuchean and the Thai authorities or because of the inevitable mechanical problems. Merely to communicate with the logistics staff in Bangkok or Singapore, therefore, involved sharing the few existing communications links.

Fifth, the magnitude of the needs of the Kampuchean people meant that no one agency could reasonably claim exclusive right to provide aid in a given functional or geographic sector. The entire aid process was one of negotiation first, between the government of Kampuchea and the various aid agencies, and then, among the aid agencies themselves to avoid duplication and wasted resources. Restrictions placed by the government on aid of certain types—on the provision of numerous experts and on direct agency participation in training programs, for example—only increased agency solidarity when an issue was important enough to contest at the highest levels of government.

Under the leadership of the Joint Mission of UNICEF and ICRC, agencies working in a given functional sector, such as industry, health, or social welfare, formed working groups to coordinate aid and share project data in that sector. Some agencies, in addition to a sectoral focus, preferred to concentrate their work in a given geographical region.

A crucial issue that further fostered interorganizational unity was monitoring. In bringing aid to a country of five million inhabitants, spread out over a wide area and governed by a sovereign state, agencies were unable to oversee the progress of their aid from port to warehouse to distribution center to village. For logistical and security reasons, the government of Kampuchea sometimes restricted provincial travel by aid-agency officials. Thus personnel confined to Phnom Penh for lack of a guide or lack of ministerial cooperation came to depend on reports from outlying areas by those able to travel. Therefore for relief-agency personnel, a journey outside the capital involved not only monitoring one's own program but the responsibility both to make a general assessment of provincial conditions and to check on particular aspects of the projects of other agencies. Such information was avidly awaited and passionately discussed in weekly meetings throughout the emergency period. Through cooperative monitoring, the agencies developed a high degree of awareness and confidence that aid resources were being responsibly used by the Kampuchean government, despite occasional but passing crises of confidence.

A few simple principles, and corresponding strategies of aid giving, continued to serve well in Kampuchea.

Self-Help. Aid giving should be predicated upon respect for the recuperative and self-help capacities of people affected by disasters. If people are viewed as partners in a process of recovery rather than as "victims," aid giving taps into a virtually irrepressible vein of hope and initiative.

Those of us who visited Kampuchea in 1979 and 1980 were as easily moved to tears by the resilience of the Kampuchean people as by their unspeakable suffering. The rapid recovery of marketplaces, the reemergence of the decimated national ballet, the readiness of farmers and fishermen to work for recovery, and the spectacle of many roadside weddings and celebrations testified to the capacity of the Kampuchean people to come back.

Most agencies inside Kampuchea began with the genuine conviction that self-help would be the energizing force of recovery and that the aid program had to be imbued with this ideal. Kampuchea was also fertile with possibilities because it had relatively abundant agricultural and fishing resources, which could be rescued from the ravages of war. Food was desperately needed, but many aid groups wanted to create the thrust of assisting self-help from the outset. The very first of the shipments of aid sent from Singapore by the Oxfam/NGO Consortium contained, therefore, not only food but also hoes, vegetable seeds, and parts with which to repair farm machinery. As the months progressed, aid for self-help action increased dramatically. Father Theodore Hesburgh, the president of Notre Dame who visited Kampuchea in 1980, remembers that everywhere he traveled in the countryside, he encountered family vegetable gardens. Thousands of vegetable-seed packets, prepared in Singapore, had been disbursed in previous months by the Oxfam/NGO Consortium.

Thousands of fishnets were likewise distributed, and the adage of "giving a man a fishing pole" to help himself was further extended by providing parts to revive two fishnet factories in Phnom Penh. In the winter and spring of 1980, the aid agencies in close cooperation with the appropriate ministries in the struggling government placed highest priority on importing and distributing rice seed, fertilizer, and other inputs for the main rice crop.

Leveraging Impact. Aid giving in a desperate and chaotic situation can often be usefully targeted upon leverage points to achieve quantum leaps in the impact of aid. If relatively small and inventive voluntary agencies have a distinctive role to perform, it is often in initiating actions and breaking bottlenecks that open the way to the effective application of large volumes of aid by the largest agencies. This will usually require that highly qualified staff members, especially those in the disaster area, be given a large measure of discretion to use their ingenuity and to obligate funds.

Examples of the use of this leveraging strategy for Kampuchea abound. Transportation for getting aid to and distributed within Kampuchea was virtually non-existent in the fall of 1979. Oxfam's Guy Stringer was dispatched to Singapore to open a barging operation from there to Kampuchea's southern port of Kompong Som. It took a heroic effort to negotiate for rights to stage sea delivery of aid from Singapore, to persuade anti-Vietnamese dock workers to commit themselves to humanitarian aid for noncombatants, and to engage a shipping firm and reliable suppliers. Under threat of high seas, Guy Stringer accompanied the first shipment of supplies by barge, arriving in Kompong Som to be greeted by a reception committee of government ministers and watchful Vietnamese soldiers. Thirty-six more barges, carrying a total of 65,000 tons of supplies were thereafter sent by the Oxfam/NGO Consortium from Singapore to Kampuchea.

The Oxfam Consortium, UNICEF, and ICRC recognized immediately that limited land transportation was a severe bottleneck for a massive aid program. The Oxfam/NGO Consortium, for example, responded by airfreighting into Kampuchea 50 trucks, spare parts, and fuel, and ultimately provided

209 trucks. UNICEF became the major supplier of vehicles, shipping over 1,600 trucks from Japan and the German Democratic Republic. Repair shops were fitted and temporarily staffed by foreign technicians.

Appropriate Technology. A third principle of aid giving is that the aid and the technology provided should be appropriate to the needs and capacities of the local people. Virtually every disaster yields shocking stories of groups providing unusable supplies, such as high heels after the last Guatemala earthquake or potato chips for those starving in the Sahelian drought. Relatively few such stories are likely to emanate from the Kampuchea experience, although the seemingly inevitable supplies of mislabeled and expired medicines certainly found their way there.

Nevertheless, the aid organizations were continually faced with such questions as: Could Kampuchean farmers effectively use this or that variety of imported rice seed? Could imported vehicles be properly serviced and would fuel for them be available? What supply-distribution needs could be met by traditional bullock carts rather than trucks? Would certain imported insecticides and rodenticides for rice production have the unintended effect of killing fish in the waters of the rice paddies? Would diesel-powered irrigation pumps make sense? We may never have a clear assessment of how well the aid agencies conformed to the unquestionably valid principle of providing appropriate technology. Our own sense is that there was a rather remarkable success in applying it, under time and logistical constraints virtually unparalleled in the history of human disasters.

Equitability. A fourth principle is admittedly political in character and should be respectfully negotiated with the host government as an agreed guiding principle for an entire aid operation. This might be labeled the "principle of equitability" and prescribes that aid should be fairly distributed to all those in need; to those, for example, living in rural as well as urban areas. Contrary to many adverse press reports, the aid teams in

Phnom Penh never encountered evidence of significant mani-
pulation of aid resources as a political tool to reward or punish
particular sectors of the society, except perhaps in the war
zone of the Thai border; but several factors, such as a poor
transportation network, contributed to an urban bias.

Toward Reconstruction and Development. A very important
principle is that aid givers can and should work with sensitivity
on the ways by which the disaster-stricken country may move
from a state of emergency through stages of reconstruction and
development. This principle unifies the others by suggesting
that a massive aid effort, such as occurred for Kampuchea, will
inescapably influence the way that country evolves thereafter,
such as in distribution of population, communications networks, educational practices, and even in its development strategies. The Kampuchean government closely regulated the aid
process to the point of severely restricting foreign technical
assistance especially from non-Socialist countries, however,
by accepting massive aid it also exposed the country to
significant outside social influences.

Communicating About Disasters. Finally, there is a cluster
of lessons to be gleaned from the near-epic experience of communicating with mass audiences about the nature and needs of
a human disaster such as Kampuchea. Oxfam America, as the
only United States voluntary agency active in the Oxfam/NGO
Consortium, and as one of the very few American groups ever
to become operational inside Kampuchea, was uniquely placed
to convey information about conditions inside Kampuchea and
to interpret events from an insider's perspective.

Oxfam America through major newspaper advertising did indeed alert the American public to the tremendous needs of the
Kampuchean people: through direct mail, by which it raised
nearly $5 million from thousands of donors, through its grass-
roots mobilization networks as in its annual Fast for a World
Harvest, through literally scores of television and radio appear-
ances, through several committee hearings before Congress,
through three national meetings at the White House, and through

a multitude of informal and formal information-sharing networks, including the Cambodia Crisis Committee founded by national leaders and organizations.

LESSONS TO BE LEARNED

There are numerous lessons to be learned from this experience. First, any aid agency should develop an explicit strategy and plan of communication, which it consciously adapts to new needs as they arise. Oxfam America, for example, established a task force of key staff members who would be communicators for various purposes and audiences. Specific objectives and audiences were targeted for attention, but always within the framework of an agreed-upon list of principles and themes. It was agreed that all communication should stress the proven capacity of the Kampucheans to help themselves; they should be portrayed as partners, not as victims. Second, communication about disasters begs for close consultation and information sharing among key organizations in a disaster aid response because the task is quite often beyond the means of a handful of organizations. For Oxfam America and the other voluntary agencies, this began simply with intensive telephone contact and emergency meetings. This networking evolved into unprecedented forms of organized cooperation through the good offices of such organizations as the Overseas Development Council, the American Council of Voluntary Agencies in Foreign Service, and the Cambodia Crisis Center administered by the Indochina Refugee Action Center. Among many noteworthy examples of cooperation, The Hunger Project arranged national newspaper advertising that netted about $1 million in contributions to 12 American voluntary agencies with operational aid programs for the Kampucheans. Finally, humanitarian-aid organizations have the responsibility of helping citizens, government officials, journalists, and diplomats to understand the preconditions for the survival and permanent recovery of people ravaged by disaster. This is a sensitive task fraught with peril, but nonetheless the obligation of those organizations who by virtue of their work in the disaster area know what needs to be done. While this, above all, means that such organizations must focus on immediate survival and basic needs, they can ignore but not escape the responsibility of proposing broad principles for lasting remedies to a crisis that goes beyond the material assistance they provide.

Kampuchea is one of the great man-made disasters of all time, and the sensitive and experienced humanitarian aid organizations know that in the end the permanent welfare of the Kampuchean people depends upon diplomatic solutions, which at the end of 1981 still seemed remote indeed. Such solutions must, to a major extent, depend upon the principles of self-determination for the Kampuchean people and upon mutual security agreements among the nations of the region that are sanctioned by the major world powers.

Furthermore, until a reasonably stable polity and economy can be restored in Kampuchea, the premature termination of Western foreign assistance for relief and development could quickly undermine the country's still precarious recovery.

The major lesson of this experience is that the world can act to save an entire nation, and accomplish this within the brief period of two years. But unless peaceful diplomatic settlements are achieved and substantial economic aid is continued, the Kampuchean people could even more swiftly return to the abyss.

MEDICAL CARE INSIDE KAMPUCHEA

Josiane Volkmar-Andre

The mission that brought my colleagues and me to Phnom Penh was the opening of a pediatric hospital with an outpatient clinic and a 60-bed inpatient unit. The hospital had originally been completed in April 1975; then when the equipment was in place and the staff on its way, the government surrendered to the Khmer Rouge. It was used by Pol Pot as a torture chamber for deserting intellectuals. In October 1980, the hospital reopened with a staff consisting of me, another doctor, a nurse, a lab technician, and 70 Khmers.

Past history assists in understanding present medical care in Kampuchea. During the Angkor civilization under the Leper King, there had been a medical faculty (medical school) and hospitals. Before the arrival of the French in the mid-nineteenth century, the practice of medicine in Cambodia was very similar to that in China: administration of roots, barks, leaves, shells, and liver, and reduction of fractures. From the time of the arrival of the French until their departure in the mid-1950s, Western medicine developed very slowly. The main center of French medicine was in North Vietnam, and the Cambodians went there to train until 1948, when the medical faculty opened in Phnom Penh. This medical faculty developed and

---

Josiane Volkmar-André, a physician, worked with World Vision International as Head of the World Vision Children's Hospital in Phnom Penh from October 1980 to April 1981. She is now a medical relief worker with the French branch of the Hospital Christian Fellowship, based in Strasbourg, France. She currently lives in Chad.

progressed to modern medicine only after independence several years later. First, there were still French professors, but gradually they were replaced by Khmers who had taken further training in France. Nursing, midwifery, dental, and pharmacy schools also started about that time. In the countryside, a network of hospitals and dispensaries was functioning well.

From 1970 to 1975, a military medical system developed with the assistance of American military advisers. In 1975, when Pol Pot took over, there were more than 600 doctors and 600 medical students. In the four years of his regime of terror, no appropriate medical care was available. No doctors, nurses, or midwives were allowed to practice. There were no medicines. So-called medical care was given by "the barefoot doctors," teenagers from 12 to 15 years old who had three months of training. They treated the sick as hopeless victims, practicing sexual abuse and experimental surgery. Without aseptic techniques, they injected patients with dirty water, coconut milk, or other concoctions; many ill people died as a result. Anesthesia was administered by the old method of a blow on the neck! After these dark years in which 350 doctors were exterminated, more than 200 physicians escaped to countries of asylum and less than 50 remained in the country. The same proportions also apply to paramedical workers and medical students.

In 1979, after the invasion of the Vietnamese, people began to come back to Phnom Penh to try to find their families, to establish roots, or to receive better food and medical care. In 1980, the population of Phnom Penh increased from 50,000 to 500,000, with another 500,000 in the surrounding province.

The 50 Khmer doctors remaining in the country were equally divided between the countryside and the capital. In Phnom Penh, they had to assume political, teaching, and practicing functions.

Answering a challenge that certainly required faith, the medical faculty reopened under the dedicated care of Dr. Me Samdee. There were no books, laboratory equipment, furniture, or teachers. The students had not received any training or education for five years. They had been broken by fear, famine, hard work, and the loss of their families. They were all five years older than medical students generally are.

The need for medical care, however, was so great and so desperate that something had to be done. Foreign help was very reluctantly accepted. Some physicians came from Vietnam, Cuba, Soviet Russia, and other Eastern-bloc countries, but the problems of adjustment, language, lack of training in tropical medicine, and the shortness of the stay of many physicians made it difficult to have any semblance of efficiency—let alone, of teaching.

Instructors were, therefore, recruited from among the Khmer doctors, many of whom had never before been involved in teaching. All of them were busy with numerous tasks—reorganizing the hospitals, treating the flood of patients, participating in politics, and finally, teaching. They had not seen a medical book for five years and hardly had access to any. They would teach from their memory and experience, mainly in French. (There is no medical vocabulary in Khmer.)

In October 1980, when I arrived, there were about 150 medical students. They had just received chairs and desks, and two vans to help with transportation. A few books were to be found in the library, but many more had yet to come. Some lab equipment had also arrived, but the up-to-date trained personnel to direct the lab sessions was missing.

Every morning, the students worked in the hospital and dispensaries. They rotated for periods of six weeks in the various units: surgery, obstetrics, medicine, TB, pediatrics, malaria. In the sixth year, they would choose one of these units for specialization. Each afternoon they joined the faculty for lectures: one-third on the Vietnamese language and politics, two-thirds on medical subjects. Political sessions on special occasions and political duties, such as harvesting or cleaning the streets before a festival, would often alter this schedule. The students had no time to read or to prepare personal works. In addition, some students and young doctors would be sent unexpectedly to Vietnam or Soviet Russia on three days' warning. This system compromised the continuity of teaching.

By October 1980, a few hospitals had reopened and were

functioning more or less efficiently. There were thousands of sick people, but the overwhelming crowds of 1979 had diminished; most of those patients had died. Now there was an average of about one bed for each patient, and mats and blankets, drugs and laboratory facilities, and surgical and obstetrical services were available.

The Cambodian doctors and students were assisted by a few foreign doctors. The pediatric facilities were all concentrated in the "Seventh of January Hospital" (Hôpital de 7 janvier) in a 100-bed unit. Some cots had recently arrived, donated by the Polish Red Cross. The OPD, run by the Comité Francais, would have about 100 consultations a day. Intravenous infusions, drugs, and oxygen were supplied by the government. The lab was barely adequate; there was much technology, but few trained people. The flame photometer had been partially eaten by rats! Besides, the necessary gas to run it was unavailable.

That same month, we visited a country hospital in Kompong Speu, which was run by the ICRC. The ICRC had had the uneasy task of setting up teams from the Eastern-bloc nations in rural hospitals and providing them with drugs and equipment. The collaboration with these Eastern European governments was difficult. In this particular hospital, a Hungarian team was working. It had just arrived for a three-month stay, but there was no continuity; the previous team had left two months before. Hospital activity had almost stopped, while everyone waited for the new team to take over. There was no Khmer doctor, but two Vietnamese doctors were doing some surgery. The obstetrical unit was well run by a good Khmer midwife, and the rest, including a TB ward, was under the supervision of a Khmer nurse.

In November 1980, I slipped into a dispensary in Phnom Penh without permission and without warning. It looked much like a drugstore. The mothers would come with their children and ask for powdered milk, cough syrup, or other medications. There were adults who came as well. Nobody was individually registered, weighed, or measured; only the total number of patients was counted. Rarely a stethoscope was put on a chest, and there was no facility in which to examine the patients.

Soon afterward, the dispensaries stopped giving out milk powder and high-protein biscuits, although tons had been brought into the country by a number of relief agencies. The reason was that some mothers had been caught selling powdered milk on the black market. The government thereafter kept the milk in its state stores, where it was available only to government workers.

In the dispensary, I met a woman doctor who was responsible for organizing the primary health care. She was tough and intelligent, and was very unhappy about the situation. She told me that she had been trying to explain and distribute the "Road to Health Chart" to the 128 infirmaries in Phnom Penh. In doing so, she had often encountered inadequate buildings, inadequate water supplies, inadequate hygiene, and inadequately trained people. Even worse was seeing nurses selling medications to the people in order to make money, instead of caring for the patients.

Before the opening of the Pediatric Hospital, we also visited the orphanages, four in Phnom Penh and one in Kompong Speu: two housed 500 orphans, ages six to 16; one housed the older ones and the handicapped and the other, the younger children. The orphans attended school and were given a thorough political indoctrination with films, loudspeakers, and lectures. Toys, games, and sports were almost unknown. Music, dancing, and painting were done mainly for the visitors. In one of these orphanages, 16 adults were assigned to the 500 children. They divided them into small families, in which the older ones took care of the younger ones. These groups were self-sufficient, and the leaders would counsel and supervise.

The nutritional state of these orphans was at the lower limit of normal. They received enough rice but very little else. The government allotted one riel per child each day. Out of the 30 riel received per month, 14 were used for rice; five were given to the child as pocket money; and 11 were left for fish, eggs, chicken, vegetables, and fruit. The children spent their pocket money buying sweets or sherbet made with water from the Mekong River; as a result, many had parasites.

The medical care in these orphanages was poor. There was

just one primary nurse with a few medications in each orphanage. There was no regular control of the children's weight; the authorities stated that the children were weighed monthly, but I never could see any record or scale.

Officially we were not allowed to visit any public building, private home, or anywhere else without permission and without the presence of our guide or driver. Nevertheless, because the work at the hospital sometimes brought me into special circumstances, I took the liberty unexpectedly to visit some of the orphanage buildings, and then I saw what is usually not shown to foreigners.

In the orphanage for older teenagers, I sensed an atmosphere of heavy depression. These young people seemed to have no interest, and no purpose in their lives. Most of them had not had any education before the accession of Pol Pot and could neither read nor write. They now were being intensely trained to read and write and to participate in politics. Our relief organization had provided them with several facilities, most notably a center for apprenticeship, but none of us was allowed even to speak to them. In mid-December, 40 were sent to Soviet Russia; they had no choice in the matter. All had experienced great trauma, all had lost their families, all had been involved in forced labor during their childhood years. They were pathetic.

The handicapped children were then also in this orphanage though later they were transferred to a shabby building in a remote part of the city. I made friends with a little blind girl who in her desperation with tears flowing from her sightless eyes, told me her story. I was never allowed to visit her again.

In November 1980, a relief agency, which had set up several centers for the handicapped in Vietnam was allowed to come to Kampuchea to study a similar project. The report was given to the government at the end of November, but by April nothing had been decided.

In January 1981, a well-built handicapped boy, about 16 years old, was brought to the hospital needing surgery of the hip. Such surgery could not be done in Kampuchea because of the risk of infection, so we worked out a plan to send him to East Germany. An agrement had been made between Kampuchea and East Germany for the transfer of ten patients a year who needed special surgery. The report, written in English, French, German, and Khmer, was brought to the attention of the Ministry of Health at the end of January; in April the boy was still in Kampuchea.

The last orphanage—for those under the age of five—was located at the corner of the street next to our hotel. Every day, from two to ten of these small children were sent to the Pediatric Hospital, so I visited this orphanage on a daily basis. It had the pompous name of Nutrition Center, but it might better have been called Malnutrition Center. One hundred children were under the care of six adults helped by 25 older orphan girls. A teacher and an orphan girl were in charge of the 32 children above the age of three. The children played, lived, slept, ate, and were taught in one big room. They never went for a walk, their small dusty garden was full of rusty pieces of metal and later was turned into a vast unprotected hole for the cellar of a new building.

The care of the babies was shared among the older girls who would usually look after six of them at a time, sleeping and living with them day and night. They lived in an old house with a leaky roof, no electricity, a run-down water supply, and clogged toilets and drainage. The girls had no training and almost no education. General hygiene and sanitation were very poor. As a result, four months after the opening, 46 of the 83 babies under six months of age had died, but the house was still full because of new admissions.

Two Khmer primary medical-care nurses would carefully follow our instructions regarding medications, but they were not properly trained to supervise hygienic living conditions. The orphan girls would get tired of being there seven days a week; some got sick, and others would play hookey (go away) for a few hours. Nothing was done by the government to improve their status or to increase the number of nurses.

Several people and organizations tried to help modify these terrible conditions. Material aid was always accepted, but teaching help was not. Many visits, a special session at the mayor's office, and coordination with the other agencies slowly improved the situation.

Apart from these orphans, thousands of other children had lost their parents. Many went to live with distant relatives or friends, but hundreds of homeless children roamed the streets, eating leftovers from markets or restaurants. Walking late at night, one would see them lying packed like sardines on the sidewalks.

THE PEDIATRIC HOSPITAL

October 15, 1980, was the opening day of the Pediatric Hospital. After the official ceremony, the OPD opened and the patients literally flowed in. After a week of free entry, with more than 250 patients admitted a day, we had to find a way of limiting the flow. We had already been pressed by events to open the inpatient unit.

There was some disagreement among us, as the Khmers wanted only those who came with an official paper from a dispensary or from a district officer to be given free admission. We, on the other hand, were afraid that because of corruption, this would limit our selection to the wealthier patients. We finally agreed to give free admission to all orphans, to the children of members of our staff, to emergency patients, and to those patients who had already been treated if they could show us their appointment cards.

The Khmer staff of the hospital increased from 60 to 90. The director was one of the two pediatricians left in the country after Pol Pot. He was gentle and kind, and overall a dedicated practitioner, in addition to being the father of nine children and foster father of three orphans. His wife was mentally ill, however, and he did not want to lose his position by standing up for the hospital, so when difficulties occurred, he just kept silent.

Besides the director, there was the hospital administrator, a hard-line Communist who had had some nursing training and been a taxi driver before Pol Pot. He was intelligent and hardworking. He was active in negotiations with the Ministry of Health to obtain the release of drugs and more personnel, food, oxygen, and money for the hospital staff. The monthly pay was 80 to 120 riels, which seemed very low, and indeed made it difficult for our personnel even to feed themselves. A typical businessman or seamstress earned 600 riels a month. Nevertheless, none of our workers would have given up their jobs because government jobs brought many advantages, especially access to the state stores. As an example, rice cost one riel per kilogram in the state stores and up to three riels per kilogram in the public market.

Fifteen state nurses (with training equivalent to a registered nurse in the United States) had been assigned to the hospital, and this was a great luxury since most hospitals only had one to three. I found it difficult to accept that some of these nurses would be assigned to work in the laboratory or in the administration of the hospital. Nevertheless, we were unable to do anything to change that. Some of the nurses were old, and all suffered from psychological problems due to the terrible fears they had experienced under the Khmer Rouge. All had lost family members. They had been properly trained to give drugs and injections, but they had been taught very little about hygiene and nursing care.

The other nurses had very little training; they had taken a hurried six-month course given by uncertain teachers. We found that they desperately needed to learn simple hygiene, cleanliness, and elementary nutrition for the first six months. Chart notes and simple graphics were usually written by the head nurse since the others were unable to do so. We rapidly discovered that the best help would come from the mothers, who were the most highly motivated individuals and never left their children alone in the hospital.

A large administrative staff was kept busy with registrations and demands from the ministries. They would request the help of operating-room personnel to make pennants for numerous special Communist events. A small staff would wash, sew, cook, and supervise the stores. The pharmacist, lab and x-ray technicians, and the operating-room and OPD nurses completed the staff of the hospital. Nobody was specifically assigned to do cleaning and gardening. The cleaning was done by everyone each morning and on Saturday afternoon after the political meeting. Gardening was also done then or in the evening if people were free. On Sundays our staff was regularly required to clean the streets or the market. The six-and-a-half-day work schedule, which included one or two night shifts, severely hindered the staff members' power of concentration, as did the heat and the aftereffects of malnutrition and suffering.

The key person at the hospital was the pharmacist. He was a very intelligent, dedicated, and honest man, and he was a great help in solving our problems with the dispensing of drugs. When we arrived, drugs had already been ordered from Singapore by our predecessor, who also had been in charge of ordering the medical equipment. Fortunately, the orders were large enough; the varieties of different drugs available were well over 200! Nevertheless, after six weeks we realized that some of the drugs had not been delivered, the stock of some had already been totally depleted, and that drugs were being prescribed in excessive amounts. By that time, we had already reordered some drugs from Singapore, but the supplier misunderstood our most important requests. So we developed an urgent approach that included establishing a drug list of 100 preparations, setting up a system of labeling boxes of medications to minimize theft and loss, and teaching the OPD staff to use fewer of them. It took six months to establish this system, and even then it did not function properly, so you can imagine how we felt during epidemics of measles or diarrhea. I suppose most relief workers go through these battles, but we certainly learned to rejoice over the arrival of any drug.

Although the Pediatric Hospital was built by a relief organization, it was considered to be one of the university hospitals with a teaching program. The dean of the faculty and the hospital director insisted that the teaching inside the hospital must be done by foreigners. This situation was somewhat contradictory, because no Khmer was allowed to speak to foreigners without being suspected of being a CIA agent. Our task was accordingly very delicate. As I was the only one who spoke fluent French, I did most of the teaching. There were several kinds of students: third- and fourth-year medical students, nurses, and health officers (former state nurses training to be doctors). Continuity in teaching was difficult because no one ever knew in advance how many students would come and for how long. The training of the Khmer staff was more regular, but as it was not compulsory, it lacked motivation.

Apart from the irregularity of the students participating in the teaching program, the daily working schedule was very much impaired by politics. One never knew how many of the staff would be present. Politics had priority over care in every respect. Day after day new slogans were nailed on the walls, but pictures, even in the children's wards, were not permitted. Strict governmental control tended to discourage good work; it led to a lack of motivation in the care of the patients, and a high rate of absenteeism.

Seasonal changes brought a number of epidemics: in the fall of 1980, viral conjunctivitis often combined with vitamin-A deficiency; in the winter of 1981, measles affecting mainly malnourished children complicated with severe laryngitis, pneumonia, and bloody diarrhea—several died; and in the spring of 1981, gastroenteritis and skin infections.

During the six-month period from October 1980 to April 1981, malnutrition was found in one-fourth of the OPD children and in two-thirds of those hospitalized. Although the general food supply was more or less adequate, malnutrition still appeared as a result of ignorance and poor social conditions. Working mothers did not breast-feed their babies long enough. Among the poorest, widows or abandoned women had a hard time feeding their families, often augmented by one or two orphans. Small children were left in the care of the elder ones while the mother tried to earn some money. Over one-third of the women had no husband to support them.

Among the less frequent diagnoses, we saw tuberculosis (still 8 percent of all cases), a few cases of leprosy, glomerulonephritis, meningitis, polio, tetanus, burns, fractures, hemorrhagic fever, heart disease, thalassemia, hepatitis, and neurologic disorders. All admitted patients had at least two or three diagnoses. Anemia was present in most of the malnourished who also had infections, diarrhea, or worms or other parasites. The multiplicity of pathology, combined with a small laboratory, made it very difficult to develop precise statistics. We were particularly struck by the number of deaths. Children were often brought from very far away to be treated at the Pediatric Hospital, and many of them reached there too late, indicating that peripheral health service was still poor.

In view of the amount of malnutrition, our first idea was to institute a supplementary-feeding unit for the poorest children on the grounds of the hospital. The need for personnel and food, the overwhelming task of starting the hospital, and the distance from the patients' homes to the hospital led us to abandon the project. We felt it must be undertaken by the city social service. We therefore tried to sensitize the government and to counsel the mothers as much as we could with talks, pictures, and personal advice. Although immunization had a high priority on our list, the program, undertaken in collaboration with UNICEF, was delayed for various reasons. We accordingly started immunization on a small scale by inoculating the children of our staff members. The "Road to Health Chart" was an entirely new concept to the Khmer staff. Their education was much more geared toward the use of innumerable drugs. It took many hours to make them aware of the need for good nutrition and to warn them against the dangerous effects of antibiotics and cortisone, which they liked to use for everything.

LATER DEVELOPMENTS

Under a joint ICRC/UNICEF operation, a medical-assistance program developed in Kampuchea in 1980. The previous year, a Swiss doctor and a nurse had started to evaluate the need for qualified medical personnel. They constituted an alliance between the Red Cross and the Red Crescent Societies of the USSR. In 1980, a Russian team arrived in Phnom Penh first, and was then followed by Hungarian, Polish, East German, and Swedish teams. They worked in the hospitals there and in most of the provinces. At the end of 1980, 31 relief workers, mostly doctors and nurses, were involved. According to ICRC, 800 village primary-health centers, 140 country dispensaries, 20 country hospitals, and 750 other medical units were provided with standardized material, drugs, first-aid kits, and when necessary, fresh blood. Nutrition assistance under medical supervision was also provided, using high-protein biscuits, sugar, powdered milk, and vegetable oil.

At the end of 1980, a medical mission sent to survey the situation reported that although the needs were still very great, they were projected as no longer qualifying for emergency aid. Thus the ICRC planned gradually to disengage and to try to coordinate this disengagement with the implementation of other organizations working in reconstruction and development.

CONCLUSION

Millions of refugees, victims of war, and malnourished people face death every day in this world. To be part of a team helping such hopeless people is the biggest reward I or anyone else could receive: *As you did it to one of the least of these my brethren, you did it to me* (Matthew 25:40).

HOSPITALS DURING THE POL POT REGIME: A CAMBODIAN MEDICAL STUDENT'S PERSPECTIVE

Seang M. Seng

In the Pol Pot regime, hospitals were not created to provide health care but to prepare the patients for death. The usual "hospital" was a big hut with torn roof and no walls. Some patients who were lucky might have their own beds, some who were less fortunate just lay on the bare ground. When the rain came, some could move to the middle of the hut, but some were too weak and could not even crawl; thus they were left wet and shaky. It was even in a worse state than a barn was in the former regime. Patients were considered lazy people; their value was given less than animals, and hence, they were treated very badly.

Ninety percent of the time, patients got two to four cups of dilute porridge per day with nothing else but a half spoon of salt. The "nurses," ranging from 8 to 12 years of age, were allowed to give intramuscular and intravenous medicines. The injectable medicines were collected in soda bottles wrapped tightly on their openings by plastic sheets and rubber bands. The nurses could tell which medicines were which by their colors: vitamin C was white; vitamin B_{12} was red. . . .

With the hospital of 150 beds, they had only one good syringe and two broken ones, which also were used. These three syringes were boiled in the early morning and used until the next day. I personally had experience with these soda bottles, labeled Quinine, once intravenously. Fortunately I survived. The treatment was based almost totally on traditional medicines, such as bark, roots, and tree leaves, or pills made from rice flour. The three common pills they had were swelling pills, diarrhea pills, and fever pills. But no one seemed to care about these medicines. First, because of their inefficacy, and second, because generally speaking, the patients were not sick but starved. The patients almost always threw the pills away after the nurses had gone. What was life but the seeking of a full stomach, the running away from starvation? Dishes did not need to be washed: the patients' tongues would lick them thoroughly until no ant could detect the leftover.

APPROPRIATENESS OF SERVICES
IN EASTERN THAILAND

Martin Barber

A concern to many of us throughout the relief operation and a particular worry of the Thai authorities was the level of services provided to the refugees. It is a maxim of UNHCR's assistance procedures that the level of services provided to refugees should be related to the standard of living of the surrounding population. Where the local population's living standards are unacceptably low, then UNHCR should try to ensure that programs provided for the refugees should also be available to local people.

Eastern Thailand is generally a poor, rather arid region. In many villages, only the most minimal health care is available. Meat and fresh vegetables are available only erratically. Many of these villages were to be dramatically affected by the sudden arrival of the vast network of aid, which brought supplies not only to the holding centers but to the thousands of Khmers living on the border. For some local people this was a bonanza; they set up every conceivable type of commerical operation to service the many relief workers. For others, the new situation meant only a rise in the prices of basic commodities and a harder life.

The Thai government had some success in persuading UNICEF, WFP, ICRC, and a number of the voluntary agencies to contribute to a program for "Thai affected villages." This assistance was nothing compared to what flooded into the holding centers. Thai villagers looked on bemused as many Khmers sat doing nothing in a huge field behind a fence and had all their necessities trucked in by those crazy foreigners, while Thai farmers sweated desperately in the hot sun to earn enough to buy a few aspirins for their headaches. It is an odd world!

THAI VILLAGE PROGRAM

Richard W. Steketee

Heidi, sitting on the porch surrounded by curious women and slightly more fearful children, was a heartwarming sight. Behind the oversized sunglasses, she persisted in chiding the women in her broken but ever-improving Thai into letting her know who actually lived there, what were the names, ages, and sexes of the children. The men seemed to stand at a farther distance, more reserved but no less curious.

It was the beginning of the hot season in early 1980. We were in Ban Ma Kok, a small village of just over a thousand people, located several kilometers north of the town of Ta Praya along the Thai-Kampuchean border. Our Filipina nurse, Heidi, was busy at her morning activity of surveying the village families and developing our medical-record system. I was wandering through the handcrafted houses, looking for their official government numbers and making a map of the village that would allow us to find our patients for follow-up care. Other members of the team were doing the same, surveying the families and mapping the village.

We were in the midst of a public-relations campaign, trying to let the people know who we were and to find out who they were. After they received their pink family card with the house

Richard W. Steketee is a family physician who worked as Director of the Mobile Medical Unit of the International Rescue Committee in Thailand from February to June 1980. He is now an Epidemic Intelligence Service Officer in the Malaria Branch, Division of Parasitology, Centers for Disease Control, United States Public Health Service, Atlanta, Georgia.

number on it that corresponded to our records, they often brought in some family member with a medical problem to be checked. We asked them to come to the afternoon clinic and joked in the universal language of smiles and handwaving. The people were accepting, and in some villages, most hospitable—and they were always curious.

The days in other villages would be similar, though each had its own character. Some had a well-organized headman who was congenial and helpful while others had headmen who were either perpetually absent or "out back," drinking rice wine with their friends. We learned to seek out certain villagers for their smiles, their kindness, or sometimes their troubles. Each day we learned a little more about who they were and what it was that we could—or should—do.

The Thai Border Village Mobile Outreach Program (often known as "the mobile medical teams") along the Thai-Kampuchean and Thai-Laotian borders began in February 1980. The Kampuchean refugee camps and holding centers had then been in existence for a few months, and the Laotian ones for about five years. Likewise, the villages on the Thai-Kampuchean border that served as the overland food bridge to those in Kampuchea had been served by ICRC for several months. By that time, much had happened for the Kampuchean and Laotian refugees, and it was apparent that the villages within Thailand were not receiving any comparable assistance. In addition, there were important considerations for the Thai government and military that the villages along the border area remain supportive of the present Thai regime. Thus, from its inception, a primary objective of the mobile outreach medical program was one of public relations—between the voluntary agencies and the Thai government, and between the Thai government and military and the villagers.

This public-relations campaign was by no means trivial amidst the large-scale relief operation that was underway. Even the relations among the voluntary agencies stood to benefit from a separate program outside the camps where each agency had its own "turf" and still had the potential of working with other agencies on large-scale projects, such as immunization or sanitation.

The Thai military, which at this time was the political force in the region, was given responsibility for assigning the voluntary agencies among the villages. The region north of Aranyaprathet and north of Khao I Dang was chosen for the beginning of the mobile medical program. The village of Ta Praya became the central location of operations. Many agencies became involved. The Thai military, which also had responsibility for the coordination of efforts, often sent one or two soldiers to accompany the medical team. Certainly, it was good public relations for the military to escort the medical teams to the villages, and the military could then observe the activities of the medical-team members as well as those of the villagers.

The medical teams, however, were left to their own devices in deciding what they would do in their assigned villages and how often they would visit them. Each team had its own style and approach. All of them provided some form of medical clinic in which they evaluated patients, and prescribed and dispensed medications. Some teams covered two or three villages; others, five or six. Thus some teams went out daily while others went out only two or three times a week. Some teams had members that rotated weekly or monthly with fellow workers in the holding center at Khao I Dang, while others had permanent members. In the first months, it was helpful to meet briefly with members of other teams and ask how they worked and what they did.

The work had a guts-and-glory sound to it: the mobile medical team out there saving lives where villagers had never before seen a physician or nurse. The aura might easily have stayed. All the other expatriates were working in the camps. They knew each other and saw each other's daily work. But the mobile teams drove off down the road, and all that those working in the holding center had were our stories.

I recall the third day out. We had received a 50-kg bag of rice and had made arrangements to take it to a Khmer settlement along the border and save lives with this food. This was the big time, driving out to the border where people carried their guns wherever they went. We arrived at a very scattered encampment with more than a thousand people living in the barest of makeshift huts. Our 50-kg bag of rice was simply a cruel joke. It was time to return to the villages.

We were not a disaster-relief team; that was neither our directive nor our intention. There was work to be done, however; but it was not being brought to us on stretchers. We were going to have to figure out what the needs were and how to address them.

We began a systematic program. We had some advantages over other teams. Our team had stability of staffing the same people each day—five or six days a week. We spent the morning mapping and taking censuses or surveys of the villages. This was no easy chore. The houses seemed to sit on top of one another; all had been officially numbered. These numbers were sometimes useful, but they often had been washed off or were in no obvious sequence. We were able to see everyone's home, to meet those that we were trying to help, and occasionally to have brought out to see us the sickly child of the family or the grandmother with TB. The work was tedious at times and took more than a month in the form of one day spent each week in each of six villages. The result, however, was pleasant: we knew the name of each village and its people, we had a record system by family and household, and the villagers knew who we were.

Lunchtime was another chance to see the activity of the village. We found the best of local restaurants. Khao Phret Poy had a "three-star" version of Thai noodles and broth. Some villages had no restaurant; in those we wandered off to the water-buffalo pool and ate egg-salad sandwiches and drank Pepsi. We heard that the price of chickens had quadrupled since checkpoints had been put on the road from Aranyaprathet. (Some of the villagers, however, were doing quite well trading on the black market with the Kampucheans on the border, bringing back gold and silver in exchange for goods and foodstuffs.)

We spent the afternoon in our medical clinic, looking over the problems. Our record system was impressive. People brought their pink cards with the family name and number, and we were able to pull out their family card from our box. It was not flawless, but it served its function of allowing us to follow our patients' courses—signs, symptoms, diagnosis, and treatment. And it would allow us to pass on the information to new arrivals on the team—a big concern in a relief program where three months was a typical length of stay for an expatriate.

There were days when few were sick, but many came just to see what we might have to offer. Other days, we would find significant illness. Rarely did anyone need to go to the hospital; besides the difficulty of getting a patient there—getting through several checkpoints on the road and past the hospital bureaucracy—tended to discourage the process. In time, one of our team members befriended one of the Aranyaprathet hospital physicians and arranged a meeting between our team and hospital staff members that solved the problems of admitting patients. We also made contact with the health center in Ta Praya to try to complement their work, rather than be blind to the efforts of the Thai Ministry of Health. The primary concern of the community health center in its village outreach was in family planning. That was a nice discovery since we had serious reservations about being a team of outsiders offering birth control—"genocide" in some people's eyes.

We found adults with tuberculosis and children with otitis, pneumonia, and diarrhea. We saw cases of leprosy, malaria, and intestinal parasite infestation. We tried to be somewhat scientific and established a stool-specimen survey in each village. We did not have the time or the expertise to do random sampling, so we simply passed out stool cups and returned the next morning to collect fresh specimens. A Dutch laboratory technician in the Ta Praya health station was most pleasant in accepting our specimens and examining them. We simply wanted to know what parasites there were and to get an estimate of their prevalence. Then we had to find someone with information on mass treatment for intestinal parasitic disease. At what prevalence should we treat everyone in the village? Or should we not waste our time, given our team's likely stay of less than two years? We did not easily find the expert with that information, even in this massive refugee-relief operation.

In the initial months, we were on our own to make decisions about our medical-care practices. Most of the medical expertise in the refugee-relief program was in curative hospital-based medicine. There were few people with outreach community-medicine experience. But our initial efforts seemed to be leading us in a reasonable direction, and the public-relations campaign had not really taken so much expertise as personal warmth. Being on our own, making our own decisions, was fun, too. That allowed us to assess the situation, see what we thought would be reasonable and what would have lasting benefit, and then set our priorities. We continued performing surveys, this time examining the problem of anemia. We took a sanitary engineer out to the villages to evaluate their water supplies. We inquired about the availability of vaccines.

A sanitary engineer from Khao I Dang joined us one day for a visit to all our villages. It was ambitious to go to six villages in one day to evaluate water supplies and disposal systems for excreta, but the water systems were simple—hand-pump wells, at least one per village. The disposal systems were likewise simple—night soil deposited in the surrounding fields. The rainy season, however, would make a latrine system difficult to maintain. An alternative was not obvious, at least not at a price that the villagers might be able to afford. We learned that the Thai government had a program planned for improving the water supply to outlying villages in the region, so we decided simply to encourage the Ministry of Health in those efforts.

After about two months of activity, CBERS—a branch of Thai Public Health—called a meeting to coordinate the effort of the Thai village-outreach teams. This was the first forum for discussion that we had had, and it was most welcome. Our team was proud of its work on the census, medical records, and simple stool and anemia surveys. (We all need to think that we are doing a good job once in a while.) The CBERS representatives had their own particular bias, and although they very much encouraged such basic organizational structures, they also wanted the teams to place emphasis on family planning and birth control. We had our reservations about this. But the meeting was the beginning of a dialogue that allowed us to hear ideas from other teams and consider ways in which we might collaborate on larger projects.

The immunization program was the most obvious area for collaboration. As we had already collected much of the information needed for the data base on which to start an immunization program in our villages, we actively pursued the issue. The vaccines were easily obtained through the Thai Red

Cross. The eventual result was the coordination of several mobile teams and the immunization of children in more than 30 Thai villages in the region north of Khao I Dang.

Our memories are not of census work, medical records, or even of stool specimens containing the Chinese liver fluke; they are of our own experiences and adventures. Our medical adventures were our contacts with traditional medical practices. For many of the people in the villages, we were the first Western-trained medical people that they had ever met. Much of their care had been based on traditional medicine. Although we were not actively seeking out or studying traditional medical methods, we frequently crossed their path.

One encounter with traditional medicine came in Ban Pang Lang. We had been to the village the previous day and had seen a child with apparent acute poliomyelitis—the second polio victim that we had seen in a month. He was four years old, and the Western medical team had little to offer but rest and aspirin for his fever. Polio was not an unknown disease to the villagers. The consensus was that the problem might have been caused by the return of his grandfather's spirit. The grandfather had recently died under "questionable circumstances." On this day, the villagers were out in number participating in what seemed to be an exorcism to chase or cajole out the evil spirit. The village band played on a variety of drums, flutes, and stringed instruments. Four women sat, knelt, or stood and wailed as the spirit moved them. Their clothes varied from old army fatigues to symbolize the grandfather's time in the military to newly made sarongs from as many families as could supply them. Candles burned and incense rose from the altar in front of the women. A final event was the eating of the candle flame that represented the evil spirit. The event occupied several hours of the afternoon and continued into the evening. The village headman had asked us to hold our clinic as planned, but we felt rather strange seeing patients at a location just down the pathway from this event. It was a juxtaposition of Western and traditional medicine, and it was *our* team that felt twinges of discomfort, not the band or the wailing women or the mother with the ailing child.

The medical events of the day were often fascinating, but not so much for the diseases as for the social structure surrounding them. We had begun trying to receive reports of births in the villages when we were told of a recently delivered infant who was having trouble. We followed the village headman to a remote hut that housed one of the poorest families in the village. The three older children in the family, aged four, two and one, stood wide-eyed outside the house as we entered to see the mother and her newborn child. The mother was lying on a mat on the raised floor under which a fire smoldered beneath the room. She would stay there for seven days with the fire below and smoke all around. The infant was in the corner, well removed from the heat. As she unwrapped the child, our nurse reported that the girl had a complete cleft lip and cleft palate. The father said that he had seen it before in other babies, and he knew the problem: such babies die because they cannot suckle. He seemed to be saying that there was no reason to try to nurture the child, and in this instance, it seemed as if his pronouncement might well be fulfilled. Try as we might to offer encouragement and hope, the child got little attention.

We organized medical field trips. We had identified several villagers with advanced tuberculosis—mostly women over the age of 50—and we had decided to get x-rays in addition to sputum specimens. This was as much for our education as for their follow-up treatment. We made all the preliminary arrangements at Khao I Dang. We stopped there in the morning to make sure that there was enough film developer and a technician to take the films. The day before, we had stopped in the village to make sure that the women had their identification papers. We gathered their names and obtained a letter from the military to allow our passage past checkpoints and into the holding centers. For one women it was her first visit past Ta Praya in her lifetime of 75 years. For all, it was their first view of the refugee camps, an x-ray machine, and a hospital. For us, it was a joy with six women, each from a different village, asking about each other's disease, age, and life. All six x-rays showed extensive lung disease. But we really wished that we could have heard the stories told in the villages that evening as they showed their x-rays to friends and families. We had made them temporary celebrities.

We began to get regular requests to have other relief workers join us, one or two a day to come out with our team. We were happy to show off our villages and our work, and the physicians and nurses in the camps seemed to enjoy the break from their routine. A professor from the Cornell team joined us one day and was a most helpful teacher. Another physician, who joined the team for a day, diagnosed 15 patients as having Bitot spots of vitamin-A deficiency (he was actually looking at benign pterygia). This was our chance to educate Khao I Dang hospital staff members that there were people other than Kampuchean refugees who had illness and poverty as part of their daily lives.

These visits brought out another difference between those who worked in the holding centers and those who worked in the villages. Within the camps, we had heard no end of stories about the terrible treatment of the refugees by the Thai people and the Thai government. In the villages, we worked with Thai people and sat daily with the Thai military, who became our friends. Anon, our Thai translator/administrator, resented the accusations against his people and strove in his silent way to be an ambassador to us for his countrymen. We learned a different perspective on the antagonisms between Thais and Kampucheans.

As a mobile medical team, we had an interesting identity. We were not part of the holding-center medical extravaganza that was developing neonatal intensive care and sophisticated surgery. We were an offshoot created because the level of care available to the refugees exceeded that available to the Thai people in the region. It was nice to be separate; we enjoyed not working in the pressure and hierarchy of the Western hospital setting. We answered only to ourselves and to the people we were trying to care for and had no higher authority than our judgment, our conscience, and the reaction of the villagers.

The simplicity of the villages was most enticing. These were places that were concerned with their future, caught in the web of someone else's conflict and changed because of it. Nevertheless, the cattle still rested lazily under the trees while chewing their cud. Men still marked logs and cut board after board to build new houses. The fields would be planted as they had been for years, waiting for the rains to bring life to the seeds once again. The people knew each other, knew what they stood for, and what to expect from one another. They were not refugees. They were in their own homes and were there for the duration. They had expectations for tomorrow and a sense that they had some control of what would come. But their poverty and illness were no less real.

The Thai village-outreach medical program was a good idea. The refugee-relief effort had been typified by a rapid response to a serious disaster. The Thai village program did not require that kind of response. It began as a public relations campaign, and medically it was addressing primary-care and preventive-medicine needs in a poverty area. The teams worked under certain constraints; activities were under the direction of the Thai military and far from Thai medical care support—and no one knew how long we would stay.

Some aspects of the work were crucial to our success. Record keeping was no less important in the villages than it was in a hospital setting, and it provided very important demographic information. The work on family records fitted well into the framework of the public-relations campaign; and when we were ready to vaccinate the children, the records were invaluable. In future community outreach programs, a good record system will be extremely important, providing information on family size, age, sex, birth, death, and morbidity of family members. Certain questions will always arise regarding what information should be gathered and how the records are to be kept. Who should keep the record—the family, the individual, or the medical team? What is its long-range purpose? Will it simply record vaccinations? or note patients with chronic illness? or will the same medical-care system be left in place, thus making the recording of regular medical-care problems a reasonable concern? In what language should it be written?

In medical care, the team tried to work within the realm of science. It was appropriate that it should seek whatever information was available before embarking on treatment. Rather than simply mass-treating villagers for intestinal parasite infestations, we looked first to see which organisms were prevalent, to what extent they were causing clinical problems, what the options were for intervention in hygiene and sanitation practices, and what medications were available for case-by-case or mass treatment. We tried to make use of existing medical-support facilities, such as the laboratory, getting important information without overusing the resources.

The issue of availability and use of medications will also arise in future programs. We adhered to the idea of using medications sparingly and appropriately. Handing out medicines ("Western magic")—even vitamins—makes one popular with the people. But, taking the time to teach simple prevention and treatment remedies that do not involve medications will be well worth the trouble in the long run. Likewise, learning about traditional treatments and the use of local herbs may be very useful. Often these traditional treatments became standard practice for a good reason.

For the time and energy spent, it remains true that an ounce of prevention is worth a pound of cure. There is little doubt that the single most effective way to lower infant mortality in this setting is to vaccinate all children under five years of age against measles. If money permits, vaccine against diphtheria, pertussis, tetanus, polio, measles, and tuberculosis may also be appropriate. Other medical problems are more complicated. The approach to tuberculosis requires case identification, patient and family education, possibly vaccination, and prolonged treatment during which noncompliance becomes a common problem. The economic status of the community may play an important role as poverty and overcrowding seem to present good conditions for the spread of this disease. Problems of nutrition, sanitation, and hygiene are other areas to be addressed in efforts at prevention. These, too, may be entangled in the web of poverty.

Perhaps the most important issue is that of training. Our

single biggest mistake was not to establish a training program for village health workers. One or two trained persons from each village with eventual connections to the Public Health Center in Ta Praya would have been a significant improvement in the health-care system at minimal long-term financial investment. Instead, there is a new hospital in Ta Praya, built and staffed by the Italian medical team. Perhaps they will stay forever, or turn it over to the Thai Ministry of Health, who will face the difficulties of enticing Thai physicians to stay, work, and take an interest in the lives of these remote villagers. But the villagers themselves did not have the opportunity to learn more, nor were they left with someone in their midst who would continue simple health care and education.

As the resources of the voluntary agencies diminished and village-outreach programs took a back seat to refugee-relief work, the infrastructure left in the villages was no better than before the mobile medical teams arrived. Something had been given and was then taken away. The first question to be asked in such a village-outreach program should be, What will we be able to leave behind? If the question is neither asked nor answered, it is likely that little will change.

RESETTLEMENT IN THIRD COUNTRIES VERSUS VOLUNTARY REPATRIATION

Martin Barber

In admitting the Khmers to the holding centers, the Thai government had had a somewhat ambivalent attitude about their long-term future. On the one hand, experience with the Laotian refugees had convinced many senior officials that resettlement in the United States and elsewhere served as a magnet, encouraging people to leave their homes. The final result was that a refugee camp could never be emptied, because there were always new arrivals keen to follow their relatives and friends to a home in the West. On the other hand, there were many husbands separated from wives and parents from children when immediate resettlement was the only possible humane option. There was pressure on the Thai government from many sides to allow large-scale resettlement.

It may seem difficult to imagine, at this distance in time and space, that anyone could have wished to prevent or delay the movement to new homes in the West of people who had just escaped from four years of hell under Pol Pot and the Khmer Rouge, people whose country had been devastated and who were still suffering in certain areas from famine conditions. It is worth sitting back for a moment and looking at the problem in a larger dimension. The Khmers who reached Khao I Dang and Sa Kaeo were escaping from the *consequences* of four years of Khmer Rouge rule. Most of them were not escaping from the Khmer Rouge itself, because by the end of 1979 all the populated areas of Kampuchea were in the hands of the Vietnamese-supported Heng Samrin regime. Those Khmers who insisted they would never return to Kampuchea were refusing to live under a regime of which they had only the most limited experience—if any at all. Khao I Dang had attracted many educated and technically qualified people who, having miraculously survived four years of brutality and oppression, were naturally keen to make contact with relatives and friends living overseas. In the first few days, few of them, except those separated from close family members, seemed to have had any idea that they might follow those friends overseas and live there permanently. As they made contact with the United States Embassy staff, voluntary agency personnel, and visiting Khmers, they began to be faced with a choice which, for all but a few of the educated families, was hardly a choice at all: whether (1) to do everything possible to get to Australia, Canada, France, or the United States, where education, jobs, and all the basics of life would be assured in ample abundance; or (2) to stay in the austere conditions of the holding centers and wait for an uncertain opportunity to return home, knowing that their country was going through the first months of recovery from devastation, under the control of a Vietnamese army of occupation that represented the most feared historical threat to Kampuchea's independence. Once the options were perceived in this way, few chose to stay.

If the choice for individuals was simple, the consequences of that choice for their nation would be severe. After the Khmer Rouge, Kampuchea had a sickeningly small number of educated and qualified people left. As more and more of these people flew out of Bangkok to Paris and San Francisco, so the chances of Kampuchea surviving as an independent nation declined, and the daily life of the five million people left behind, without doctors, teachers, or engineers, became that much harder.

Of course, those who left did not see it that way, and perhaps we ought not to have viewed it that way either. Nevertheless UNHCR's mandate was to promote satisfactory durable solutions to refugee prbolems. I could never quite see how we were contributing to the solution of Kampuchea's refugee problem by flying its few remaining qualified people to new homes thousands of miles away. The debate as to whether or not resettlement was an appropriate solution for the Kampucheans has been long and intense. Different departments within the United States government even took up different positions on whether or not most Kampucheans had a genuine claim to refugee status. The debate continues to this day.

Initially the Thai government tried to control the movements of the refugees, and we in UNHCR, hopeful that a realistic and safe program of voluntary repatriation might be established, urged the resettlement countries to concentrate their attention for the moment on moving Vietnamese and Laotians, many of whom had been sitting in refugee camps for four years. There were initial restrictions on the degree of family relationship required with a sponsor overseas, then there were temporary freezes, and finally, once-and-for-all quotas. After months of haggling, the resettlement countries and most of the individual refugees got what they thought they wanted—and Kampuchea lost.

My own personal opinion remains that the best interests of most individual Kampuchean families, and certainly those of the Kampuchean nation as a whole, were not served by massive programs of resettlement in the Western world. In the end though, one incident brought home to me the futility of our efforts to try and think of Kampucheans in general, rather than of the desires of each individual. In Paris in 1980, I met a Khmer family. One of the family members told me in great detail how he had a female cousin in Khao I Dang. Since she had no closer relative outside Kampuchea, he was arranging that a friend in Paris should claim to be her husband, so that she would come within the resettlement criteria and be admitted to France. In his situation, I would certainly have done the same myself.

* * * * *

The biggest storm faced by ROKU was over the program of voluntary repatriation which took place from Sa Kaeo in June 1980. This involved returning 8,000 Khmer Rouge supporters to the point on the border from which they had been rescued in October 1979. From the Khmer Rouge point of view, they were simply taking back followers who had had eight months of useful rest and recuperation. From the Vietnamese/Heng

Samrin point of view, 8,000 fresh guerrillas were being launched at them from within the safe sanctuary of Thai bases. From the United Nations point of view, we were simply enabling 8,000 Khmers to exercise their right to return to their homeland.

It was not, of course, as simple as that. At the outset, serious fears were expressed that many of the 25,000 Khmers in Sa Kaeo who did *not* want to return to Kampuchea would be coerced by the Khmer Rouge elements into going against their will. It was also feared that the Vietnamese would see the move as an act of aggression. The first fear proved in the end unfounded, thanks to an elaborate organization that saw every single adult among the 8,000 declare, while standing alone in a tent with a United Nations official and an interpreter, that he or she was returning voluntarily. From that point of view, our success lay in the 17,000 Khmers in Sa Kaeo who were able to decide *not* to return to the Khmer Rouge areas.

Unfortunately, however, the fear of Vietnamese retaliation proved justified. A sharp two-day assault in the area of Non Mak Mun caused a number of casualties; it seems likely that this incident was connected with the repatriation. The repatriation issue prompted passionate discussions that continued long after the events were over. In the end, of course, there was no choice. The Khmers asked to return to the area of Kampuchea controlled by the internationally recognized legitimate government of their country—Democratic Kampuchea. The Thai government, as was clearly its right, insisted that they be allowed to return. UNHCR's sole function was to ensure that those who went did so voluntarily. We exercised that function as well as we could, but all of us were moved to give an unusual amount of thought to the nature of man's exercise of his "free will." How much are we "coerced," "persuaded," or "encouraged to volunteer" by our leaders, particularly in times of apparent national emergency? In such circumstances, these three terms would seem to differ little.

THE STRUGGLE CONTINUES: IMMIGRATION AND RESETTLEMENT

Chhang Song

A 43-year-old former Cambodian farmer named Uon came to my office this morning (September 19, 1985) with his three young daughters to secure some emergency clothing for his family's needs. This clothing had in fact been given to us at Save Cambodia, Inc., by sympathetic American donors for distribution to the newly-arrived Cambodian refugees. Uon and his family had themselves only arrived in the United States just a few days ago after having languished in Cambodian refugee camps inside Thailand for the past six years. Tragically, this one family alone had lost 23 relatives during the Pol Pot regime. Uon's children had grown up mainly in a camp environment and were consequently almost entirely uneducated.

As I looked at these youths seated across from me, however, my ten years of experience with refugees told me that they

---

Chhang Song, who served as Minister of Information in the Lon Nol government, left Cambodia as a refugee in 1975. In 1980, he helped to found Save Cambodia, Inc., (SCI) an organization he continues to direct. Based in suburban Washington, D.C., it assists Cambodians who have immigrated to the United States and (as of 1985) continues to serve as a rallying point for the Cambodian cause.

would soon be not only able to speak English as fluently as any American, but also would be earning good marks in their studies at the neighborhood school and would perform well at their future jobs. As a matter of fact, some Cambodian refugees whom we had sponsored who came to the United States in 1980 are now economically self-sufficient.

Unquestionably, some if not many of these survivors of the Cambodian holocaust are doing well in their new culture; but, unfortunately, there are others—250,000 in fact—who still experience immeasurable suffering today in the Thai refugee camps with no hope of resettlement to the West since having made their perilous flight from Communist Cambodia into Thailand. Many of them have been abused, robbed, beaten, raped, and often left in a deprived condition—hungry, sick, and without clothing and proper shelter.

There have been times in which, when all creative thought has abandoned me, I have wondered why, as a refugee in the United States, I had chosen to struggle on behalf of other long-suffering Cambodians. Ten long years now after the fall of my homeland to the Khmer Rouge Communists, I still find myself being touched deeply by story after story as they are recounted to me by newly-arrived refugees. One of those stories told to me after my arrival in the United States explained how, after having failed in their obsessive desire to arrest me, the Khmer Rouge captured my younger brother instead and clubbed him to death. The account went on to say, moreover, that my mother had had her feet tied together by her captors and had been left in a nearby paddy field to die of starvation and the elements. . . . The stories of my people's sufferings continue to afflict me day and night; so that the only solution I could think of to save them was for me to assist in whatever ways I could to evacuate to safety in the West those compatriots of mine who could not remain in Cambodia without jeopardizing their lives.

This inner moral imperative to help these victims of war and genocide to rebuild their shattered lives in America impelled me to commence speaking out publicly as well as privately on the Cambodian issues. Actually, it first began in my conversations with bus drivers and tourists in Hawaii. Then my vocal concern spread to college campuses, civic clubs, rallies, social and political gatherings throughout the United States and abroad. In addition, I gave interviews for television and radio, wrote newspaper and magazine articles, and spoke out on Capitol Hill and at the White House. In these ways, I contributed to the public awareness of Cambodian refugees and appealed for their assistance.

Starting with only a few friends, I soon witnessed our efforts beginning to mushroom. By 1980, we were in a position to incorporate ourselves as a non-profit, self-help organization known as Save Cambodia, Inc. (SCI). We did so with the encouragement and assistance of such leaders as Senator Robert Dole, Congressman Stephen Solarz, Assistant Secretary of State Elliott Abrams, and many others—both Cambodian and American.

Our efforts have continued as always to focus on assisting refugees to be resettled in the United States. The basic difficulty for our organization in appealing for relief was initially due to Cambodians' being practically unknown to the American population. I well remember that at the height of the Vietnam War in the 1960s, when a handful of us young Cambodian students came to study in the United States, few Americans even knew that Cambodia was located immediately adjacent to Vietnam! Hence, making the Cambodian problems a matter of interest and concern to Americans was a major task indeed. Nevertheless, from the start of our activities those Americans from every walk of life who have listened to us—of every race, creed, color, and political persuasion—have responded positively and generously to our appeals for help. And it is this kind of grass roots reaction to the plight of the Cambodian refugees that has kept our struggle for Cambodian survival alive.

In 1977, for example, there were only 25 Cambodian refugees admitted to the United States during the entire year. It required the combined efforts of Senator Dole (Republican from Kansas), Representative Solarz (Democrat from New York), and the active support of Senator Edward Kennedy (Democrat from Massachusetts) to convince the United States Congress in 1978 to mandate admission into the country the

15,000 Cambodian refugees then waiting in Thai refugee camps for some relief. Since that landmark legislation, the flow of Cambodians to the United States, despite troublesome problems along the way, has paralleled that of their Indochinese neighbors—the Vietnamese and Laotians. For example, from October 1983 through September 1984, the Reagan Administration admitted nearly 18,000 Cambodians. Although the 124,710 Cambodian refugees admitted into the United States from April 1975 to July 1985 constitutes only one-fourth of the 482,447 Vietnamese refugees and is less than the 148,574 Laotian refugees admitted into the United States within the same period of time, this number nevertheless demonstrates the fact that America has welcomed over two-thirds of the total number of Cambodian refugees resettled throughout the Western world since mid-1975.

Cambodian refugees trying to immigrate to the United States over these years, however, encountered a number of serious obstacles: (1) persons and things Cambodian were largely unknown to the American public; (2) refugee admission criteria, stressing family affiliations of those in refugee camps with those in the United States and connections to the United States war effort in Indochina, excluded almost all Cambodians from being admitted; (3) refugee policy was ambivalent, based on a misguided hope of the success of voluntary repatriation back to Cambodia; (4) ambiguity of the political situation in Southeast Asia has prevented Cambodians from obtaining their legitimate refugee status, thus denying escapees international protection; and (5) the difficulty of American immigration field officers in separating bona fide refugees from culpable Khmer Rouge.

Most Cambodians in the United States are from rural Cambodia. They are predominantly illiterate or semiliterate in their own language because the Pol Pot regime singled out the educated for extermination. Moreover, because the 1975 evacuation plan for Cambodians devised by the Lon Nol government failed at the last moment, very few members of the educated class escaped. Basically, there are three groups of Cambodians who have been resettled in the United States since 1975:

1. The few government officials, military officers, and business and professional people who arrived in the United States in 1975 immediately following the fall of Phnom Penh. Most left Cambodia by military plane or boat. About 7,000 of these people have been resettled and have found employment.
2. Rural and uneducated Cambodians who crossed the border and fled to Thailand in 1975, at about the same time as the educated urban and professional people did. But these people, lacking family ties in the United States and having no connections with the past United States war effort in Indochina, were detained in Thai camps until 1979, when the United States Congress called for their admission as a special group (under the provisions of the Dole-Solarz Amendment). About 10,000 of these rural Cambodians were resettled in late 1979 and early 1980.
3. The rest of the Cambodians have been admitted into the United States since 1980. They consist of a heterogeneous mix of urban and rural, educated and illiterate refugees; and all carry with them the scars of the hardships and inhumane trauma of the Pol Pot years. Many Cambodian youths and teenagers in this group—not unlike the ones I saw and listened to this morning—have not had any formal education since 1975. Those educated Cambodians, who by some miracle managed to survive, have been further alienated by the subsequent Vietnamese occupation of their land, which began in January 1979.

For the past ten years now, those Cambodians in the United States—in particular the new arrivals and those who have fallen through the existing social safety net—have continued to seek out assistance from SCI. In order to respond to these critical needs, we mobilized an effective volunteer network in both the American and refugee communities. The needs of these refugees are numerous. Almost immediately after the refugee's arrival, an appointment is necessary with the Department of Social Security to file for a Social Security card. Next, the refugee must be taken to the county health department to have his/her health rechecked. Refugees usually arrive in this country with a clean bill of health; nevertheless, rechecking at the local health unit is a must and needs to be taken care of as soon as possible. Some of the health problems frequently detected after the refugee has received such a clean bill of health are tuberculosis, gonorrhea, intestinal parasites, dental problems, and anemia. Children and adults need to be registered at a school (especially for the purpose of English-language training). Then, too, important documents relative to any legal, medical, or cultural problems need to be prepared and filed properly.

Housing looms as one of the biggest problems facing new arrivals. Too often housing arrangements have not taken into account the typical lifestyle of a Cambodian family. Although most Cambodians have large families, modest living accommodations are adequate. Moreover, new arrivals are not familiar with the complexities of modern American housing (e.g., the use of gas and electricity for heat and lighting, use of the telephone, indoor plumbing, and garbage disposal) as well as police, bank, and transportation services.

Now after an initial period of adjustment to these and other aspects of American life, the final and most vital need of the Cambodian refugees must be met—that of employment. It is in this field that SCI has been most helpful and effective in the past five years with our Refugee Employment Support Project. This project has aimed to place illiterate and semiliterate Cambodian refugees in jobs by using American and Cambodian volunteers. Through a series of employment demonstration projects, we have succeeded in proving that the refugees—even those with only limited language ability and job skills—are employable. Moreover, when properly coached, these refugees maintain their jobs and meet employers' expectations. A few have excelled in their performance, and many of those we had placed in jobs during the early 1980s have since bought their own homes!

Nevertheless, the tragedy in Cambodia runs on seemingly unabated. As long as human needs arising from this tragedy persist, those of us at Save Cambodia, Inc., will continue to respond to those needs in whatever modest form possible.

PART 5

BROADER PERSPECTIVES:
PAST, PRESENT, AND FUTURE

THE CAMBODIAN BORDER RELIEF OPERATION IN THE CONTEXT OF OTHER RELIEF OPERATIONS

Frederick C. Cuny

The emergency operation for Kampuchean refugees along the Thai border was in itself an extraordinary event and outpouring of international aid. Yet coming as it did, at the end of a decade in which international relief to refugees in the developing countries moved from obscure, ad hoc assistance into major prominence, it marks a milestone in the development of relief approaches and provides a yardstick by which to measure progress in the emerging field of emergency humanitarian assistance.

There is a saying among disaster and relief specialists that every operation defines the state of the art. Relief work is characterized by a high turnover of personnel, and few people with field experience work in more than one operation. This, when combined with the fact that there has been little documentation of lessons learned, nor extensive research into emergency operations and the impact of different methods and approaches commonly used, has contributed to the frustrations of the few

---

Frederick C. Cuny, affiliated with Intertect, worked in the Cambodian relief operation from September 1979 to February 1980 as Emergency Operations Advisor to the United Nations High Commissioner for Refugees. He returned briefly to this work in July 1980 and February 1981. He is at present an emergency management consultant and Chairman of Intertect, Dallas, Texas.

relief workers who continually respond to disasters, as each operation has often appeared to be starting from square one. During the 1970s, however, a few experienced relief personnel began to take a closer look at emergency operations and propose alternatives to the normal practices. Some large relief agencies also began to retain people as disaster specialists, and their experiences have started to pay off. Thus, the Kampuchean relief operation provided an interesting gauge of what impact research and experience has had on the state of the art at the end of the 1970s.

In order to understand the importance of what the Kampuchean emergency operation was, one must first understand what it was not. It was *not* the largest influx of refugees; in fact, by the standards set in the decade, the Kampuchean border operation would not even fall into the top ten. Even in comparison with refugee crises during the same period in other parts of the world, such as Somalia and Afghanistan, the crisis was relatively small. Kampuchea was also *not* the worst in terms of physical magnitude. The area where the relief operation was conducted was relatively small, and the refugees were in large clusters and not dispersed over a remote or rugged terrain. The operation was *not* even the hardest to respond to. There were good roads, an excellent transportation network, plentiful supplies in Thailand and nearby countries, excellent accommodations for relief workers, and a generally cooperative government in the country of first asylum.

Yet the money spent by the international community was the largest amount ever spent on a relief operation during the decade. More voluntary agencies responded and committed more staff and cash than in any previous emergency. The volags reported the largest response to appeals ever received (as of late 1981, some had still been unable to dispense all the money they had acquired during that period). Overall, the response devoted to the Kampuchean operation outweighed all other contemporary refugee situations and buried them in the surrounding publicity.

CONTRASTS WITH PAST OPERATIONS

Concentration of refugees in disputed territory. The one distinctive feature of the Kampuchean border operation was the extremely large number of refugees who remained inside the Kampuchean border in disputed territories not under the control of the occupation government. This presented a series of unique problems for the relief agencies. UNHCR, by its mandate, could not work with the refugees until they actually crossed the border (in United Nations terms, the refugees inside Kampuchea were classified as "displaced persons"). This situation, coupled with security problems, necessitated the development of special cross-border relief-operations procedures and techniques. The situation prevented agencies from duplicating the approaches being used in the Thai camps and prevented successful and thorough follow-up so that even today it is difficult to assess thoroughly the impact and performance of the programs.

Level of funding. Funding was never a major problem for the agencies providing assistance on the border. The UNHCR had an adequate supply of funds throughout the operation, and many agencies experienced a surplus. In past operations there had rarely been enough money to go around. Indeed, for the relief operation for Kampucheans in Thailand, UNHCR committed more money in the first three months than it expended in an entire year in Somalia, though approximately three times the number of refugees were present in the latter operation.

Experts in key roles. Experienced experts in many different fields converged on the Kampuchean border, and many found themselves in key posts in UNHCR and the voluntary agencies during the initial stages. Many of these experts had worked together in prior operations, and this provided an experienced and complementary core of staff.

Manageable levels of new arrivals. Throughout the operation, the number of refugees always remained at a manageable level. More important, the number of daily new arrivals rarely exceeded the capacity of the reception center's ability to process and register the newcomers. The average number of crossings of new arrivals during the most intensive period was somewhat less than 4,000 per day. On the worst day, an estimated 27,000 people crossed the border from Kampuchea to Thailand. In India, in 1971, at one reception center, approximately 80,000 people crossed the border every day for three weeks.

A manageable geographic distribution. The Kampuchean border operation occurred along a relatively short distance and the concentrations of refugees, both in Thailand and inside Kampuchea, covered fairly small areas. In addition, refugee camps in Thailand were easily accessible by road, and the refugee concentrations in Kampuchea were close enough to paved roads so that most supplies could be trucked to within a few kilometers of the distribution points. By comparison, in contemporary relief operations in Afghanistan and Somalia, camps were often several days' journey apart and on roads that were impassable several months of the year.

Adequate supplies in neighboring countries. The vast majority of the provisions and materials needed to supply the refugees could be obtained in Thailand or in other nearby countries, unlike many relief operations in which the neighboring countries are in almost as bad a situation as the refugee-generating state. Thailand and other Asian countries had adequate surpluses from which relief supplies could be drawn without adversely affecting their economies. In fact, there were so many suppliers available that relief agencies had the luxury of being able to use competitive bidding. Furthermore, the basic items, such as food and building materials which were available in the surrounding countries, were compatible with the lifestyle of the refugees. Thus, overall logistical operations were greatly simplified.

Adequate transportation systems. Thailand enjoys one of the most advanced road systems in Southeast Asia. Furthermore, trucking companies with large capacity vehicles, water tankers, and other equipment were readily available at all stages of the relief operation. This, coupled with the locally available supplies, further enhanced logistical capabilities.

A fairly supportive host government. After initial official ambivalence and early rejection of the refugees, the attitude of the Thai government changed to one of generally constructive support. Especially during the critical period—the first three months—the Thai authorities cooperated extensively with the UNHCR and voluntary agencies to an extent rarely seen in other host countries. Few restrictions were placed on refugees other than general confinement, and UNHCR and the volun tary agencies were permitted a great deal of flexibility in providing assistance. While the Thai government did not go out of its way to help, it certainly did not go out of its way to hinder.

Strong, central role of UNHCR. UNHCR played a strong central role in the operation on the Thai side during the initial stages. To a large extent, this was because there were strong personalities in the field who recognized that a leadership vacuum existed that only UNHCR could fill. This leadership paid dividends, and even while UNHCR was not active across the border, the style that was set and many of the programs that were initiated in the Thai camps were duplicated by those operating across the border. Many inexperienced observers, who have no basis for comparison, have criticized UNHCR's leadership in the early phases of the operation. Yet to those who have observed and participated in past operations, the unprecedented and active leadership role of UNHCR was welcome, for it greatly reduced the amount of confusion and duplication usually present. (This operational involvement has had a profound impact on UNHCR. A thorough evaluation of the experience has been conducted and a new emergency unit has been organized to facilitate UNHCR emergency response in similar situations.)

SIMILARITIES TO PAST OPERATIONS

The major differences notwithstanding, the Kampuchean-border relief operations were similar to many earlier operations. The following are the major similarities:

Lack of preparedness. At the outset, UNHCR and the voluntary agencies were totally unprepared for the arrival of the refugees. No actions were taken until the refugees actually reached the border area, despite the fact that signs and indications of a mass movement of refugees had been present for several months. Indeed, several months previously large numbers of refugees had attempted to cross into Thailand and been pushed back across the border. While political maneuvering commenced at that point, operational preparedness was minimal. When the refugees actually crossed the border in October 1979, none of the responding organizations was logistically or operationally prepared.

Competition between the agencies. For the voluntary agencies involved in the operation, competition rather than cooperation was the rule. To an extent, UNHCR was able to promote more effective cooperation through its coordination efforts, especially at Sa Kaeo and Khao I Dang. In the other camps and in the cross-border operations, competition between agencies severely hampered the relief efforts and caused untold wastage in supplies and resources.

Inequities in distribution of aid. In the early stages of the operation, assistance was marred by inequities in the overall assistance program. Each agency undertook its assignment with a different approach. This resulted in some refugees receiving a substantially higher level of assistance than others. A case in point was found in the supplemental-feeding program in Khao I Dang. In one sector, the voluntary agency in charge provided a high standard of service, which included outreach, registration, nutrition education, surveillance for disease or health-related problems, and a high degree of refugee participation in the management of the program. In a feeding center in an adjacent section of the camp, another agency provided only additional rice and some powdered milk to anyone who came to the feeding center when it was open. The more experienced and professional agencies, such as CARE and Concern, cooperated extensively in standardizing operations, but many of the newer agencies lagged far behind, and it fell to UNHCR to prod them toward a higher standard of care.

Overemphasis on medical aid. It is common in emergency operations for inexperienced relief organizations to focus on medical assistance to refugees, and the Kampuchean border operations were no exception. One month after the start of the operation, UNHCR conducted a survey of the agencies involved. Not counting the Red Cross and organizations directly under the ICRC banner (which accounted for more than half the personnel on the border), approximately two-thirds of all expatriate personnel working in the camps were with medical teams—this despite the fact that only an estimated 2 to 5 percent of the refugee population required medical assistance. Furthermore, most of the medical personnel were serving in surgical or curative medical roles, rather than concentrating on preventive medicine or public-health needs. Numerous studies of past operations have concluded that the most prevalent health threats to refugees can best be addressed through preventive rather than curative approaches.

Poor execution of nutritional programs. In the emergency phase of the operation, many of the agencies that offered to conduct feeding programs lacked any practical experience in supplementary or intensive feeding. Extensive literature has been developed, and lessons from past experience are well documented, as to what works and what methods should be employed; yet with only several exceptions, most of the agencies involved appeared unaware of this information.

Overemphasis on charity. The majority of the relief organizations, especially the relatively new organizations, adopted approaches that stressed maximal participation by expatriates and minimal-to-zero participation by the refugees themselves. Unfortunately, the Kampuchean border operation was similar to previous situations in that such opportunities and approaches to the refugees were largely ignored. Few agencies developed self-help opportunities, and many ignored the obvious fact that the refugees were not only able to but eager to participate in measures for their own welfare. Only after UNHCR field officers asked the agencies to emphasize self-help measures and maximum participation by the beneficiaries was there a move in this direction.

Failure to assess long-term impact. The actions of the agencies often contributed to development of unrealistic expectations on the part of the refugees and contributed to delays in the development of permanent solutions. For example, many organizations began teaching the refugees English. The refugees thus came to believe that if they could speak English their chance for resettlement in the United States was virtually assured. This, in turn, may have contributed to an overall reluctance on the part of the refugees to consider repatriation or resettlement in a country within the Southeast Asian region.

It has been argued in some circles that many of the relief activities contributed to the stagnation of the situation on the border. While more research is needed to verify these claims, it is certain that few of the relief agencies considered the implications or possible consequences of many of the programs that were instigated, and few agencies were even aware of what the options for permanent solutions were.

COMPARISON WITH OTHER CONTEMPORARY SITUATIONS

As mentioned earlier, the Kampuchean relief operation took precedence over all other international relief efforts. The reasons for this are many, and must include world revulsion at the horrors that had taken place inside Kampuchea and the outpouring of sympathy which it engendered. This humanitarian concern, however, resulted in a disproportionate amount of assistance and attention being concentrated on Kampuchea and a resulting reduction in the amount of assistance being given to other refugees during the same period. A comparison of border operations in Kampuchea, Afghanistan, and Somalia provides some interesting statistics:

Level of commitment. The Kampuchean border operation received a much higher level of initial financial commitment than the operations for the Afghani refugees or for the refugees in western Somalia. In terms of funding, the Kampuchean border operation received three times as much as Afghanistan and eight times as much as Somalia during the first three months. Even taking the different operational modes into consideration the overwhelming amount of aid and attention given to Kampuchea is evident.

Degree of sophistication. Because of the much higher level of commitment, it was natural that a greater degree of sophistication in programs and approaches was achieved along the Kampuchean border than in the other operations. Better staff and equipment and more resources contributed to a willingness to experiment with new ideas, and the availability of sufficient cash and personnel gave agencies the flexibility they needed if they were to experiment. Thus, programs in every conceivable area were formulated and executed, and many approaches which had previously only been proposed were finally tested.

Standard of service. The greater degree of sophistication contributed to a higher standard of service than in any previous refugee relief operation and far surpassed anything in the Afghanistan or Somalia operations. The services that the Kampuchean refugees received were more diverse and comprehensive, and virtually every human need was addressed.

While it can be argued that the international relief system was incapable of handling more than one large relief operation at a time, or that the Kampuchean refugee operation was the first to erupt and thus drained the available resources of the period, the simple fact remains that there was little public interest in the other operations and that there thus was a lower level of commitment and response. It is also interesting to note that many of the resources later committed to the Afghani operation and to Somalia were surpluses from the Kampuchean operation.

SIGNIFICANT DEVELOPMENTS IN THE KAMPUCHEAN BORDER OPERATION

In the Kampuchean border operation, a number of significant developments in the field of emergency relief are noteworthy. Some represent the implementation of proposals developed as a result of the analysis of previous relief operations. Others are an adaptation of programs developed for natural-disaster relief programs. Still others were simply original ideas that proved successful. The following is a summary of the state of the art, as defined by the Kampuchean border operation:

Management and coordination. The Kampuchean operation demonstrated, once again, the need for a strong central lead agency to serve as coordinator for operations. Ideally, this agency is UNHCR, and in Thailand, in the early phases of the operation, UNHCR assumed this role. The need for changes in UNHCR's operating procedures during emergencies has been discussed elsewhere, and in fact, many changes are currently taking place. Whatever organization is selected as the lead agency, it must have authority to impose basic minimal standards of service; otherwise, inequities in relief will continue.

In the Kampuchean border operation, a series of uniform standards for relief aid were developed for use by UNHCR as a means of affecting better coordination and of standardizing services to refugees in the UNHCR-operated camps. A number of personnel from the voluntary agencies, many of whom were recognized experts in their respective fields, participated in the development of these standards. The standards were then incorporated in a comprehensive manual, which was to be distributed to the field officers of UNHCR and the staffs of the voluntary agencies in each camp. The standards were meant not only to equalize services within the camps but also to provide inexperienced agencies with a guide for effective program planning. The most important standards were for supplementary feeding, intensive feeding, and minimal space requirements for shelters.

Initially the standards were welcomed by many of the voluntary agencies, for they recognized that competition and unequal services were counterproductive. Unfortunately, UNHCR decided not to use the documents as standards per se, but rather as guidelines, and failed to encourage actively any meaningful compliance. In the camps, however, the UNHCR field officers did encourage compliance and often used the standards as a means of supporting their own arguments for increased services in various areas. In addition, many of the more professional organizations quickly adapted to the standards and could proudly proclaim compliance in their reports to donors. Those agencies which met the standards also found that they received much more support from UNHCR and were assigned more responsibility than those that did not.

The Kampuchean experience with standards has led to their application in several other instances, with varying degrees of success. Most disaster specialists have concluded that internationally recognized minimum standards for basic services are long overdue, but the difficulties in achieving international agreement are certainly recognized. Differences in refugee populations and in the regions in which operations may occur must also be factored into the standards, and adaptation for each specific operation must, of course, be made.

Camp planning. A number of innovations in refugee-camp planning were successfully employed in the Thai camps. First, a basic minimal standard of 3.5 square meters per person was accepted as the minimal space requirement for the purposes of camp planning. This proved to be a good minimum standard and could be used in both multifamily units and family shelters.

After an initial fiasco at Sa Kaeo, where thousands of refugees arrived before the camp layout had been considered, more attention was given to camp planning and a number of innovative layouts were attempted in the subsequent camps.

At Khao I Dang, the largest of the camps (approximately 140,000 people maximum), a checkerboard master plan was used with adequate open space left throughout the camp to provide relief for the more dense housing sectors. With the exception of the hospital facilities, all other services were dispersed throughout the site, and each sector had its own outpatient clinic, supplementary-feeding center, water batteries, sanitation units, and other facilities and services.

Decentralizing sites and services contributed to providing more thorough services for the refugees, and enabled the agencies in charge of each sector to deal with a manageable number of people. Because dispersion requires more staff, agencies were compelled to use refugees as part of their work force, thus contributing a needed self-help element to the operation.

In later camps, planning techniques were even more advanced. In the construction of Sa Kaeo II, community units consisting of four to eight shelters surrounding an open square were used as the basic planning unit. Each square provided the refugees with a common ground for washing, cooking, and even gardening, and each square had several individual sanitation units immediately adjacent.

The innovative layouts and integration of sites and services were made possible by the installation of fiberglass Aqua-Privys as the primary sanitation unit. While these were not without problems, especially in the initial stages, the importance of the unit in terms of the flexibility it afforded planners cannot be ignored.

Sanitation. As in all refugee operations, sanitation and adequate latrines remained a problem throughout the operation. At Khao I Dang three different approaches were tried in six months, none of which was satisfactory. It is a bit disconcerting that more efforts have not been expended in this particular field and that pit latrines are still the primary means of handling excreta in large refugee populations. As sanitation is a primary link to refugee health, those organizations that continually respond to disasters should devote more attention to this area. While the Aqua-Privy is a significant step in this direction, more effort is required, and stockpiles of low-cost, rapidly deployable sanitation units need to be purchased and stored for emergency use.

Children's centers. A unique concept in the care of unaccompanied minors was developed at Khao I Dang. Instead of placing the children in a central orphanage, individual "families" of children of different ages were created. Mothers who had lost their own children were sought as surrogate mothers for each of the new families, which were dispersed throughout the camp. From an operational standpoint, however, these centers were an innovation that should be noted for future operations.

Supplementary-feeding programs. Even the best of the supplementary-feeding programs carried out in the Thai camps showed few improvements over approaches developed in past operations. While the programs moved smoothly and provided an excellent range of services, there was still too much emphasis on institutional-type feeding, with recipients standing in line for long periods of time. Decentralization of supplementary feeding can be achieved, but it requires that sufficient space be provided in camp layouts for decentralized services and that the volags develop a capacity to provide nutritional education.

Intensive feeding: Intensive feeding procedures were established along the lines suggested in de Ville de Goyet et al., and they proved to be generally effective. The complete feeding centers with all the suggested wards were not, however, built immediately and did not go into operation until the majority of cases had already received extensive attention.

Cross-border therapeutic feeding. Special procedures for cross-border therapeutic [intensive] feeding were developed to provide assistance to refugees inside Kampuchea. Full therapeutic feeding proved impractical due to security problems and the inability of the staff to remain in the centers overnight. During the initial stages of the operation, it was difficult to ascertain how effective these cross-border programs were as follow-up registration, and other parts of the operation were extremely difficult under the circumstances. Additional research is needed to determine the effectiveness of the approaches used and to modify them as required for future operations.

Shelter. A variety of different approaches were used to provide shelter for the refugees. In the emergency stages, people were provided with bamboo and thatching materials and encouraged to build large, linear, multifamily shelters. These units produced a harsh environment and created a fire hazard. Because of their density, they also increased the dangers of fostering communicable disease. In later stages, more permanent buildings, made of a fire-resistant fiberboard, were erected in some of the smaller camps. Duplex, triplex, and even quadruple shelter units proved workable, but when the number of families in a shelter was increased to more than four, problems induced by density occurred. Planners argued for single-family units, and cost estimates showed that certain designs were feasible, but space and other economic practicalities prevented construction.

The most innovative designs were erected in Sa Kaeo II and Kamput. These shelters were made of a fire-resistant wallboard and could be subdivided according to the number of families and individuals assigned to each unit. Families were provided with bamboo and other materials in order to divide the shelter and enclose the front of the house. This encouraged individual design and style, while assuring basic fire-resistant construction for most of the shelter. In the initial planning stages, many experts criticized these shelters as being too expensive and not in keeping with the traditional houses found in Kampuchea. In retrospect, however, the decision to erect these structures appears to have been sound, and the durability of the buildings has justified the initial expense. By raising the houses on stilts, one or two feet off the ground, localized flooding problems during the rainy season were overcome. In addition, their wooden floors proved much more acceptable to the refugees than either the bare ground or the cement floors found in shelters in other camps.

Use of sanitarians. One of the most innovative public-health measures employed in* the camps was the utilization of sanitarians—professionals involved in public health, sanitary engineering, and vector control—to advise on vector control and other measures to reduce the likelihood of contamination or the spread of disease. At Sa Kaeo, where they were first employed, the sanitarians effectively reduced flies in the hospital area and are credited with having identified unsanitary water supply procedures that were contaminating the water in the camp. The sanitarians also proved invaluable in selecting chemicals for mosquito control and for recommending measures for controlling vectors around kitchens, latrines, and solid-waste disposal areas. The IRC should be lauded for bringing these trained specialists to the border area.

ASSOCIATED ISSUES

Quite a few issues arose during the conduct of the border operation which are interesting to note, and require more research in order to evaluate effectively methods for addressing them. These issues were not completely new and have arisen in other operations, yet the Kampuchean-border operation provides an excellent laboratory for studying the situation and developing information that might be useful in the future.

Linkage between refugees in Thailand and on the Kampuchean border. As mentioned earlier, large numbers of refugees remained just inside Kampuchea. The reasons these refugees had for not crossing the border were many and varied. Some simply wanted to wait and see how the situation would develop. Others remained for purposes of trying to reestablish contact with their families, others to participate in supply operations for the interior, and many were reluctant to cross for fear of not being able to repatriate. (The occupation government of Kampuchea had made it clear that those who crossed the border would not be welcomed back.)

Because of the dual situation on the border, UNHCR felt especially constrained to ensure that services on the Thai side should not surpass the levels of services provided to refugees on the other side of the border, lest it draw more refugees across. (It should be noted that the UNHCR mandate prohibits any activity that might encourage more refugees to leave their homeland.) Thus the concept of linkage—that is, equating services and supplies provided to the refugees in the camps in Thailand to the assistance refugees received on the Kampuchean side of the border—was established.

Linkage is an issue that arises in many refugee operations and has become a source of propaganda or provides an explanation by the national government of the refugees as to why so many people are leaving. There is no conclusive evidence to show, however, that this actually occurred on the Kampuchean border. Assistance levels throughout the operations were scarcely such that refugees would be encouraged to leave their homeland simply to take up residence in a refugee camp. A far greater inducement to border crossing was the chance of permanent settlement in a Western country, an activity upon which those in the holding centers soon launched.

The whole question of linkage is one that needs to be addressed in future research on refugee operations. The objective should be to determine at what levels of service and for what nonmilitary considerations or conditions—such as famine—refugees will "immigrate" across a border in search of relief.

Linkage to surrounding villages. Refugee operations are often criticized for failure to consider the impact of the operation on the communities surrounding the refugee camps. In Thailand, the government continually expressed its concern that the level of assistance given to the refugees should not be more than that normally received by the neighboring Thai villagers. Thus, UNHCR instructed its field officers to reduce services to the level of the surrounding villages.

The trouble with this decision was twofold. First, the village standard was not determinable. Was it the level of a poverty-stricken peasant or was it a basic—but unspecified—minimal level of services to which the Thai government aspired? Second, the needs of refugees confined in a camp without free access to, or means to participate in, local markets were very different from those of the villagers.

It would be hard to show that the refugees in the camps received better food or lived in better conditions than the surrounding villagers. While certain services, such as medical aid and supplementary feeding were far better than in any rural area in Thailand, the health problems of the refugees were far different from those of the rural Thai population. (Of far greater concern should have been the impact and inflation caused by the large influx of refugee workers, yet this was never manifested either by the Thai government or the operational agencies.)

These arguments, however, did not satisfy the Thai government, and unfortunately, few agencies offered to undertake village development work which could have lessened the objections.

There are two ways in which these concerns might be addressed. The first is through the adoption of the basic minimum standards mentioned earlier. These standards could be shown to be tailored to meet the needs of the refugees and equated to the average services found in rural villages. Another means of lessening criticism would be the basing of some of the major health facilities, such as hospitals, in the surrounding communities, not in the camps themselves. They would thus serve not only the refugees but also the surrounding communities. The refugees would continue to receive a high standard of service, and there would be permanent improvement to the communities' facilities, which would endure after the refugee operation terminated.

Finally, the fact that there is some impact on the surrounding environment must be recognized by relief agencies and sufficient plans and approaches for lessening the negative aspects of this impact must be developed.

Assistance as a disincentive to repatriation. Because of the unusually high standard of services in the Thai camps, many observers felt that such a "good life" would serve as a disincentive to repatriation, or would discourage resettlement within other Asian countries. These sentiments have also arisen in other refugee operations, yet in those, few took them seriously because the level of service was so inadequate. Inside the camps in Thailand, however, observers could see flourishing markets, an adequate water supply, excellent feeding facilities, schools, recreational facilities, and even a local Khmer dance academy. Thus, a false image of easy living was often projected to short-term visitors. Actually, while the standard of service was high and a variety of supportive activities were provided, the basic plight of the refugees remained such that few wanted to stay in the camps any longer than was absolutely necessary.

In order to provide relief officials with the tools necessary to combat these false impressions, and to continue to provide a high standard of service without undue criticism, more sociological evidence on camp life and on the aspirations of refugees under different sets of circumstances is needed.

SUMMARY AND CONCLUSIONS

The Kampuchean-border operation has shown that the international relief system still has many weaknesses and problems to overcome. Coordination continues to loom as the major problem, especially with the proliferation of agencies. Professionalism and sophistication in approaches are still not highly developed, especially in the newer and inexperienced agencies. The disparities in the services provided and the measures used to correct them illustrate that uniform standards should be developed to effect more equitable assistance to refugees. A further concern should be the development of measures to equalize assistance levels in operations occuring at the same time.

The state of the art, as defined by the Kampuchean border operation, shows considerable improvement since the beginning of the 1970s. The retention of experienced personnel is beginning to pay off in more effective programs and the lessons learned are beginning to be incorporated in overall planning. Alternative approaches, however, are still required. More documentation, training, and professionalism are needed, and more funds are required for programmatic research, as well as for development of specific relief items, such as sanitation systems.

Finally, the Kampuchean operation illustrates that developmental concerns and approaches can successfully be incorporated in emergency refugee-relief programs. More effort must be expended by the relief organizations in order to capitalize on these opportunities and to move away from pure relief into more developmental activities.

THE CORNELL MEDICAL TEAM

Cynthia S. Weikel and Donald Armstrong

In late 1979, some third-year medical residents, fourth-year medical students, and nurses at The New York Hospital Cornell Medical Center began a combined humanitarian and academic project, supported by the leaders of the medical center. Subsequently, the IRC agreed to fund and help manage the group. This cooperative effort was unusual because an academic center became directly involved in disaster relief, and created a successful alliance with a private voluntary agency's funding and administrative skills for health-care delivery to refugees.

A program was developed which had three objectives: (1) to provide assistance by many physicians, nurses, and medical students; (2) to expose health professionals to the challenges and educational opportunities of health-care delivery in the developing world; and (3) to initiate training programs for Khmer health workers concentrating on preventive medicine and common medical problems. In January 1980, the first members of the Cornell medical team arrived in Thailand to organize and begin 24-hour coverage of the emergency [admissions] ward at Khao I Dang.

Cynthia S. Weikel, a physician, was a senior medical resident at The New York Hospital Cornell Medical Center when she served on the Cornell Medical Team of the International Rescue Committee from March to June 1980 and from January to March 1981. She is now an Assistant Professor of Medicine, Division of Geographic Medicine, University of Virginia Medical School, Charlottesville, Virginia. Donald Armstrong is Chief of the Infectious Disease Service at the Memorial-Sloan Kettering Cancer Center, and Professor of Medicine, Cornell University Medical College, New York. He served as an attending physician of the Cornell Medical Team at Khao I Dang in April and October 1981.

By February 1980, a full team of 17 members had been established [see the chapter, "Working at Khao I Dang: A Physician's Experience" by Barry S. Levy, a member of the Cornell team]. It consisted of several graduate nurses, most of whom were very well-trained in critical-care medicine—the nurses worked for three- to six-month rotations, with some extending their rotation to a year; a few fourth-year medical students from Cornell and other medical schools who were taking two-month clinical electives; a few second- or third-year medicine and pediatrics residents who were taking an elective for two to three months; on occasion, a fellow in infectious diseases for two to four months; and generally one attending internist or pediatrician on leave from a medical school, usually Cornell, for a month or longer.

In general, the basic university teaching structure of student, physician-in-training, nurse, and attending physician was maintained. Although rapid turnover of personnel is unusual in relief work abroad (usually commitments of six months or longer are expected), this arrangement proved to be viable. The schedule led to certain administrative strains, particularly in respect to transportation arrangements. Benefits, however, arose from a continuous supply of enthusiastic workers from a single source. Thus, there was a team approach to the functioning of the admissions ward, vital to the smooth delivery of health care and the achievement of its original objectives.

The transition from a university base to a low-technology, foreign setting was eased by the establishment in January 1980 of a comprehensive orientation program for students, physicians-in-training, and nurses. This program consisted of seminars on every aspect of medical care. The information collected from the field indicated that the critical medical problems of the refugees were not exotic, thus both common problems (pneumonia, otitis, and gastroenteritis) and illnesses unusual in the United States (malaria and dengue) were discussed. There were lectures on the history and culture of the Cambodian people and on Thai traditions and culture. Logistical matters, such as food and housing, were also addressed. An opportunity to learn the basics of the Thai and Cambodian languages was provided.

(The simple thoughtfulness of being able to address our Thai neighbors with "Good morning" in their own language helped later to increase team members' acceptance into the community.) Lastly, a concise and informative packet of the applicable literature was provided to each prospective worker.

In Thailand, IRC's administrators met arriving team members at the airport in Bangkok, welcomed and briefed them, and took full responsibility for all housing and transportation. The medical team lived together in groups of six to eight in rented houses in Aranyaprathet, about a half hour by minibus from Khao I Dang. At the camp, the ward was jointly managed by the IRC field administrator; a senior medical resident, or fellow designated as "team leader"; and the head nurse, chosen by colleagues. The IRC field administrator played a critical role in the smooth functioning of the ward by relieving the physicians and nurses of such responsibilities as trying to locate and insure the delivery of needed supplies. Thus, within the ward, the attention of medical staff members was essentially undiverted from the delivery of care. In addition, mandatory team meetings involving all members of the medical and administrative staffs were held every one to two weeks, providing a forum for open discussion of any problems that the team was encountering. These sessions were invaluable in maintaining team spirit and improving the team's understanding of the policies of the Thai government with respect to the Khmers. Due to this continual reevaluation of the ward's activities, ideas for improvements in health care were frequently made, and "quality-of-care" standards were set.

Within the ward, our medical team was joined by indispensable Khmer co-workers. The Khmers, with their graciousness, ingenuity, and multilingual talents, helped in numerous capacities. Many worked as translators who were learning the health-care skills of physician's assistant by working side by side with a specific doctor or medical student.

The necessity to talk to patients through translators posed limitations in the taking of histories. The English skills of the interpreters were variable. Sometimes physicians speaking

Chinese or French found more meaningful histories could be obtained in those languages than in English. Staff members learned by carefully watching the exchange between the patient and translator when the latter's desire to please overcame the search for actual truth, or when the translator made the judgment that something a patient said was not important enough to relay to the doctor. One patient mentioned that his father was sick, but an inexperienced translator thought that this was not worth repeating. The doctor, hearing the statement not translated, asked for a translation and found that the patient's father had tuberculosis, an important fact since this is what the patient had and it was surely contracted from his father with whom he lived.

Another obstacle was the team members' limited understanding of the culture, a gap that the translators were often unable to fill because there were at least three different ethnic groups in the camp—Chinese, Vietnamese, and Cambodian. Each of them had their own traditional medicine practices, which were unfamiliar to the ward staff, and there were many "black-market" drugs. These drugs were apparently taken according to the color and configuration of the pill. One example was a patient who took multiple "black-market" pills in a suicide attempt and was brought into the admissions ward apparently comatose. The pills turned out to be tetracycline which have no central nervous system effect and the patient's response was hysterical. Usually the physician did not know what pills had been taken or what other procedures had been followed.

The workday was scheduled into two shifts, the day shift being from 7 A.M. to 6 P.M. The work week for each team member was generally six days. In the event of illness, it was understood, however, as it is in any university medical center, that full coverage would be maintained. Illness—generally manifested by fever and diarrhea lasting from two days to two weeks —was frequent among team members and other hospital workers.

At Khao I Dang, the admissions ward served a myriad of functions and was central to the organization of the hospital.

First, during the daytime, it acted as a referral center from the outpatient departments. Once referred, patients often received follow-up through the admissions ward. In fact, with time, this became more common as outpatient departments were closed. It also was the holding center's emergency room and served as a consultative source for both the wards and the outpatient departments. In the admissions ward, all referrals for admission and all emergency cases were triaged by a nurse and fully evaluated by a medical student and a physician. Appropriate diagnostic testing and therapeutic intervention were initiated.

Initially, diagnostic work-up in this low-technology setting consisted of the most simple and basic of laboratory testing. At nighttime, laboratory work was performed by the admissions staff. This provided an excellent opportunity and the motivation to learn how to prepare slides to diagnose malaria. For many students, it was the first experience in doing a manual white blood count. No bacteriological cultures were available. X-rays (of suboptimal quality) were limited to plain films and were available only nine hours a day. In general, this lack of sophisticated laboratory testing was not viewed as detrimental. Rather, it served as a stimulus for sharpening our clinical skills.

Therapy also posed its own set of intriguing problems and revelations to physicians-in-training accustomed to free choice from the plethora of medications in a university setting. It was soon clear that the most crucial medications were antibiotics, especially penicillins. Fortunately, these were available in abundance. In contrast, there was a limited availability of other drugs and changing suppliers. Team members learned to use available medications effectively. Open-mindedness and flexibility were the keys to providing good medical care.

During the daytime, patients clearly requiring inpatient evaluation were transferred as quickly as possible from our ward to the appropriate inpatient ward. Those with less severe medical problems, yet too ill to go home immediately or with an unclear but unsettling clinical presentation, were kept in a holding area in our ward. While waiting for the results of diagnostic tests, patients were carefully observed, and vital signs monitored. When appropriate, initial doses of antibiotics were administered, and fever control and rehydration therapy begun. Prior to discharge from the admissions ward, patients and family members were carefully instructed in the importance of compliance with prescribed medications, control of fever, and careful medical follow-up.

At night, the admissions ward served to evaluate any end-of-the-day overflow from the outpatient clinics. Because there were no hospital admissions at night, except for acute surgical problems, the admissions ward also served as an inpatient acute-care facility as well as a short-term holding area. As the camp size was reduced through the resettlement of thousands of Khmers, the physician on nighttime duty became responsible for emergency care on the inpatient medical and pediatric wards. The "holding area" function of the admissions ward proved particularly valuable in providing an opportunity to let those illnesses in which the diagnosis was initially unclear evolve, and start treatment for certain conditions such as convulsions. Much unnecessary discomfort and suffering were alleviated (for example, by providing short-term rehydration) by short stays (up to 12 hours) in the admissions ward.

During the first four months of operation when the camp's population was more than 100,000, more than 8,000 patients were seen and examined by the admissions ward staff. The day shift then evaluated approximately 60 to 80 patients; the night shift, 30 to 40. These numbers sometimes transiently rose, taxing the ward's facilities. When the camp population was approximately 60,000 in late 1980 and early 1981, approximately 40 patients were evaluated per day shift and 20 at night.

The Cornell team's personnel were also involved in educational and teaching programs for the team, the hospital, and the Khmers. Customary university-teaching habits were maintained through morning and evening rounds where problem cases were discussed after research in available texts and consultation with team members or others particularly knowledgeable on a specific topic. Standard medical and pediatric textbooks were available in the ward, as well as tropical-medicine and emergency-medicine books and guides. Grand rounds for the entire hospital were organized in February 1980 by Dr. Tom Jones, Chief of the Division of International Medicine at Cornell. During these rounds, cases were presented and a carefully prepared discussion was given by a member(s) of the Cornell team or other health workers in the camp with special experience in or knowledge of such topics as meningitis, tuberculosis, cholera, or leprosy. Weekly ward "walk rounds" were established and conducted by the hosting ward, with physicians and medical students gathering at the bedside to discuss patients with difficult diagnostic or management problems. Finally, either the team leader or attending physician would meet once a week with other camp physicians and administrators to determine when patients should be transferred to Bangkok for more specialized care after local resources had been exhausted.

Educational programs for the Khmers included lectures on common medical problems given primarily for the interpreters and ward helpers. Topics included those diseases most frequently seen in the ward: otitis (ear infection), pneumonia, and gastroenteritis. Techniques for the clinical diagnosis of pneumonia, evaluation of hydration status, and basics of therapy were taught. The book *Where There Is No Doctor* was an excellent supplement. Due to the ward's one-Khmer-to-one-staff-member working arrangement, the Cambodians became skilled in the initial evaluation, triage, and therapy of common and uncomplicated medical problems. With time, they successfully undertook more and more ward responsibility. After the establishment of a program for training Khmer nurses, these lectures were expanded to include topics relating to emergency-room nursing [see the chapter "Medical Training Programs for Refugees" by Barbara Bayers].

There were unique aspects to the process of self-education and teaching in this refugee-camp setting. First, an extraordinarily heavy work load compelled the attending physician to work primarily side by side with all the other workers. The attending physician could not serve only as a consultant. He or she had to keep seeing patients plus discussing with other team members patients having difficult problems or unusual findings. In addition, doctors from other wards frequently consulted with the attending physician. Second, entirely different professional relationships, either student-teacher or nurse-physician, existed both on and off the ward. The team worked, traveled, ate, and lived together. The hours were long and physically taxing. The patients were consistently sicker than patients in outpatient settings in the United States. This, combined with the matter-of-fact discussion of the gruesome brutality witnessed by the Khmers in Cambodia, was emotionally taxing. Because of these factors, student, teacher, nurse, and physician became true colleagues, respectful of each other and of each other's efforts in working together toward common goals. The team was unhampered by the hierarchy of a university setting. It seemed as if each individual's clinical skills flourished. In particular, nurses were drawn into the mainstream of medical care. They learned to recognize rales, inflamed eardrums, and many other physical signs.

Under the circumstances, a high quality of medicine was practiced. Consultations, as already suggested, were frequently sought. Histories, physical findings, and laboratory studies were documented in brief notes on small charts. Plans for the management of patients were recorded whether they were to be admitted to the hospital or referred to the outpatient department. Continuous discussions of and concern for precise diagnosis and therapy stimulated appropriate medical care for a refugee camp setting.

An important deficit of the admissions ward originally, however, was the lack of proper documentation of diagnoses and follow-up as to what happened to those patients admitted to the various inpatient wards. At least one team member, preferably the attending physician, should have made rounds on the various wards to find out what happened to those admitted. In the early months, this was seldom done; but later, when the camp population was smaller and better nourished and when fewer epidemics occurred, such rounds were made and were rewarding.

Team members learned about the medical, political, and economic realities of working in an underdeveloped setting. They also could see that their medical care made a substantial difference in an individual patient's sense of well-being.

Educationally, the benefits were mutually shared by the

Western staff and the Khmers. The evaluations of this unique program by medical personnel have been overwhelmingly laudatory. For many of us, it was clearly the most rewarding and stimulating clinical experience to date in our careers. New priorities in our medical education were recognized. Career objectives were changed.

Within the admissions ward, the Khmer translators and helpers became progressively more adept at the skills of health-care delivery. These individuals latched onto their particular job areas and constantly sought to increase their knowledge base. The result was that in February 1981, there was a ward managed by the Khmer staff and supervised by the Cornell team. The Khmers did the initial triage, and began to recognize critical findings that needed immediate presentation to either a Cornell physician or a Khmer translator who functioned as a physician's assistant. Trained Khmer nurses were usually able to carry out a physician's orders correctly and efficiently. These individuals, oppressed for so long, were beginning to achieve independence and a sense of accomplishment in a working situation. Close supervision by members of the Cornell team was still necessary, but progress was being made.

Initial objections to the concept of a university team working in a low-technology setting included the idea that such a team would be inept—primarily due to a lack of previous experience in the Third World. In truth, the transition was easily made for two reasons. First, both the Division of International Medicine at the New York Hospital and the IRC took commendable steps to alleviate gaps in team members' education and to organize the practicalities of day-to-day life. Second, all those involved made a strong commitment to both the program and our team approach. From early on, team members recognized that being flexible was key. But, more important, several hundred new individuals now have had on-site experience in an underdeveloped area. These people as they spread throughout the United States will serve as a potential indoctrinated source of manpower in future crisis situations. In addition, since the medical aspects of the program were organized essentially through one office, there is an "institutional memory" of the problems that were encountered, particularly problems related to preventive medicine, so that they are less likely to occur in future relief operations [see the chapter, "A Medical Student's Perspective" by Patricia F. Walker]. For example, the children at Khao I Dang should have been immunized earlier against measles and polio virus; vitamin A to prevent xerophthalmia should have been administered as the refugees entered the camp. The failure to initiate rapidly such programs in Khao I Dang led to considerable morbidity and mortality. These lessons have been retained for future application.

In conclusion, the alliance of a university hospital and a private voluntary agency for the delivery of health care in a refugee camp was successful. The admissions ward, as organized and administered by the Cornell medical team and the IRC, achieved its original objectives. Hopefully, it will excite and motivate other university training programs, voluntary agencies, and medical personnel to respond to new crisis situations where such combined efforts are so sorely needed.

AN AMERICAN MEDICAL STUDENT'S PERSPECTIVE

Patricia F. Walker

Ban Nong Samet is a tiny village straddling the border of Thailand and Cambodia. Just north of the settlement, over the preceding months, thousands of Cambodians had gathered in an area dominated by tall grass, rice fields, and sparse clumps of trees, where they eked out a precarious existence on the minimal supplies of water and rice provided by international relief agencies. When we arrived, a German team of five physicians and nurses was working desperately to keep alive the severely malnourished infants. ICRC and Thai Red Cross doctors arrived and left on a sporadic basis. We were asked by a Cambodian doctor, obviously swamped with patients, to help staff an OPD.

Our "clinic" was a long bamboo-frame, thatched building, the interior of which was divided into three examining rooms. We had bamboo examining tables, a large box filled with various medications—primarily antibiotics, vitamins, and iron—and what instruments we brought with us—stethoscopes, bandages, syringes, and some minor surgical equipment. Crowds formed before our van pulled in each day; most people were in need of medical care, but some came simply out of curiosity. We saw four hundred patients a day: case after case of malaria, anemia,

Patricia Walker, who was raised in Thailand, was a medical student at Mayo Medical School in Rochester, Minnesota, in November and December 1979, when she served as a member of the American Refugee Committee's second medical team in Thailand. She is now a general internist, currently working as Medical Director of the Emergency Department at Mt. Sinai Hospital, Minneapolis, Minnesota.

malnutrition, tuberculosis, mothers' inability to nurse their babies, vitamin deficiency, and bloody diarrhea. We saw many patients who had obtained antimalarial medication on the black market and injected themselves, creating huge hip abscesses. One doctor ran an obstetrics clinic. Another pulled dead and infected teeth. Two young men came in with gunshot wounds, reminding us of the occasional distant shelling and much closer small-arms and automatic-weapons fire we heard daily. After working on the border for three days, our team was given the job of staffing an intensive-care ward at Khao I Dang, which had just opened.

Our ward was a 110-bed bamboo structure covered with a blue plastic roof. The beds, which we set up on the first morning before patients began arriving, consisted of a piece of plywood mounted on a metal frame and covered with a thatched mat. We admitted 85 patients that first day, and as we were the only ward then open, we accepted everyone from malnourished infants to elderly TB patients. Patients walked in or were borne in, either on stretchers or by their relatives. Families (that is, the surviving family members—I never met an intact family during my entire stay) would sleep in the one bed provided for the patient. Family members took care of feeding, giving baths, and cleaning up diarrhea and vomit. Relatives watched over the patients night and day, telling us when IV lines infiltrated and suggesting good sites for new lines. They were always strong, quiet, and accepting of our limited help. With the exception of orphans, I never saw a patient die alone at Khao I Dang.

Malaria with temperatures from 105 to 106 degrees was common, as were anemia, beriberi, dehydration, diarrhea, malnutrition, and tuberculosis. We admitted a few unusual cases— leprosy, liver cancer, a fungal infection called "madura foot," and occasional land-mine or bullet-wound injuries.

What was it that was so different about medical work in a less-developed country? The weather, the primitive medical conditions, the tropical diseases? No, it was much more pervasive than that. It was an attitude, a feeling, engendered not by the doctors and nurses working in Thailand, but by the refugees themselves. As in most Eastern cultures, death was so much a part of life for these people that they did not seem to go through Kubler-Ross's stages of grieving. Instead, I saw only quiet acceptance, and in that acceptance, sitting on a cot with a dying husband, wife, mother, father, child, an attitude enviable in Western society. In our culture, intrusive technology and aggressive care make it difficult for even well-adjusted families to let a beloved relative die with dignity. Instead, they die in intensive-care situations, often alone, hooked up to monitors and lines.

I asked a Cambodian doctor working with us about discussing with patients their impending death. He explained that this was not done in his culture because it was believed to hasten the death. How ironic! Back home, I often talked with patients about not being resuscitated, and they often ended up dying alone with unaccepting relatives. In Thailand, I could not tell patients when they would die, yet they seemed to know and rarely died alone.

The most gratifying experience was to watch our patients improve almost before our eyes. I was reminded of Dr. Tom Dooley's work in Laos and the comment in his book *Deliver Us from Evil* about the power of antibiotics, vitamins, soap, and cleanliness.

Thinking afterward of my experience, I realized that while I was in Thailand I had never cried. Since I had grown up in Southeast Asia, I felt that in many ways my fellow countrymen were being destroyed by war and genocide, and I was immensely saddened. Yet each night at our communal house we were too tired to talk much, or when we did, we spoke only of the refugees' incredible strength and will to survive. I could not cry when they did not. Since then, during my residency training, frustrated by the indignities of modern medicine and the inappropriate prolongation of suffering, I have cried.

It is hard to convey the richness of medical relief work to those who have not been involved in it. As a student, I learned through confrontations with situations for which no course in medical ethics could prepare me. I learned much tropical medicine. I learned the importance of preventive medicine over acute care, even in a crisis situation. I learned self-confidence, sensitivity, ingenuity, and a sense of perspective about Western medical care—both its advantages and its shortcomings. I also learned the nuances of administration of such a massive relief program and had a chance to interact with stimulating professionals from all over the world.

Very importantly, a relief work experience helps to break many "limits" about health care and the attitudes toward it imposed by medical training. Inevitably, the necessary working as a team in crisis situations helps to erode the competitiveness so deeply ingrained in traditional Western medical training.

The morning we left Thailand was full of emotional, strained good-byes. Our interpreter, Rith, had become very close to the team, living and working in the ward. I had watched his sad eyes begin to soften over the course of the month, crinkling at the corners as he smiled. The day we left, as I saw him standing in the crowd saying good-bye, his eyes filled with tears. I remembered what he had once told me, "I want a mother and father and sisters. I think it will be very hard to find a mother and father like mine." Then he asked me, "What is the word for very, very sad?" and I watched as he recorded my quiet answer in his notebook. "Tragic."

THE NEED FOR THE DEVELOPMENT
OF AN "INSTITUTIONAL MEMORY"

Dieter Koch-Weser, Joseph Wray, and James Traver

Throughout this century, more-fortunate individuals have been moved to action by the plight of refugee populations; there has been a continuous record of humanitarian efforts to assist refugees. Most refugee relief and permanent integration efforts have, however, been carried out on a case-by-case, ad hoc basis. There needs to be planning for not only short-term but also long-term needs. With academic institutions, including their health-care-providing institutions, being increasingly involved in national and international public-policy investigation and action, it seemed appropriate for us in 1980 to evaluate if the Harvard health professional schools could play a role in the refugee relief operation in Thailand.

In early 1980, Dieter Koch-Weser was Associate Dean for International Programs at the Harvard Medical School; Joseph Wary, the Director of the Office of International Health at the Harvard School of Public Health; and James Traver, a third-year student at the Harvard Medical School. At the invitation of the International Rescue Committee, they visited, in 1980 and since, a number of Cambodian refugee camps on the Thai-Cambodian border and two Laotian and Hmong refugee camps in northern Thailand. They also had discussions with the staffs of many relief programs. At present, Dr. Koch-Weser is Lecturer on International Health, Harvard School of Public Health, Boston; Dr. Wray, Professor of Clinical Public Health, Columbia University School of Public Health, New York; and Dr. Traver, Medical Director, East Providence Health Center, Providence, Rhode Island. All are physicians.

Our main objective was to investigate the potential for involvement of academic institutions. The two programs we observed that impressed us as highly successful were run by the Cornell group at Khao I Dang and the pediatric group from the University of Minnesota at Nong Khai, a Laotian refugee camp. Both were of great value to the students, broadening their horizons, making them aware of the social and cultural influences on health, and giving them a view of health care for the underprivileged and underserved. The faculty and residents also had an experience they could have had nowhere else, which made them more broad-minded and mature.

Acutely aware that some problems, as we observed them, might be temporary, were observed several years ago, were present only in one setting, and are subject to our misinter pretation or use of inaccurate information, we now describe some of the problems we observed in the hope of making a modest contribution to a highly successful relief operation. Our uncertainty has led us to mention these problems in very general terms.

1. There was no effective way of involving Thai institutions and individuals in the planning and implementation of refugee-related activities performed by agencies from other countries. We discussed with many Thai health professionals their attitudes and ideas, and found that, in contrast to the often quoted "hands-off" position of some official Thai groups, virtually all realized that the problem would be with them for years to come and were eager to cooperate. The School of Public Health of Mahidol University, for example, was actively engaged in refugee programs, but with little, if any, coordination and cooperation with the expatriate agencies.

2. The health-education programs for the refugee population were either completely lacking or insufficient. The refugees often did not know rudimentary personal hygiene and healthy behavior, particularly important under the crowded and relatively primitive living conditions in the camps.

3. It seemed to us that the health professionals and health

workers among the refugees were not sufficiently included in the delivery system, given that they far better understand the ethical, cultural, and social factors impinging on the health status of their compatriots.

4. There were essentially no programs in community mental health, a prerequisite for sound community development and an absolute necessity for those populations living under confinement in a strange, sometimes hostile country, mostly without work and without a future.

5. There seemed to be a lack of ready plans available for the physicial facilities of refugee camps at the time they were built. Although each camp had to be adapted to the prevailing local conditions, previous experiences with mass disasters should have created some expertise. But apparently there were no blueprints for safe and sanitary housing, including some possible measures for fire protection. (The hospital at Khao I Dang and most of the houses in a Laotian camp in Thailand were later destroyed by fire.) There was insufficient knowledge about water supply and distribution and about sanitary facilities.

6. With all the efforts and dedication resulting in spectacular successes in curative surgery and medicine, the planning and implementation of an overall preventive medical program lagged far behind. Well-organized immunization programs were introduced only sporadically, and there were debates over the usefulness of BCG vaccination.

7. Food supplies, particularly supplemental foods, were often culturally highly inappropriate. We witnessed many discussions about "dry milk" products. Should they have been banned completely, even though large quantities already were in storage in Thailand? Should they have been freely distributed, even though the possible harm done due to diarrhea and dehydration if they were used as substitutes for breast feeding was well known? A policy of prudent and controlled use seemed indicated, considering the advantages and disadvantages.

8. Even more heated was the debate about indications for a methodology of family planning. While the Thais naturally

were worried about high fertility in the camps and strongly promoted birth-control programs, including the controversial drug DepoProvera, some of the relief workers, strongly objected to the use of a drug not approved for family planning purposes by their own governments or the United States Food and Drug Administration. American agencies seemed to have an ambivalent position on this very sensitive issue.
9. The preparation—medical, social, and cultural—of the relief workers could have been better. For example, physicians working in the relief operation often came directly from a tertiary academic setting or from a private practice in a well-to-do neighborhood in a developed country. Without specific training, it could not be expected that they would know how to deal with a third-degree malnourished child or drug-resistant cerebral malaria. On the other hand, it is surprising how rapidly almost all of them adapted and become effective in a relatively short time. Equally difficult to achieve is an understanding of the cultural, religious, moral, and other social factors in a strange culture that impinge on such issues as life and death, child care, contraception, drug taking, and nutrition. Appropriate preparation could and should have been offered all relief workers both in their own home countries and after their arrival in Thailand, probably with the help of the Thai academic health institutions. To many highly motivated health workers, the treatment and prevention of previously unknown diseases in a culturally strange environment must often have seemed overwhelming.
10 The necessary change from relief to development planning was only beginning to take place.
11. The practice of selecting "the fittest" for immigration into other countries, leaving the "least desirables" in Thailand, needed negotiation and clarification, particularly if this practice depended on the goodwill of the Thais.
12. While there was no reason to complain about the quality of curative care in the camps, the continuity and uniformity of care could have been improved. This admittedly is difficult if health workers from various backgrounds are thrown together for varying and overlapping periods. Stronger

overall leadership, better record keeping, and enforced coordination would have helped.

13. Information gathering, evaluation, and surveillance were very well performed by the epidemiologists of the CDC whenever and wherever they were present. These activities should have definitely been expanded.

14. Malaria, tuberculosis, and other diseases were being diagnosed and treated by widely differing methods in different camps and even within the same camp by different teams. There should have been standardization of diagnostic procedures, therapy, and protocols.

15. It should have been carefully investigated if the largely hospital-based care programs were cost-effective, and if the more peripheral, ambulatory clinical activities would not have been preferable in many cases.

16. The longer the various refugee camps are in existence, the more their relationship to the surrounding Thai population must be a matter of careful attention. In the development phase (after the relief phase), planning for health care—in the sense of WHO's "physical, mental, and social well-being"—must be undertaken for refugees *and Thais* if ultimate integration is the goal.

We reiterate that this listing of possible problems and some suggested solutions in no way implies a critical attitude toward the total relief operation in Thailand. On the contrary, we left Thailand with clear admiration for the dedication and skill exhibited by the numerous agencies and workers in every category.

CONCLUSION

We believe that there is a definite role for the organized participation of academic institutions in international refugee and disaster relief.

Writing in 1982, we feel it will be necessary to remedy the remaining problems, particularly recognizing that this tragic acute situation undoubtedly will be transformed into a chronic responsibility for the world community. Already now similar man-made disaster areas exist in Pakistan, Afghanistan, East Timor, Palestinian camps, and Somalia, and undoubtedly additional man-made and natural disasters, such as floods, earthquakes, droughts, and famines, will require assistance. It can be predicted that international refugee-aid and disaster-control activities will be necessary, not only in the expected long-lasting situation in Thailand, but also in many other areas of the world.

Large multidisciplinary institutions, such as universities, with many thousands of health and health-related professionals, are in a very favorable position to create programs to prepare experts, ready on short notice to confront such situations of need. They can also develop an "institutional memory" so that skills and knowledge acquired during one operation can be adapted and transferred to subsequent ones.

Academic faculties with expertise in the health, social, behavioral, and political sciences and with experience in virtually all parts of the world could cooperate with the international, national, and voluntary relief agencies in educational activities, including the preparation of manuals and materials and the development of appropriate education and training programs. Both for their proven enthusiasm and the opportunity to expose them to international refugee and disaster relief, students from health-professional schools should be included in these teams. Overall coordination of such academic participation should be performed by a respected national organization, such as the National Council for International Health.

PART 6

EPILOGUE

AT THE BORDER:
LATE 1982 AND EARLY 1983

Robert C. Porter, Jr.

A deceptive feeling of security, calm, and permanence pervaded the border area in December 1982. The border camps were then neat, clean, well run, and orderly—a remarkable change from the dirty, insecure, near anarchic camps of 1979 and 1980. The houses were well built and substantial. Lush fruit and vegetable gardens were everywhere. The raising of pigs, ducks, chickens, and other livestock was increasing. There were well-functioning schools and clinics. Most of these changes were due to the efforts of the Khmer who lived there, supplemented by the efforts of the international organizations and voluntary agencies. Camp residents seemed to have learned to ignore the presence of the heavily armed Vietnamese and Heng Samrin soldiers only a few kilometers away. Most of the warlords who formerly controlled the border camps had been killed, had disappeared, or had gone to Bangkok or France to live on the wealth they had acquired through control of the border gold and silver market. Since all the refugee camps had been brought more or less under the control of one of the three main resistance groups, internecine warfare had almost disappeared.

The border camps remain, however, as of March 1983, extremely vulnerable. Most camp leaders and residents realize that when a period of calm and stability occurs, it is only a temporary lull, and that it is easy for the Vietnamese to disrupt or destroy the camps and send their residents fleeing into Thailand. The camp residents in late 1982 were also aware of the hardening Thai attitude toward refugees residing temporarily in Thailand and were worried that in the event of a strong Vietnamese military attack, the Thai might be slow in allowing them to seek refuge on the Thai side of the border.

The continuing vulnerability of the border camps were demonstrated in January and February 1983, when, during their annual dry season offensive, the Vietnamese forces, backed by heavy armored tank and artillery support, attacked and destroyed the camp at Nong Chan. The Vietnamese attackers deliberately burned the primitive homes, hospitals, markets, and schools of the camp's civilian residents and continued to fire artillery rounds at them after they had fled the camp and sought refuge along a large ditch within Thai territory. In March and April 1983, Vietnamese troops appeared to be maneuvering to attack other refugee settlements north of Aran. During the surge in military activity in 1983, the international organizations and voluntary agencies demonstrated that they could handle sudden emergencies with efficiency, speed, and professionalism. They quickly arranged for those who had fled Nong Chan to be fed, sheltered, given medical assistance, and later moved to a safer location.

Despite the occasional increase in military activity, the work of the international organizations and voluntary agencies has become routinized. There is very little of the pressure international workers encountered in 1979 and early 1980, and except for periods when they must take care of those injured or displaced during increased military activity, most seem to work a very leisurely eight-hour day. The bustling Wild West atmosphere of Aranyaprathet in 1980 has given way to a calmer, businesslike pace. Personnel from the foreign embassies in Bangkok are no longer a frequent sight on the border, and the embassies seem to take a less activist, less interested role.

Of the UNHCR holding centers, the Khao I Dang "Hilton" is no longer as comfortable a place to live. Following its policy of "humane deterrence," the Thai government has implemented several restrictions on life in Khao I Dang in order to make it less of a magnet for those Khmer still on the border. The atmosphere of the holding center at Sa Kaeo, formerly a tightly ruled, Khmer Rouge-influenced, regimented place to live, became much more relaxed, free, and easy-going before it closed in December 1982; and its residents seemed content not to worry about their future.

AT THE BORDER:
LATE 1984

Rebecca A. Parks

The dry season has started early this year. It's only mid-November; I'm sitting in my quiet, air-conditioned office in Bangkok. The news from the border is not good. Nong Chan was attacked yesterday—November 16—and more than 10,000 people have beem moved to "Evacuation Site 6," where the United Nations Border Relief Operation (UNBRO) team was waiting for them. Our collective experience with emergency evacuations has become so great over the past five years that we are now much better prepared to cope. We have honed and developed our "disaster preparedness" to a fine art. That in itself is a blessing, although it is painfully little reassurance to be good at coping with something that annually involves such a tremendous amount of human suffering.

Perhaps the news coverage of the latest Vietnamese military offensive will refocus some of the world's attention on a problem that is no longer fashionable, no longer in the public eye. Our relief effort has been overshadowed by many more dramatic, seemingly more acute human disasters—Ethiopia, Somalia, Chad, Pakistan—and with the concomitant decrease in news coverage of the Khmer situation, the world assumes that we no longer have a problem on our hands. It is a classic journalistic case of "out of sight, out of mind." The world's

Rebecca A. Parks has worked in the Cambodian relief operation in Thailand since May 1980, initially as Medical Coordinator and then as Director of American Refugee Committee activities there, a position she currently holds.

attention span for disaster situations is characteristically short. Short memory for troubles in this part of the world has resulted in concrete financial limitations: decreased willingness to contribute to aid for this ongoing disaster has meant that each year fewer resources are available.

Ironically, fewer resources are available over the long term, while the problems on the border seem only to increase. The official border population remains at nearly 250,000. The total number of people do not change from year to year, only their locations. In five years, many have gone on to Khao I Dang, Phanat Nikhom, and third countries where their dreams can be more or less fulfilled. Their places have been taken by ever-increasing numbers of new arrivals from the interior of Kampuchea—political and economic malcontents, hungry people—who come to the border seeking freedom and a better life. Their dreams, also, are more or less fulfilled.

But every dry season brings nightmares. Long days of shelling, nights of no sleep, waiting with everything packed to be told at any moment to leave home for an evacuation site. Parts of Nong Chan's population have moved no less than six times since the dry season of 1983. The 1984-1985 dry season began yesterday, and they have again moved one more time. Most border camps served by UNBRO have already moved at least once this year.

Five years out from the start of this relief situation, we are involved in a strange hybrid of "emergency" and "development." A child who was born in Nong Samet in 1979 is now five years old. Normally he should be offered school, literacy, and socialization. Personal and institutional role models should have already shaped his preschool years, laying the crucial foundation for the good "citizen of the world" he has a right to become. Despite every humanitarian effort, where are the appropriate role models in a Khmer border refugee camp? Long-term development programs proceed within situational constraints during the rainy season—schools, women's associations, public-health campaigns. They are all interrupted with the first shell that signals the start of the dry season. Annually, and now semiannually, our illusions of participating in the normal development of the Khmer people are shattered as we are forced to drop all "nonessential" programs and switch back to the emergency, life-and-death mode of the dry season. What about the Khmer "citizens of the world" we were developing? For now they must wait, sleepless at night, packed to leave for an evacuation site. "World citizen" development cannot continue until the rains start and the fighting stops.

In the past five years, thousands of people have participated directly and through their donations in the relief effort, which many have called the best ever organized. All who contributed and those of us who have worked here have spared no amount of humanitarian effort and devotion to the Khmer people. The task has been approached creatively, collegially, religiously, and persistently. A solution has been sought for every new problem that has arisen. Fresh new ideas and new dedication has arrived with every new relief staff. More difficult problems have been met with longer work hours and even more dedication on the part of the staff. For the first several years, most of us felt that our efforts could directly influence the outcome for the Khmers. We believed that sufficient "good works" could actually save the Khmer people.

Five years into a formerly acute emergency situation, it is apparent that we are deadlocked and are now evolving into a chronic state. Several hundred thousand people are still caught in no-man's-land without any immediate hope of resolution. Many hundreds of thousands more remain inside Kampuchea, a place no longer their home, but occupied by foreign invaders who appear to be settled there for a long stay. No amount of devoted humanitarian effort has *truly* changed the ultimate outcome for the future of Cambodia. For five years we have narrowly succeeded in protecting an endangered Khmer population and prevented their rapid, total, and outright extinction. Now we must acknowledge our helplessness and admit that the final solution for Cambodia is out of our hands. Higher political powers hold all the cards for the final match. We can only be satisfied that our part of the job was well done—and continue to hope.

REFLECTIONS: SPRING 1985

Daniel C. Susott

The news is horrifying. Rebecca Parks was right. The Vietnamese attacked on Christmas [1984] with devastating brutality, destroying Nong Samet and Ban Sangae and sending 80,000 refugees scrambling for their lives. The Khmer hospital medics arrived at "Red Hill" [just outside Thailand] without even their shoes; they watched in despair as the sky darkened with smoke from their homes and the hospital. Their whole village camp was burned. Dozens of innocent people died, and many more were wounded. The fighting continues to rage, as the Vietnamese seek to eliminate the bases of the Khmer resistance on the border. In a few months, the monsoon rains will begin, bogging down the Vietnamese tanks and troops. The advantage will then return to the [Khmer] guerrillas, if they survive. The harvest in Cambodia is dismal this year [early 1985], as it was in 1979, when thousands of starving staggered into the consciousness and conscience of the world.

And through all this, the people suffer. The basic conditions of life are not changed from the summer of 1982, when I was summoned back to Thailand to serve as medical coordinator for UNBRO. Responsible for coordinating the volag health aid to the border population, I had the uncomfortable feeling that the United States was continuing to fight the Vietnam War, this time in the guise of international relief.

My assistant Barbara Bayers and I hiked nine hours into Sok Sann, an encampment of 8,000 KPNLF supporters, which the Vietnamese had overrun a few months earlier. After burning

the camp, the Vietnamese stayed only a short time, driven out
as much by the deadly drug-resistant malaria as by the KPNLF
forces. The utter deprivation and hardship these people endured
was made painfully real when 400 mothers implored us—the
first foreign medical workers they had seen in months—to help
their infants, each with a belly swollen from severe malnutrition and malaria. When I asked the leader of Sok Sann village
why his people chose to stay in such a malaria-infested place
where food and medical help were so difficult to obtain, he told
me that they would never leave until Cambodia was free of the
Vietnamese. His small village was crucial to the Khmer resistance in the south.

Then I learned that some of the surviving family of Chan Thy
Yi, my foster son, had made their way to the border and were
in Nong Chan camp, hoping to enter Khao I Dang and be resettled in America. There were six people, including his elderly
mother who was going blind and in pain; and his older sister,
a widow, with two small sons, both of whom had been so malnourished in the Pol Pot years that they could not walk. Their
camp was the site of regular Vietnamese shelling, and I feared
for their lives as the prospects of bringing them across the border through legal channels (Thai military/United States govern-
ment/UNHCR) dimmed. In desperation, I used my position to
attempt to smuggle them to safety across the border, but my
ploy was discovered and I lost my job, threatened that if I
ever returned to the border I would be put in prison. Shortly
thereafter, Nong Chan was wiped off the map by the Vietnamese, only weeks after Chan Thy's family had been led to safety.
Joy over the safety of "my" family was overshadowed by
sorrow at the fate of the thousands of others who were scattered to the winds.

Chan Thy Yi is now preparing to graduate from Hawaii's
best high school; part of his family, including his mother,
joined him in Hawaii in January 1984. Seang Meng Seng [see
"Hospitals During the Pol Pot Regime: A Cambodian Medical
Student's Perspective" and "One Person's Story"] is a second-year
medical student at the University of Hawaii; he and his lovely
wife, Kimly, arrived in America just ten days before their child,
Sakona, was born. These happier stories make the more painful

memories easier to bear, but always there are the letters: letters from the camps, "Help me—I'm still here after all these years"; letters from the United States and France, "My mother and my cousin are in the camps. They are in danger every day. They have no money and no food. How to help them?"; letters from Phnom Penh and the Cambodian countryside, smuggled out through the border camps, telling of the continuing privation and suffering inside Cambodia.

Cambodians, resettled in lands far from their home, struggle to carry on, are tortured by memories of the past. The survivors fill their days with their new lives—school, work, friends, cold weather—but at night when all is quiet, they cry in their sleep or sit bolt upright in bed, remembering.

I cannot help thinking of the children I know, forced into the mountain jungle with their parents, foraging desperately for something edible—a leaf, a sprout, a scorpion, a worm. Imagine their anguish as their elders and siblings weakened, day by day—·their panic and helplessness, their sorrow and guilt—each death leaving them more alone, to scrape graves out of the mud with sticks and plates. Wondering what they have done to merit such punishment.

I cry again for all those people who have to carry on alone. I cry for the people blinded or crippled or orphaned or widowed—yesterday and tomorrow—by the land mines and the shelling. I cry for the little people who will always carry the guilt of having survived, of not being able to have done more for those most dear to them, enduring torture that will not end. How can wounds like these ever heal?

I want the world to cry again for the Cambodians, to cry and understand and feel, and hopefully to help—to help not only the Cambodian people but all people everywhere who have suffered and been displaced from their homes by famine and by war.

AFTERWORD

Barry S. Levy

Much of this book has been about refugee relief activities in late 1979 and 1980. As I write [early 1985] Sa Kaeo is closed, and Khao I Dang now has far fewer people—about 30,000—than it did in 1980. Many Cambodians have been transferred to less crowded camps inside Thailand or on the border, and thousands of others have emigrated to other lands. Several Cambodians mentioned in my earlier chapter have emigrated: Mrs. Mom Kamel and Chu Pheng now live in the United States, Hong Gau in Switzerland, and Bun Heang Ung in Australia. Siphana Sok, Sichanth̆a Neou, Pheng Eng By, Chhoeunly So, and Keo Sambath, whose chapters appear in this book, now live in the United States. Some of them have struggled to adapt to their new lives; for example, the Cambodian health professionals among this group have met with many difficulties and frustrations in becoming licensed practitioners in the United States. Others have been remarkably successful; for example, Siphana Sok completed college in two years, and is now both studying for a master's degree in business administration and working as a marketing director for a real estate developer.

Although there have been some improvements since the height of the crisis in late 1979 and early 1980, the picture of life on the Thai-Cambodian border and within Cambodia is a mixed one. While the overall situation in Cambodia has improved since late 1979, the continuing occupation by approximately 200,000 Vietnamese troops has created problems. The situation of the Cambodian refugees requires a political solution, but none is in sight. Some dream that peace and neutrality could be brought to Cambodia through the United Nations or the superpowers. If so, many refugees might willingly return to rebuild their homeland; but this seems unlikely—at least in the foreseeable future.

It is all too easy to say that there is no way to influence this seemingly hopeless situation. Many of us who worked at Khao I Dang and other camps believe, however, that the situation is not hopeless and that a political solution can be found. There remains an opportunity for all to help by participating directly, by encouraging and supporting workers who are doing so, by contributing to relief organizations, by writing those in power to urge continuation of governmental support for the relief operation and for initiatives to achieve a lasting peace in Southeast Asia, and by sponsoring or otherwise assisting those Cambodians who are immigrating to third countries.

Many health professionals and others continue to work in the relief operation, which since 1980 has placed a much greater emphasis on educational programs than before, including a program on the border to enable Cambodians to be responsible for almost all their own medical and health needs. Thousands of others have been involved in other emergency relief projects, such as in Somalia, Ethiopia, and Pakistan (each of which has had many more refugees than there were in Thailand), and in the longer-term development projects to end hunger and unnecessary suffering in the world.

GLOSSARY

Aranyaprathet, or Aran: Thai town near border with Cambodia, center of Cambodian refugee relief activity.

ARC: American Refugee Committee. Minnesota-based private voluntary organization involved in refugee relief.

CBERS: Community Based Emergency Relief Services. Thai-based public-health and development organization, which, in part, operated a family-planning program in refugee camps in Thailand.

CCSDPT: Committee for Coordination of Services to Displaced Persons in Thailand. Bangkok-based organization that coordinated all services for Cambodian, Laotian, and other refugees in Thailand.

CDC: Centers for Disease Control of the Public Health Service, a branch of the United States Department of Health and Human Services.

Concern: Ireland-based private voluntary organization primarily concerned with maternal and child care.

CRS: Catholic Relief Services. United States-based private voluntary organization involved in relief.

FAO: Food and Agriculture Organization. United Nations agency responsible for food and agriculture development and other related activities.

Heng Samrin: Vietnamese-supported Chief of State of Cambodia since 1979.

ICEM or ICM: Intergovernmental Committee for (European) Migration. A consortium of more than 30 governments, founded in the 1930s to transport refugees from Nazi oppression; currently based in Geneva and responsible for the medical screening and transport of refugees.

ICRC: International Committee of the Red Cross. Switzerland-based, politically neutral international organization involved in relief of man-made disasters.

IRC: International Rescue Committee. United States-based private voluntary organization involved in refugee relief, founded in the 1930s to facilitate migration of Jewish refugees from Nazi oppression and currently working in many countries to serve displaced populations.

IV: Intravenous

Kamput: Small refugee holding center("camp") for Cambodians in Thailand.

Khao I Dang: Largest refugee holding center ("camp") for Cambodians in Thailand.

Khmer: Cambodian; also, the Cambodian language.

Khmer Rouge: Communist force in power in Cambodia from 1975 to 1979.

Khmer Serei: "Free Khmer." Non-Communist resistance group.

KPNLF: Khmer People's National Liberation Front. Anti-Communist resistance group.

Lon Nol: Sihanouk's prime minister who gained control after a right-wing coup in 1970 and remained leader of Cambodia, with United States support, until 1975.

LRCS: League of Red Cross Societies.

MHD: Malteser Hilfsdienst. German-based private voluntary organization.

MSF: Médecins Sans Frontières. France-based private voluntary organization.

OPD: Outpatient department or ambulatory clinic.

Phnom Penh: Capital of Cambodia.

Pol Pot: Leader of the Khmer Rouge.

PVO: Private voluntary organization (synonymous with volag, see below).

ROKU: Refugee Office Kampuchea Unit of the United Nations High Commissioner for Refugees.

Sa Kaeo: Large refugee holding center ("camp") for Cambodians in Thailand.

SAWS: Seventh-day Adventist World Service. Private voluntary organization.

Sihanouk, Prince Norodom. Ruler of Cambodia from 1953 to 1970.

Soforthilfe: German-based private voluntary organization.

Son Sann: Leader of KPNLF.
TBM: Thailand Baptist Mission.
Third country: Eventual country of asylum for refugees.
TMC: Traditional medicine center.
UNBRO: United Nations Border Relief Organization.
UNHCR: United Nations High Commissioner for Refugees.
UNICEF: United Nations Children's Fund.
VOA: Voice of America.
Volag: Voluntary agency, or private voluntary organization (see PVO, above).
WFP: World Food Program. The operational arm of the United Nations Food and Agricultural Organization.

BACKGROUND READING

Books and Monographs

Allegra, D., Nieburg, P., and Grabe, M. *Emergency Medical Refugee Relief: The Cambodian Operation, 1980-1981.* Washington, D.C.: U.S. Government Printing Office, 1985. Details the role of epidemiology in refugee relief operations, drawing examples from the Cambodian relief operation.

International Committee of the Red Cross. *Kampuchea: Back from the Brink.* Geneva, Switzerland: ICRC, 1981. Brief account of the relief operation from the perspective of this international organization.

Mason, L.A., and Brown, R. *Rice, Rivalry, and Politics.* Notre Dame, Indiana: University of Notre Dame Press, 1983. An interesting book describing the origins of the Cambodian relief crisis, abuse and reform of rice distribution, the beginning of the seed rice program, feeding of the Khmer Rouge, and the management of the relief operation.

National Council for International Health. *Cambodian Refugee Relief: Lessons Learned and Future Directions.* Washington, D.C.: NCIH, 1980. Proceedings of a two-day 1980 workshop on the administrative, political, and technical aspects of the relief operation.

Shawcross, W. *The Quality of Mercy.* New York: Simon and Schuster, 1984. A well-written book detailing the sociopolitical aspects of the relief operation, and examining the ways a catastrophe in the Third World evokes a response in the developed world as well as the modern conscience toward victims of disaster and persecution.

Periodical References Specific to Khmer Refugees

Adler, J., Bodner, E., Bornstein, S., et al. Medical mission to a refugee camp in Thailand. *Disasters* 1981; 5:23-31.

Buist, N.R. Perspective from Khao I Dang refugee camp. *Brit. Med. J.* 1980; 3:36-37.

Centers for Disease Control. Follow-up on the health status of Kampuchean refugees—Thailand. *MMWR* 1980; 218-225.

Centers for Disease Control. Health status of Kampuchean refugees—Sakaeo, Thailand. *MMWR* 1979; 28:546-547.

Centers for Disease Control. Health status of Kampuchean refugees—Khao I Dang. Thailand. *MMWR* 1979; 28:569-570.

Centers for Disease Control. Measles, Khao I Dang holding center, Thailand. *MMWR* 1980; 29:133-134.

Dahlberg, K. Medical care of Cambodian refugees. *JAMA* 1980; 243: 1062-1065.

Ebena, K. Lack of vaccines and water among refugees from Cambodia. Report from Khao I Dang, Thailand. *Lakartidningen* 1980; 77:1101-1102 (No. 18).

Glass, R.I., Cates, W., Jr., Nieberg, P.I., et al. Rapid assessment of health status and preventive-medicine needs of newly arrived Kampuchean refugees, Sakaeo, Thailand. *Lancet* 1980; 1: 868-872.

Goldenring, J. Cambodian journal. *The New Physician* 1980; 25-31.

Grabe, M. Report from Khao I-Dang, Thailand. *Lakartidningen* 1980; 77: 1765-1768 (No. 18).

Gunn, S.W.A., Arita, I., Doberstyn, E.B., Nieburg, P. Health conditions in the Kampuchean-Thailand border encampments. *Report of the WHO/UN Health Mission to the Kampuchea-Thailand border.* Geneva, Switzerland: World Health Organization, 1983.

Hurwitz, E.S., Johnson, D., Campbell, C.C. Resistance of *Plasmodium falciparum* malaria to sulfadoxine-pyrimethamine (Fansidar) in a refugee camp in Thailand. *Lancet* 1981; 1068-1070.

Johnson, D.E., Williams, R.G., Burke, D.S., Murray, B.E. Observations on medical care in a refugee camp in Thailand. *Military Med.* 1981; 146: 842-845.

Reacher, M., Campbell, C.C., Freeman, J., Doberstyn, E.B., Brandling-Bennett, A.D. Drug therapy for *Plasmodium falciparum* malaria resistant to pyrimethamine-sulfidoxine (Fansidar). A study of alternate regimens in eastern Thailand, 1980. *Lancet* 1981; 2: 1066-1068.

Refugees health. *MD Magazine* 1980; 24: 49-57.

Smilkstein, G. Refugees in Thailand and short-term medical aid. *JAMA* 1981; 245: 1052-1054.

Smilkstein, H. Short-term medical assistance overseas: a point of view. *Consultant* 1981; (Sept.) 191-200.

Spanier, R. ". . . a very present help in trouble." *Forum on Medicine,* March 1980; 190-195.

Swenson, D. Oregon sanitarians help Cambodian refugees in Thailand. *J. Environ. Health* 1980; 42: 335-337.

Weiss, R. The second holocaust. *JAMA* 1980; 243: 2161.

Williamson, J. Centers for unaccompanied children. Khao I-Dang holding center. *Disasters* 1981; 5: 100-103.

General Reference List

Assar, M. *Guide to Sanitation in Natural Disasters.* Geneva, Switzerland: World Health Organization, 1971.

Benenson, A.S. *Control of Communicable Diseases in Man.* 14th ed. Washington, D.C.: American Public Health Association, 1985.

Cairncross, S., Feachem, R. *Small Water Supplies.* London: School of Hygiene and Tropical Medicine, 1978 (Ross Bulletin, No. 10).

Centre for Research on the Epidemiology of Disasters. *Medico-nutritional Information on Disaster-prone Countries and Glossary of Common Illnesses.* Brussels: University of Louvain, School of Public Health, Epidemiology Unit, 1979.

de Ville de Goyet, C., Seaman, J., Geijer, U. *The Management of Nutritional Emergencies in Large Populations.* Geneva, Switzerland: World Health Organization, 1978.

Feachem, R., Cairncross, S. *Small Excreta Disposal Systems.* London: London School of Hygiene and Tropical Medicine, 1978 (Ross Bulletin, No. 8).

International Disaster Institute. Medical care in refugee camps. *Disasters* 1981; 5: 171-336.

Protein-Calorie Advisory Group of the United Nations System. *A Guide to Food and Health Relief Operations for Disasters*. New York: United Nations, 1977.

Taylor, A.J. Assessment of victim needs. *Disasters* 1979; 3: 24-31.

Taylor, A.J., Cuny, F.C. The evaluation of humanitarian assistance. *Disasters* 1979; 3: 37-42.

Torjesen, H., Olness, K., Torjesen, E. *The Gift of the Refugees*. Eden Prairie, Minnesota: The Garden, 1981.